THE CITY IS OURS

THE CITY IS OURS

Spaces of Political Mobilization and Imaginaries of Nationhood in Turkey

Muna Güvenç

CORNELL UNIVERSITY PRESS   ITHACA AND LONDON

Furthermore:
a program of the J.M. Kaplan Fund

Publication of this book was supported by a grant from Furthermore: a program of the J. M. Kaplan Fund.

Copyright © 2024 by Cornell University

All rights reserved. Except for brief quotations in a review, this book, or parts thereof, must not be reproduced in any form without permission in writing from the publisher. For information, address Cornell University Press, Sage House, 512 East State Street, Ithaca, New York 14850. Visit our website at cornellpress.cornell.edu.

First published 2024 by Cornell University Press

Library of Congress Cataloging-in-Publication Data

Names: Güvenç, Muna, author.
Title: The city is ours : spaces of political mobilization and imaginaries of nationhood in Turkey / Muna Güvenç.
Description: Ithaca [New York] : Cornell University Press, 2024. | Includes bibliographical references and index.
Identifiers: LCCN 2024002195 (print) | LCCN 2024002196 (ebook) | ISBN 9781501774355 (hardcover) | ISBN 9781501776373 (paperback) | ISBN 9781501774362 (pdf) | ISBN 9781501774379 (epub)
Subjects: LCSH: Built environment—Political aspects—Turkey—Diyarbakır. | City planning—Political aspects—Turkey—Diyarbakır. | Kurds—Turkey—Politics and government—21st century. | Kurds—Turkey—Ethnic identity.
Classification: LCC HT169.T92 G884 2024 (print) | LCC HT169.T92 (ebook) | DDC 307.1/2160956677—dc23/eng/20240221
LC record available at https://lccn.loc.gov/2024002195
LC ebook record available at https://lccn.loc.gov/2024002196

Cities, like dreams, are made of desires and fears, even if the thread of their discourse is secret, their rules are absurd, their perspectives deceitful, and everything conceals something else.

—Italo Calvino, *Invisible Cities*

Contents

List of Illustrations	ix
Acknowledgments	xi
List of Abbreviations	xv
Note on Transliteration, Translation, and Pseudonyms	xvii
Introduction: Urban Maneuver	1
1. Whose City?	19
2. Building the Frontier: "We Will Not Surrender"	39
3. Seeing Like a Movement, Acting Like a State: "We Will Administer Ourselves"	70
4. Branding the City: "Diyarbakır Is Our Capital"	94
5. Sculpting Violence, Activating the Street: "Freedom or Freedom"	124
6. Dismantling the Kurdish Landscape: "Hey, You People—Dreams Canceled"	159
Conclusion: Wiggle Room	192
Notes	201
Bibliography	219
Index	235

Illustrations

FIGURES

1.	Political map of Turkey	xviii
2.	Map of the city's expansion in four phases	6
3.	Aerial view of Diyarbakır in the 1930s	24
4.	Diyarbakır People's House in the early twentieth century	26
5.	View of squatter settlements in Sur	52
6.	Proposed relocation of residents from Lalebey and Ali Paşa in Sur to Çölgüzeli	57
7.	Map showing expropriated properties of Lalebey and Ali Paşa neighborhoods in Sur	65
8.	Typical street view of squatter settlements in Sur, 2009	74
9.	Graffiti in the Hasırlı neighborhood of Sur	75
10.	Meeting room of the Free Compatriot Association in Sur	78
11.	Women distributing *tandır* bread by a laundry house in Sur	83
12.	View from Kayapınar of high-rise apartments and billboard advertising new gated community	104
13.	Gate of Med City Mahabad in Kayapınar	111
14.	Turkish coffee bags rebranded as Kurdish coffee at a sidewalk stand	117
15.	Souvenir shop in Hasan Paşa displaying decorative tapestries	119
16.	Street shop in Sur displaying jerseys and scarves for the Diyarbakır soccer team	120
17.	Trees growing in the median strip veiling Diyarbakır gateway sign	125
18.	*Right to Life* memorial	129
19.	Wall panel depicting victims of bomb blast	130

20.	Wall panel depicting Kurdish society engaged in *halay* dance	130
21.	Civil Friday Prayer in Dağkapı Meydanı	137
22.	Uğur Kaymaz memorial and Sur municipality building	140
23.	Roboski memorial	142
24.	An "unnamed" park	144
25.	Kurdish politicians leading march to the city center	149
26.	Cemil Paşa Museum	152
27.	Aerial view of Sur in 2018	161
28.	Censored art in Koşuyolu Park	164
29.	Censored detail of wall panel	165
30.	Vandalized *Right to Life* memorial	165
31.	Salahaddin Ayyubi Mosque (Diyarbakır Central Mosque)	170
32.	AKP municipality's advertisement on roadway	171
33.	Tigris Valley Recreation Area Mosque	174
34.	Map of expropriated properties in Sur	177
35.	Map showing demolished and redeveloped areas in Sur	181

TABLE

1.	Percentages of pro-Kurdish party support between 1999 and 2019 in Diyarbakır	107

Acknowledgments

This book is woven from countless threads of love and friendship that have spanned many years. I want to express my gratitude to all who supported this project and made it possible.

This book could not be accomplished without the kindness and generosity of the people of Diyarbakır (whose names are disguised here for obvious reasons). Countless times, over fifteen years, many Diyarbakırians admitted me into their communities and opened the doors of their homes and offices. I remain forever indebted to them for their years-long friendship, here and there, together and apart. Even though I am not from Diyarbakır, there is no other city I am constantly inspired by. I acknowledge, above all, my gratitude to activists, mayors, artists, students, parliament members, architects, planners, academics, homemakers, merchants, businesspeople, laborers, teachers, and municipal employees of Diyarbakır—to all who shared their lives with me, helped me understand a little of what Kurdishness meant to them. They guided me through the delicacies and challenges of being Kurd in Turkey, navigating the complexities of urban mobilization.

At the University of California Berkeley, many wonderful friends, mentors, and colleagues had a tremendous influence on the early stages of this book. I thank Nezar AlSayyad, whose critical insights have been a great source of support, inspiration, and encouragement for the earlier phases of my research. He has contributed immeasurably to my appreciation of the politics of architecture and urban planning. I owe special thanks to Cihan Ziya Tuğal, who pushed me to develop the theoretical implications of my arguments with his exceptional scholarship and engagement. His insightful suggestions and thought-provoking questions about "the puzzle" have shaped this book tremendously. During the first phase of my research, Greig Crysler helped me to develop a more complete sense of national and memorial architecture. The analyses were enriched by discussions with Laura Nader and Teresa Caldeira. My friends Nadia Shihab, Carolina Cabello, Amina Al-Kandari, Pat Seeumpornroj, Kah-Wee Lee, Tiago Castela, Cecilia Chu, Rielle Navitsky, and Ayda Melika contributed immensely to numerous engaging discussions and unforgettable moments filled with joy. Thanks especially to Nadia Shihab, whose careful readings of numerous early drafts significantly enhanced the text.

At the University of Pittsburgh, the collegiality of Drew Armstrong, Gretchen Bender, Barbara McCloskey, and Kirk Savage made writing much more pleasurable. At Brandeis University, Aida Wong, Charles McClendon, Carina Ray, Ulka Anjaria, Dorothy Hodgson, Elaine Wong, Joel Christensen, and Wendy Cadge were my circle of support. I thank Jennifer Stern for her dedicated administrative support. My gratitude goes to Janelle Joseph for our weekly accountability conversations for writing plans. Along the way, I was fortunate to meet with Sibel Bozdoğan, who provided thorough feedback on the final versions of this book. All along, I have carried Nicole Watts's "Activists in Office" with me wherever I go and am deeply grateful for her critical questions and input during the conclusive stages of refining this book. I express my gratitude to Güneş Murat Tezcür for providing me with his insightful and thorough feedback. I thank Andy Manos, who did a terrific job in helping me prepare the maps. I extend my gratitude to my copy editor Glenn Novak, and to Jim Lance and Jennifer Savran Kelly at Cornell University Press.

Several grants and fellowships have made this book possible. At UC Berkeley, the financial support of the Al-Falah Program at the Center for Middle Eastern Studies, the Spiro Kostof Award, and the Dean's Normative Time Fellowship facilitated my early fieldwork in Diyarbakır, my visit to presidential archives, and my writing in Berkeley. Later, the University of Pittsburgh's Postdoctoral Fellowship at the History of Art and Architecture Department of the Kenneth P. Dietrich School of Arts helped me rethink the first phase of my research. At Brandeis University, the Theodore and Jane Norman Awards for Faculty Scholarship, the Tomberg Funds, the Summer Research Grant at the Crown Center for Middle East Studies, and the Perlmutter Excellence Award facilitated the second phase of my research. I am also thankful to Furthermore grants in publishing, a program of the J. M. Kaplan Fund, for their support for the publication process of this book.

I revised and wrote several final sections during the lockdown of the COVID-19 pandemic. I thank Juan Sebastián Ospina León and Martha Heinemann Bixby for their dedicated elementary home-school initiatives, which lent me the space and time to write during the challenging moments of the pandemic.

I express my heartfelt gratitude to Haşim Haşimi and his extended family for their steadfast and continuous support over the years. I dedicate this book to my parents Zühal and İzzettin Güvenç, for their belief in me, their endless support, and the invaluable life lessons they've imparted. I am especially grateful to them for teaching me the virtue of resourcefulness in every situation. This book owes much of its essence to Juan Sebastián Ospina León, who meticulously commented on earlier drafts, and to Ali, a constant source of love, inspiration, and unique joy in my life, shaping its very fabric. JuanSe's sophistication, encouragement, and unwavering camaraderie played pivotal roles in the completion of this book.

Sections of chapter 5 are derived in part from an article published in *CITY: Analysis of Urban Change, Theory, Action*, July 31, 2019, Taylor & Francis, available online at https://doi.org/10.1080/13604813.2019.1648037, and another article, in *TDSR, Traditional Dwellings and Settlements Review*, Fall 2011, available online at https://www.jstor.org/stable/41758881.

Abbreviations

AKP	Justice and Development Party (Adelet ve Kalkınma Partisi)
ANAP	Motherland Party (Anavatan Partisi)
BDP	Peace and Democracy Party (Barış ve Demokrasi Partisi)
CHP	Republican People's Party (Cumhuriyet Halk Partisi)
DDKD	Revolutionary Eastern Cultural Associations (Devrimci Doğu Kültür Dernekleri)
DEHAP	Democratic People Party (Demokratik Halk Partisi)
DEP	Democracy Party (Demokrasi Partisi)
DİAY-DER	Religious Scholars Solidarity Association (Din Alimleri Derneği)
DİP	Revolutionary Workers' Party (Devrimci İşçi Partisi)
DTK	Democratic Society Congress (Demokratik Toplum Kongresi)
DTP	Democratic Society Party (Demokratik Toplum Partisi)
Göç-Der	Immigrants' Association for Social Cooperation and Culture (Göç Edenlerle Sosyal Yardımlaşma ve Kültür Derneği)
HADEP	People's Democracy Party (Halkın Demokrasi Partisi)
HAK-PAR	Rights and Freedoms Party (Hak ve Özgürlükler Partisi)
HDP	Peoples' Democratic Party (Halkların Demokratik Partisi)
HEP	People's Labor Party (Halkın Emek Partisi)
HEDEP (DEM)	Peoples' Equality and Democracy Party (Halkların Eşitlik ve Demokrasi Partisi)
İHD	Human Rights Association of Turkey (İnsan Hakları Derneği)
KADEM	Women Support Center (Kadın Destek Merkezi)
KCK	Kurdistan Democratic Communities Union (Koma Civakên Kurdistanê)
KDP-Turkey	Kurdistan Democratic Party of Turkey (Türkiye Kürdistan Demokrat Partisi)
KURDSİAD	Association of Industrialists and Businessmen of Kurdistan (Kürdistan Sanayici ve İş Adamları Derneği)
MAZLUM-DER	Association of Human Rights and Solidarity for Oppressed People (İnsan Hakları ve Mazlumlar için Dayanışma Derneği)
OHAL	Emergency Rule Law (Olağanüstü Hal)
PÇDK	Kurdistan Democratic Solution Party–Iraqi Kurdistan (Partî Çareserî Dîmukratî Kurdistan)

PJAK	Kurdistan Free Life Party—Iranian Kurdistan (Partiya Jina Azad a Kurdistanê)
PKK	Kurdistan Workers' Party (Partiya Karkerên Kurdistanê)
PYD	Democratic Union Party (Partiya Yekîtiya Demokrat)
RP	Welfare Party (Refah Partisi)
SHP	Social Democratic Populist Party (Sosyal Demokrat Halkçı Partisi)
TİP	Workers' Party of Turkey (Türkiye İşçi Partisi)
TKDP	Kurdistan Democrat Party of Turkey (Türkiye Kürdistan Demokrat Partisi)
TKSP	Kurdistan Socialist Party of Turkey (Türkiye Kürdistanı Sosyalist Partisi)
TOKİ	Housing Development Administration of Turkey (Türkiye Toplu Konut İdaresi Başkanlığı)
TZP-Kurdi	The Movement for Kurdish Education and Language (Tevgera Ziman û Perwerdehiya Kurdî)
YDG-H	Patriotic Revolutionary Youth Movement (Yurtsever Devrimci Gençlik Hareketi)
YSP	Green Left Party (Yeşil Sol Parti)

Note on Transliteration, Translation, and Pseudonyms

The text includes some Turkish names. The Turkish alphabet has several letters with diacritical marks. For readers unfamiliar with Turkish pronunciation: *c* is *j*; *ç* is *ch*; *ğ* is a silent *g* (like the *gh* in *through*); *ı* is pronounced like the *e* in *summer*; *i* is pronounced like the *i* in *it*; *ö* is like *ö* in German; *or* is like *ea* in *earth*; *ü* is like *ü* in German (often transcribed as *ue* in English); *ş* is like *sh* in English. In English-language contexts I have used the familiar spellings for the major cities of Istanbul and Izmir, rather than "İstanbul" and "İzmir."

To protect individuals' identities, I've employed pseudonyms in the text for those I've spoken with, except for the mayors or experts who have explicitly granted consent for the use of their names.

All English translations are by the author.

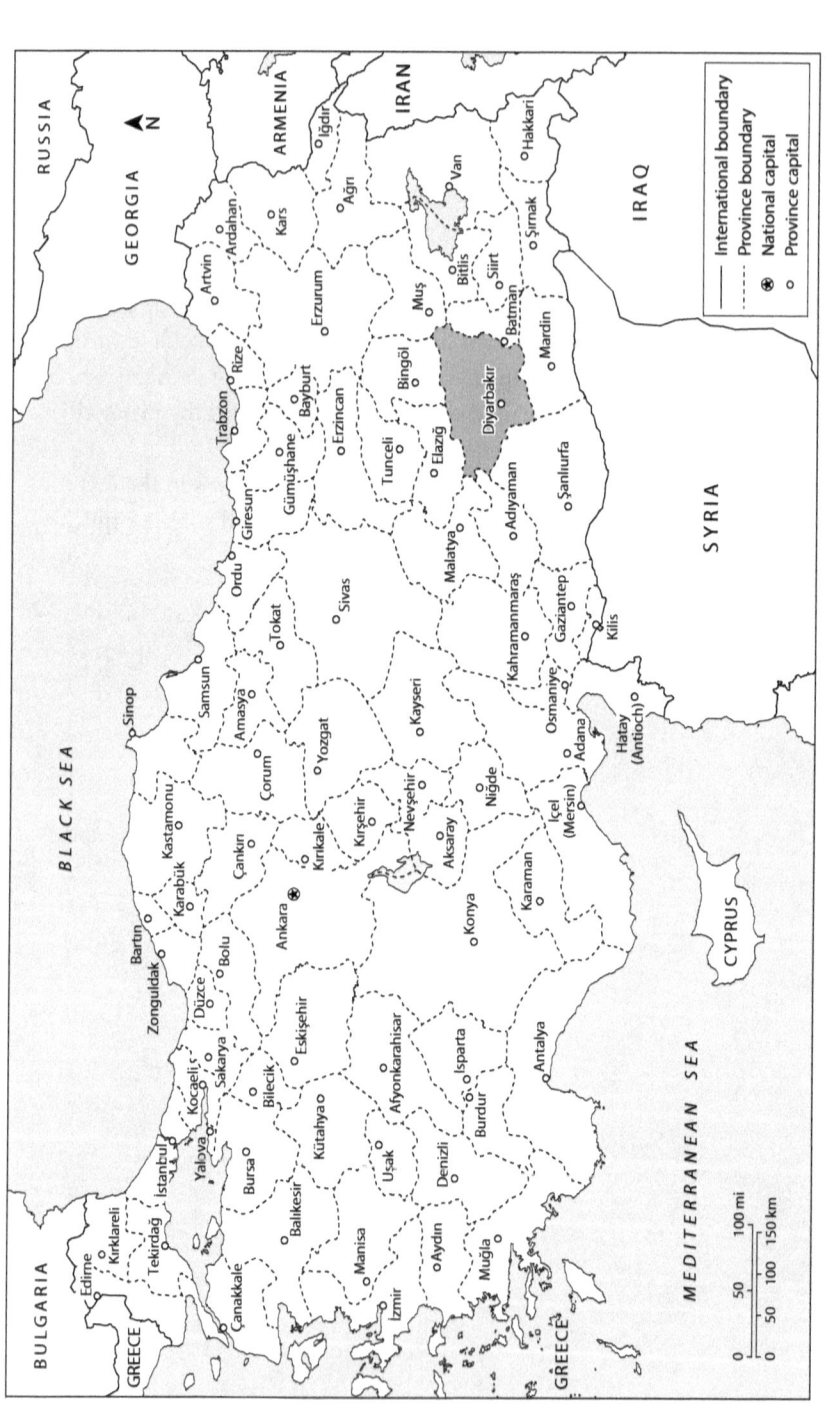

FIGURE 1. The political map of Turkey. Diyarbakır is marked in gray.

Source: Map re-created based on the Turkey maps in the Perry-Castañeda Library Map Collection, University of Texas.

THE CITY IS OURS

INTRODUCTION
Urban Maneuver

Kurds constitute one of the few communities of over thirty-five million persons without a nation-state. When national borders were remapped in the Middle East in the aftermath of World War I, Kurds were relegated to minority status in four separate countries, between northern Iraq, far northern Syria, western Iran, and southeastern Turkey. Almost half the Kurds of the Middle East live in Turkey.[1] Since the foundation of the Turkish Republic in 1923, a range of state policies exposed Kurds, the largest minority in Turkey, to ongoing campaigns of coercion, violence, and assimilation. For almost one hundred years, Kurds have frequently been barred from representation at the national level and exposed to myriad forms of violence.

The Kurdish movement has used a variety of channels to defend Kurdish identity and achieve territorial autonomy and recognition. An explicit recognition of "Kurdishness" in Turkey, however, did not become a topic for legally permissible nationalist claims until the late 1990s. Despite an ongoing campaign of coercion, oppression, and state violence, Diyarbakır—often called the informal capital of Turkish Kurdistan—became more "Kurdified" and more mobilized between 1999 and 2019 than at any time in the history of the Turkish Republic.[2] In this context, the country's largest Kurdish-populated city rose in stature to become the center of Kurdish mobilization.

By the early 2000s, a trip across Diyarbakır afforded the visitor a view of the city's entire historical trajectory. At the journey's beginning, a silent yellow prairie extends before the visitor's gaze, across which several small villages appear on the horizon. As the visitor enters the city's rural outskirts, small areas of farmland dispersed across the plateau catch the eye. After passing over the Tigris River, the visitor is greeted by the old Diyarbakır fortress. The rural hush ends here. The landscape changes abruptly as one enters the ancient inner city, Sur, with its historic quarters. For the remainder of the journey, the visitor passes through informal settlements, business districts, and low-income areas, eventually arriving at the well-off gated communities and large parks at the city's western extremity. Altogether, the forty-five-minute road trip from east to west offers a view of Diyarbakır's contrasting layers—as a frontier city, a city of farmlands, an ancient city, a city of migrants, a city of displacement and conflict, a city of political activism, a site of persistent poverty and informality, and an experiment in neoliberal urbanism. Yet, however diverse their character, each of the districts through which the visitor passes evinces a strong sense of Kurdishness—thickening these imbrications while revealing Diyarbakır's distinctiveness from the rest of Turkey.

I first went to Diyarbakır in 2007. During the first few days after I arrived, I met with Havin, a twenty-four-year-old student of electrical engineering at Dicle University.[3] Havin was born in a pious family, originally from Batman, Diyarbakır's neighbor city to the east. Even though he was not from Diyarbakır, he was a Diyarbakırian; one could feel that he owned the city. When we first met, he loved talking about the history of the city and about his experimental energy-saving projects for the city's benefit. With Havin, I enjoyed walking in the narrow streets of Sur, the historic quarters of Diyarbakır, eating out in cafés and chatting. Throughout my fieldwork spanning several years, we continued to meet. Havin's journey in the succeeding years was in many ways like those of other residents in Diyarbakır as their sense of Kurdishness and activism grew. Two years after my first arrival, in 2009, I met with Havin again. By then, he regularly attended the seminars of pro-Kurdish youth organizations and argued that political activism was the only way to achieve "recognition of Kurdish identity." In one conversation, he said: "Before, I didn't know I was a Kurd. We were all Turks. As I grew up, as I lived here, I learned that I was a Kurd. Kurd is my identity."

I never forgot what Havin told me—how he became aware that "he was a Kurd." For Havin, like many others I met throughout my fieldwork in Diyarbakır, Kurdishness goes beyond fixed ethnic identity. Kurdishness is a political claim, a learned identity spawned by sharing in the everyday life of the city.[4] How does one own and wear this identity? How does one turn into an activist by living in the city? What is the power of cities in identity struggles, the struggles against persistent racism, and inequality in the twenty-first century? In answering these questions, this book demonstrates how urbanism may provide opportunities otherwise unavailable to opposition political organizations that lack—or have been denied access to—more conventional channels of representation. This book studies the agency of the built environment and urbanism for political mobilization in the twenty-first-century city.

One August afternoon in 2009, I was having dinner with Havin and chatting about the aftermath of the local elections and the issues related to municipal services. Once again, with 65 percent of the votes, the pro-Kurdish party had a sweeping victory in Diyarbakır during the March local elections.[5] Havin was commenting on their victory: "Of course, DTP [the Democratic Society Party] would have won. It's alright if the municipality doesn't collect our trash or doesn't bring service to our neighborhoods.[6] The only thing we want is our Kurdish identity back." For Havin, the party did not win the local elections because it would provide better service to the city. More crucial was its "struggle for Kurdish freedom," a phrase Havin would use frequently. For Diyarbakırians, the pro-Kurdish party municipality went beyond being service providers. In the eyes of several residents, the pro-Kurdish party and the municipality were defenders of Kurdish rights and central to the future of their freedom and recognition. Havin, who migrated to the city from a rural area to pursue a university education, was one such resident who wanted to reclaim a Kurdish identity. What may be most compelling about his case, however, and about those of many like him, is how urban space provided the inspiration to "know" and "claim" Kurdishness in the absence of a Kurdish state. During my research in the city, I repeatedly heard similar comments from people: "We want our own freedom" and "We want our Kurdish identity."

This book demonstrates how the deliberate creation of urban networks and the spatial practices of the pro-Kurdish municipalities were essential to conjuring a sense of national unity and articulating the Kurdish bloc in Diyarbakır. The words of the mayor of Diyarbakır, Osman Baydemir, who was in office from 2004 to 2014, attest to this point. Mayor Baydemir was initially a lawyer, and he had a background in human rights activism. He and the Peoples' Democratic Party, the HDP, were very aware of the influence of local administration on social and political change. I first met with him in 2010 at the Diyarbakır Metropolitan Municipality. Osman Baydemir was a straightforward person. He wouldn't avoid speaking his mind and had a poetic and emotional way of speaking. In one interview I conducted with him in 2011, he passionately expressed the power of urban politics compared to parliamentary politics:

> Inside the parliamentary system, you may have twenty or thirty parliament members, but in the general legislation, you don't have the power to change the law. However, you can only do active opposition. With twenty people in the parliament [of five hundred fifty], you do not have the power to change the spirit of the parliament, as you don't have the

power to change the law. But through local authorities, you have the power to change the spirit of the city, its people.... The city is yours; the city board is yours.... The municipality is yours.

This claim over the city is not necessarily a territorial one. Rather, it is a strong acknowledgment of the significance of urban planning in shaping politics, in what Mayor Baydemir calls "changing the spirit of the city." It is an expression of a struggle for justice and equality, an aspiration for autonomy. In fact, for the mayoral elections of 2019, the HDP's campaign slogan asserted ownership of the city with the proclamation "It is ours," which produced a distinct victory for the party. During my research, I witnessed how the pro-Kurdish party creatively turned state coercion and violence into opportunities for opposition and mobilization through distinctive urban maneuvers—strategies of planning and even conscious unplanning. Like sailors maneuvering in the sea, oftentimes party officials and mayors managed to use the wind of coercion to which they were exposed. They used it to their advantage to proceed with Kurdish mobilization in the city through urban projects. The pro-Kurdish party purposefully carved out fresh avenues for urban opposition and the articulation of a politicized Kurdish identity in the face of state oppression. Under such challenging circumstances, the party repeatedly had to develop a new urban strategy or find a loophole and maneuver to open up a new operating space—what I called the wiggle room.

Studying Diyarbakır convinced me that cities cannot be wholly hijacked by capitalism, neoliberalism, extremisms, or other selfish agendas of authoritarian powers. There is wiggle room—wiggle room for solidarities and the fight against injustice. By wiggle room, I not only mean when millions of people take to the streets and protest, demonstrate, and resist inequality and injustices—actions that are already very powerful and valuable urban tools. I mean urban opportunities that include diverse strategies that empower citizens and provide larger opportunities to all for opposition. This book is about that wiggle room. The creation and use of that wiggle room is what I saw in the pro-Kurdish party's urban governance. Especially, this book illustrates how, in the early 2000s, pro-Kurdish parties, either banned by the state or denied access to parliament by targeted legal restrictions, used municipal power and urban planning to resist state coercion and foster Kurdish nationhood in Turkey.

Diyarbakır: A City with a Contested Future

Diyarbakır is the largest Kurdish-populated city in modern Turkey. With a population of more than 1.8 million and spanning around 15,000 square kilometers (around 5,790 square miles) Diyarbakır is the most symbolically important city for Turkey's Kurds today. Diyarbakır's turbulent history dates back to 3500 BCE. Indeed, the city has long been one of the most prominent cities in Mesopotamia. The city saw Hurrian, Hittite, Assyrian, and Urartian rule before being incorporated successively into the Roman, Byzantine, and Ottoman Empires.[7] Under siege by different civilizations, the city had its name changed from Amida (Amed) and later to Diyarbekir, and finally to Diyarbakır in 1937, by order of Mustafa Kemal Atatürk, a prominent Turkish military officer and statesman who became the founding father of Turkish Republic.[8] When the Ottoman Empire first conquered the region in the sixteenth century, it established an *eyalet* with its center at Diyarbakır.[9] Although its borders changed over time, the *eyalet* of Diyarbakır corresponds to contemporary Turkey's Kurdish southeastern cities—the area spanning from Lake Urmia to Palu and from the southern shores of Lake Van to Cizre, to the beginnings of the Syrian Desert. The city's growth can be parsed into four main phases. By the beginning of the republic, Diyarbakır consisted only of Sur, the walled city, surrounded by villages. Owing to migrations from rural areas, little by little, villages turned into districts of the city. Early rural migrants first filled out the vacant homes of Sur and built squatter settlements on any empty lot they found. Then the settlements flooded over the walls and created two new major squatter settlement towns: the Ben-u Sen and Bağlar neighborhoods. Ben-u Sen, developed in the 1970s on the backyard of Yenişehir, adjacent to Sur, is known as the first squatter settlement of the city. From 1965 to 1990, the population of Diyarbakır nearly doubled, increasing from about 476,000 to about 1.1 million.[10] As the population grew, especially during the forced migration of the 1990s, the city amalgamated to Yenişehir a new district, Ofis, which takes its name from "office," as a business district.[11] As Ben-u Sen grew, it was followed by Bağlar, a former orchard quarter turned into a migrants' destination in the 1980s and 1990s. Two-story houses were quickly replaced by illegal multistory apartment blocks. Diyarbakır's borders subsequently pushed even farther, to Kayapınar, a peripheral village that became a new home to residential blocks of the middle and upper-middle classes. By the 2000s, while Sur, Ben-u Sen, and Bağlar housed the urban poor, Kayapınar became the new destination for the rich and middle classes (figure 2).

The majority of Diyarbakır's economy is based on agriculture. There are around 750,000 hectares (almost 2,900 square miles) of farming area. Industrial activity is growing but is still limited. Historically, one of the significant problems in the city has been unemployment, which reached 29 percent in official figures by 2020. The lack of industrial development is seen as a root cause for high

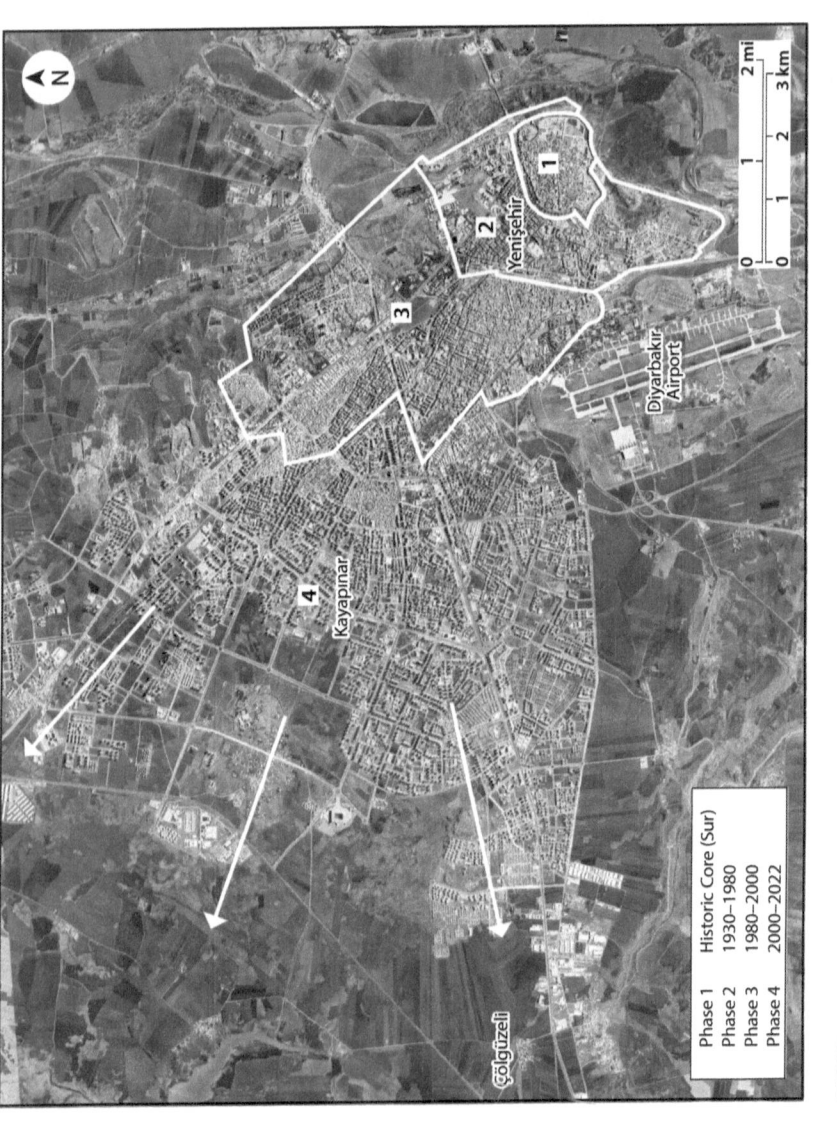

FIGURE 2. The scheme shows the city's expansion in four phases.

Source: Adapted from urban development maps provided by the Diyarbakir Metropolitan Municipality (for until 2000) and later based on Google Maps, 2022.

unemployment, particularly among young people.¹² As of 2022, the city's average household income is one of the lowest in Turkey.¹³

When Diyarbakır was established as a province of the Republic of Turkey in 1923, the city experienced drastic changes. It became a site of modern nation-state building based on processes of Turkification. Government actions included banning the use of the Kurdish language, changing village and street names from Kurdish to Turkish, and the forced displacement of Kurds. Nevertheless, the Kurdish nationalist movement in Turkey has mapped Diyarbakır as a part of a greater Kurdish nation and as the center of the movement since the beginning of the twentieth century.¹⁴ In 1925, Diyarbakır witnessed heavily armed clashes between army and rebels in what was later known as the Sheikh Said Rebellion, one of the largest uprisings. The city mobilized about fifteen thousand fighters.¹⁵ Beginning in the 1980s, the rise of armed conflict between the PKK (Partiya Karkerên Kurdistanê) and the Turkish military forces drove the migration of rural Kurds to cities as well as the formation of a series of pro-Kurdish political parties. With electoral victories, after the late 1990s pro-Kurdish politicians in Kurdish-majority cities began to control municipal administrations, creating new circumstances for the development of Kurdish movement. The pro-Kurdish parties have used urban space to transmit a pro-Kurdish narrative that challenges the state's discourse on security, violence, and identity and have successfully strengthened their popular base in the city.

Throughout the years, Diyarbakır reinforced its central role for the Kurdish movement, as pro-Kurdish parties conducted their larger campaigns and demonstrations. Also, major pro-Kurdish NGOs opened in the city. Diyarbakır has also played a leading role, particularly since the late 1990s, as an urban model in symbolic and cultural projects of Kurdishness for other Kurdish-populated cities in Turkey, such as Batman, Bingöl, Hakkari, Muş, and Van. At the same time, Diyarbakır has been a turbulent site of Kurdish mobilization. In urban politics, while pro-Kurdish mayors, NGOs, and civil society organizations occupy one end of the political spectrum, the state-appointed governorship, with its chief officers tied to the governorship and a large military presence, occupies the other. The confrontation between two power sources in Diyarbakır revealed the city as a site of contestation. In the city, antigovernment demonstrations were part of everyday life, with mayors and party officials marching at the head of crowds, delivering speeches on Kurdish rights, organizing public protests, and—on several occasions—even clashing with the police forces. Urban interventions of the pro-Kurdish party officials were not limited to mass protests but included organizing Kurdish cultural festivals, naming streets for prominent Kurdish figures, opening public parks, installing public monuments, and commemorating Kurdish rebellions, as well as promoting various cultural heritage projects addressing the Kurdish past.

While they were in power, the pro-Kurdish municipal administrations in Turkey sought not only to bring new public services to cities but also to channel—even re-create—Kurdish society through such services. Services ranged from micro-entrepreneurship projects for the urban poor to lucrative contracts for local businesspeople, to the removal of Turkish symbols from public space and the installation of new Kurdish memorials. While providing examples of an alternative government, these diverse initiatives also allowed pro-Kurdish political forces to forge a larger, urban Kurdish political bloc. The bloc encompassed a wide spectrum of society, including students, merchants, civil servants, housewives, the unemployed, teachers, businesspeople, university professors, farmers, and members of pious communities. Particularly between 1999 and 2015, these diverse groups, often from incompatible backgrounds, united as politicized Kurdish activists. These pro-Kurdish parties and their local administrations were often contested and confronted by provincial governors, prosecutors, security forces, and other authorities tied to the central government in Ankara. For instance, in 2016 and 2019, elected mayors of Diyarbakır were repeatedly detained, and state officials were appointed instead. Following the 2016 urban war between Turkish military forces and armed militias in the middle of the city, the rush to destroy the Kurdish urban landscape, to demolish and change the Kurdish built environment and arrest the elected Kurdish mayors of the city, once again marked the crucial role of architecture and urban planning in the political battle between the Turkish state and the Kurdish movement.

On the Architecture of Nationness

What is urban about nationalism in the twenty-first century? How do we study nationalism in the absence of a nation-state? How do we examine the spaces of nationhood when there is no clear distinction between the state and civil society? How have architecture and planning been caught up in this process? And how do they operate? This book specifies urban mechanisms and spaces by which nationalist struggles and national identifications are formed within coercion and in the absence of state power.

The relationship between the built environment and nationalism has been studied since the early twentieth century. Most prior research has focused on nationalism as an ideological artifact of a nation-state for which, usually, the term *state* carries a fixed meaning as an absolute entity and the sole owner of "political power."[16] This approach, adopted by several architectural and urban historians, such as Lawrence Vale, Abidin Kusno, Sibel Bozdoğan, and Zeynep Kezer, has aptly relied on state-centered understandings and viewed states as the prime actors of social, architectural, and urban transformation.[17] Further, in the same realm, nationalism has been studied as a top-to-bottom intervention in which it is frequently associated with traditional or totalistic regimes or with modernist attributes in postcolonial states.[18]

Usually, those who study nationalism through the analytical framework of the state have largely relegated space to a cursory role and tended to view capital cities, memorials, squares, and monumental buildings as powerful and fixed representations of the national regime. Within this realm, from the postcolonial era to the establishment of new nation-states in the early twenty century, nationalism and modern architecture have frequently been linked in the construction of national identity.[19] In this context, modern architecture and planning were instrumental in the building of a new nation-state along with a national identity and capital city. As I discuss in chapter 1, this phenomenon appears in the early years of the Turkish Republic, in the construction of Turkish national identity and in the making of modern Turkish cities.

But cities like Diyarbakır test the limits of such a framework. Diyarbakır is a very nationalist city—the center for Kurdish nationalism in Turkey—as made very clear in urban politics, planning schemes, planning decisions, and urban networks. But it has never fit the mold of the "modern city." Modernity has never dictated the contours of urban life in Diyarbakır. Even during the early years of the Turkish Republic, Diyarbakır was not a city like Lucia Costa's Brasilia or Clemens Holzmeister's Ankara, created with ideals of emerging modern architecture and planning. Since the early 1920s, sterilizing and paternalistic claims of official republican modernism have been constantly challenged by the plurality, fragmentation, and potency of local popular culture. In Diyarbakır, the incorporation of vernacular and historical references in architecture, of popular hybrid forms symbolically emphasizing the Kurdish past, along with assorted expressions of popular culture like *arabesk* or *dengbej* music in everyday life in the city, dispute with the homogenizing claims of modern architecture and planning. Diyarbakır is a postmodern city frequently in the midst of conflict and, more recently, caught in the rise of neoliberal urbanism. From the watermelon seller in the street to the people sleeping on their balconies at their multistory apartments during a hot summer night, from the way the city accommodated informal housing at the center to the highly decorated style of its gated communities at the peripheries, Diyarbakır didn't bother itself to be bound with any rule or style, even for serving the purpose of representing homogenized Kurdish national identity. Such postmodern identification in Diyarbakır was also comfortable and strong because the notion of "modern" was associated with the republican in the eyes of its local residents. Often, antirepublican translated to antimodern in the city. Therefore, what is at stake when we study nationalism in a postmodern, highly contested, and fragmented city? This book studies nation building and political mobilization in just such an uneven postmodern city. By showing how urban space can allow for—or undermine—nationalist aspirations, this book extends the recent scholarship by investigating the power of place making to incite large societal transformations in the absence of the nation-state.

A few contextual remarks: I do not take nationalism to be a fully developed model in a vacuum. Rather, I take it as a political process constantly being shaped and changed in the city. My approach to nationalism is specifically informed by the works of scholars such as Rogers Brubaker and Lisa Wedeen, who have demonstrated how national identifications can be generated in everyday political experience, rather than merely by national regimes.[20]

When contemplating nationhood and nationness, Brubaker suggests that one should think about nationalism without nation. He contends that one "should focus on nation as a category of practices, nationhood as an institutionalized cultural and political form and nationness as a contingent event or happening, and refrain from using the analytically dubious notion of 'nations' as substantial, enduring collectivities."[21] We must understand the practical uses of the category "nation"—the ways it structures perception, informs thought and experience, and organizes discourse and political action.[22] Accordingly, I do not ask who the Kurd is but how the Kurdish identity is articulated in the political context of Turkey. Following Brubaker, I do not treat Kurds as an ethnic entity or as an "enduring collectivity" but rather as a political category that stems from distinct political discourse and collective action and not solely from ethnic factors.[23] Because, as this book shall demonstrate, I argue that Kurdish nationhood in the last twenty years in Turkey did not develop in a vacuum as an "ethnocultural or ethnodemographic fact"; rather it developed as an urban-political process in diverse settings created and governed by the pro-Kurdish parties in the city.[24] In examining Kurdish nationhood, for instance, I am interested in how and where Kurdishness happens in the city; that is, who are the actors in these events of Kurdishness?

In this regard, the articulation approach offers critical tools for analysis of pro-Kurdish parties and the development of Kurdishness in the city. Laclau and Mouffe define *articulation* as "any practice establishing a relation among elements such that their identity is modified as a result of the articulatory practice."[25] In their work on social change and political parties, Cedric de Leon,

Manali Desai, and Cihan Tuğal study *political articulation* "as the process by which parties 'suture' together coherent blocs and cleavages from a disparate set of constituencies and individuals, who, even by virtue of sharing circumstances, may not necessarily share the same political identity."[26] Thus, political parties, rather than "absorbing or rechanneling popular pressure," are "usually the most influential agencies that structure social cleavages."[27]

Moreover, I argue that, in the post-1999 period, despite the different interests across the society, the pro-Kurdish party cultivated and shaped a new sense of imagined Kurdish identity via urban practices. The municipalities' urban projects drastically helped the pro-Kurdish party to integrate distinct elements of Kurdish community into a "larger entity and forged unity."[28] Channeling the activity of NGOs, civil society, and political society, the pro-Kurdish party brought the constituents of the social together and articulated the social formations with a new discourse of Kurdish nationhood in everyday urban practices, such as festivals, protests, demonstrations, funeral ceremonies, activities in urban parks, several network organizations in political and civil society, reading nights, art exhibitions, and so on. In fact, since the early 2000s, the pro-Kurdish party not only capitalized on existing networks of civil society but also creatively established new urban networks and sites of engagement bound by specific spatial and urban activities.[29] As successful examples of alternative government action, such activities have allowed the pro-Kurdish party to forge a formidable Kurdish identity within a coherent political bloc. This book shows how these specific sites of engagement helped party leaders develop communities, informal networks, and associations to mobilize and politicize hundreds of thousands of Kurds. In these sites—in funeral houses and public parks, for example—members of seemingly incompatible identity clusters were able to find common ground in Kurdish identity.

Recent research signals the crucial role of urban analysis in examining identity politics and political mobilization.[30] Urban analysis illuminates the Kurdish mobilization in Diyarbakır both from above, through the urban practices of a sequence of pro-Kurdish political parties and their controversial relationships with the state, and from below, as experienced and enacted in the quotidian life of the city among diverse segments of society.

Toward an Alternative Urban Analysis of Political Mobilization

This book expands on current discussions in urban theory focused on the contested spaces of the Global South. Over the past few decades, scholars have looked at spaces of inequality through the lens of urban despair and deprivation, under the broad frameworks of capitalism and neoliberalism.[31] Other scholars—among them Victoria Watson, Faranak Miraftab, Ananya Roy, and Oren Yiftachel—have stressed urban theory's disregard for the relationships between power, design, and politics beyond these frameworks. In response, they have called for a "Southern Perspective," resorting to "cities of the Global South" to develop a planning theory for inclusive and just urban societies.[32] These views from the southern perspective highlight diverse structural logics of urbanization, which include but are not limited to struggles for human and urban rights, identity regimes, and racial conflicts. Taking up this call, this book explicates new forms of urban regimes that promote and seek to create opportunities for opposition and political struggle.

To date, urban scholars have either theorized the planning of urban space as a domain of state power, or they have taken the state mostly out of the formula and focused on the role of "nongovernmental actors."[33] Relevant as these positions are, we must consider whether such exclusive categorizations preclude the elucidation of underlying mechanisms of urban space such as the interplay among the state, civil society, and organized political factions. In debates about the future of statehood, theorists have questioned state-centered models of political space as the basis for national identity and have begun to develop new understandings of the politics of space.[34] While effective in examining the structure of the state and its institutions, state-centered understandings remain inadequate to explain diverse political mechanisms and reciprocal sociopolitical practices. In particular, they fall short when it comes to explaining the everyday dimensions of political space. Most critiques of state-centered theory are devoted to rejecting its tendency to treat the state as an isolated unit of analysis—an organic, fixed entity and a cohesive actor driving society. Thus, they argue against views of state and society as free-standing objects or domains.[35] In understanding major political and social transformation, such scholarship has instead focused on the reciprocal relations between state and society. In general, the critiques of state-centered approaches have offered new theoretical directions integrating the political practices of state and society, in which "the line separating the state from society is not given, but can be redetermined in different political contexts."[36] As political theorists have come to see these diverse groups as increasingly intertwined, a conceptual overreliance on the divide between "nongovernmental" actors and "the state" cannot fully capture the complex dynamics shaping the twenty-first-century city.[37]

This book takes a capacious and exploratory approach to explicating how political society (the state, political parties, municipalities, and governors) and civil society (informal networks, women's groups, and cultural and religious associations) align, interact, and confront or evade one another in urban space. In this sense, I want to move beyond the premise that the built environment is merely the finished product of a political trend or a reflection of the broader culture. I examine the unstable nexus among state, political parties, and society in the city. Rather than merely seeing urban space as a manifestation of established conditions of power, I show how fluid conditions of control over urban space—through constantly shifting planning schemes and power relations, land speculations, informal housing practices, and appropriations of public space—allow a variety of actors to contour new political fields and national identification in the city.

The pro-Kurdish party in Turkey embodies characteristics of both a social movement and a political organization. By analyzing the transformation of a popular left-wing guerrilla movement into an urban-based nationalist mobilization effort and the relationship of this change to the political order as well as to civil society, I demonstrate how the rise of Kurdish nationhood was not simply the result of a top-down intervention (as a Weberian might think) but an outcome of an articulation of urban politics interwoven across various institutions and civil and political society actors.

In this sense, Diyarbakır is ideal for scholarly analysis of political mobilization and identity struggles in a highly contested city. But here Diyarbakır is not set forth as a unique case but rather as an example of power struggles, identity conflicts, and urban mobilizations occurring in several other cities across the globe.[38] I study how political identifications may be re-created in a variety of urban settings—among sidewalk squatters, in the shadow of a memorial in a public park, in the tight quarters of a women's laundry house, in migrant vocational courses, amid informal debates at luxurious shopping malls, and through the investments of urban real estate developers. I demonstrate how conditions of conflict may be characterized not only by dispute and disillusionment but also by contradiction and creativity.

An Ethnography of Urban Maneuvering

My methodology in this study can be best understood as an ethnography of urban maneuvering in which I trace and document strategies of urban planning the pro-Kurdish municipalities develop, especially when exposed to bureaucratic and urban coercion. I investigate how control of urban space and urban practices may enhance political mobilization and movements for social change. In preparing this book, I conducted more than twenty-eight months of fieldwork in Diyarbakır, between 2007 and 2023. This work entailed spatial analysis and in-depth ethnographic work as well as over 150 open-ended and semi-structured interviews in Diyarbakır with mayors, governors, parliament members, community leaders, religious leaders, urban planners, architects, and activists, as well as ordinary city residents from diverse political and class backgrounds. When I could not record my interviews, I immediately jotted field notes at the end of the day. Then, when I returned to Istanbul or to the US, I transcribed and expanded these observations into complete field notes. To understand the level of political articulation in the city—and the ways in which people unite, mobilize, or oppose—I socialized, circulated, and interviewed residents from diverse backgrounds with distinct and opposite political views.

Throughout the ethnographic phase of this project, I adopted an extended case method rather than a large-N study. The extended case method, according to Michael Burawoy, is based on observing how the same norms and rules are employed differently over time and in different situations, extending from the micro to the macro.[39] The extended case method enables the researcher to extract the general from the unique and to connect the present to the past in anticipation of the future, all by building on preexisting theory.[40]

In this light, rather than simply reporting or identifying social and political practices, the extended case method allowed me to link my findings to the existing theoretical discussions as well as to critically examine received political and intellectual discourses. Hence, the logic of focusing on Diyarbakır is not to tell a representative story about the practices of nationalist mobilization or of a large Kurdish population in the city but rather to engage in theoretical discussions to contextualize and understand urban maneuvering in the face of political violence. In this sense, Diyarbakır, which has long been prominent in Kurdish politics and has acted as the center of Kurdish mobilization, is informative because of its significant role as a model in determining the discourse of Kurdish articulation in Turkey.

For this effort, I collected material through participant observation at the municipalities, the local headquarters of political parties (the BDP, HDP, and AKP), electoral campaigns, coffeehouses, associations, cultural centers, NGOs, rallies, workshops, festivals, homes, street protests, demonstrations, and daily activities of ordinary people of Diyarbakır, including social and funeral gatherings. The materials addressed local politics, diverse forms of nationhood practices in the city, and interactions between politicians, activists, and ordinary people. This gathering of material enabled me to examine the development of nationness in the city, the organization (and workings) of the networks between political party members, activists, and the citizens of Diyarbakır, and the experience of nationhood from both above and below.

The examination of informal and formal network organizations—from the small scale of the streets, neighborhoods, and districts to the large scale in the city—has been crucial for building my analysis on the articulative role of the pro-Kurdish party in Diyarbakır. This information led to specification of how the pro-Kurdish party channels the activities of NGOs and ordinary citizens, sets the vocabulary of national attachments, and organizes social interaction—and in turn, how people and organizations behave with commonsense knowledge and national attachments.[41]

Almost each time I visited the city, I stayed with different acquaintances at different neighborhoods during my fieldwork. I stayed with an urban planner in Ofis, then in turns with a human rights activist, a pious widow with four children, and an architect who works on restoration and renovation, all in Kayapınar. I stayed with two migrant families, one in Sur and the other in Peyas. At different times, especially during winter and early spring, I stayed at the guesthouse of the State Hydraulic Works at Yenişehir, and at a hotel in Sur (especially during fairs and festivals, to observe the participants coming from outside the city). Living among individuals from diverse backgrounds allowed me to observe how different constituents of society engaged with politics, particularly how they perceived the urban projects and actions of the pro-Kurdish municipality in comparison to the actions of the central government. In subsequent years I revisited these various families and individuals and observed the changes in people's daily lives and their changing relationships with the pro-Kurdish party as well as with the state.

I participated in the daily life of Diyarbakırians through ordinary conversations and interactions, by observing and taking part in activities including dropping and picking up children from school, cooking, grocery shopping, attending social gatherings, eating out, going to festivals and protests, witnessing momentous reactions to political news—all the while recording data in field notes. I frequently approached people through snowball sampling, whereby initial contacts generated new ones, which allowed me to capture changes both profound and subtle in society, alliances, conflicts, and public networks in the city. Open-ended interviews lasted between one and five hours. Over plates of food and glasses of tea and on road trips, I learned about distinct individuals' sense of Kurdishness.

Almost every day there was an event or an organized activity happening in the city. Several times during my fieldwork political events unfolded so fast I would find myself running from one demonstration to another, from one meeting to another. Because my methodological priority—the ethnography of urban maneuvering—was to understand the ways in which the party creates urban strategies in the face of atrocity, instead of following my own schedule I moved in response to the schedule of events and demonstrations. I attended urgent party meetings and municipal gatherings, urban and political debates, and closely observed the ways in which the party and the municipality make decisions, how they organize or network in the city in the face of crises, and especially how events (e.g., a protest or a demonstration) are orchestrated from beginning to end.

In this project, rather than taking nationalism and urban space as fixed categories of analysis, where nationalism is simply imagined, taught, and learned in the city, I bring them into conversation so that reciprocal interactions between nationalisms and urban space do not simply reproduce the relations between them but incrementally transform both actors and relations and shift the political fields. Therefore, I combined participant observation with spatial analysis at sites and events such as electoral campaigns, memorials, festivals, public demonstrations, and informal settlements, to examine how the built environment produces new ways of conducting political mobilization and nationhood. My ethnographic fieldwork in Diyarbakır covered a time of deep conflict between the Turkish state and the Kurdish movement, one in which the city underwent dramatic physical, political, and social transformation. For comparative purposes, in following the fluctuating conditions of politics and democracy in Turkey, I repeated my interviews with several of my local informants, revisited the same sites, and documented changes in the built environment with over one thousand photographs. If my visit was during summer, I would photograph either very early in the morning around six or seven o'clock or late in the afternoon at four or five, to escape from the scorching heat.

Although this methodological approach was developed largely around participant observation and spatial analysis, contextualizing the Kurdish national movement required historical analysis. Accordingly, I incorporated analysis of a wide variety of primary and secondary documents in my research. Source materials include the annual municipality reports, newspapers, party conferences, maps, urban workshop booklets, and land registry records; constitutional law documents regarding local administration, mapping, and city planning projects; official correspondence between local administrations and the central government in Ankara; excerpts from the Turkish Grand National Assembly's debates; and political party programs, pamphlets, and elections. I accessed some of these materials at the National Library, the Presidential Archives in Ankara, the archives of newspapers and magazines published by both mainstream media and left-wing associations, the offices of the Human Rights Association, and the municipal archives in Diyarbakır.

Outline of the Book

Chapter 1, "Whose City?" elucidates the urban context for the ethnographic analysis to follow and situates the political and sociological importance of

Diyarbakır as a main site of political articulation and contestation. The chapter begins by outlining how the Kurdish movement developed historically amid multiple entanglements, including Turkish nationalist modern planning, land expropriations and mass expulsions, and waves of forced migration. Next, it outlines the early efforts of pro-Kurdish parties in Turkey—how they began to use mayoral politics and designed an alternative local governance in cities beginning as early as the 1970s. The chapter maps out the main urban actors and the organization of pro-Kurdish political society (e.g., political parties and municipal organizations) and the networks of Kurdish civil society (e.g., immigrants, merchants, and associations) in the city.

Chapter 2, "Building the Frontier," considers large-scale urban strategies that pro-Kurdish municipal administrations developed in the face of state coercion of housing in Diyarbakır. This chapter takes the reader from heated city council meetings in municipal halls to public-housing projects on the outskirts of the city, from international planning workshops on housing in municipal offices to the daily resistance in squatter settlements. By examining cases of urban renewal, urban informality, and public housing in Diyarbakır, the chapter demonstrates how the succession of pro-Kurdish parties, using strategic urban actions, creatively turned state coercion into opportunities to generate Kurdish collectivity and mobilization.

Chapter 3, "Seeing Like a Movement, Acting Like a State," discusses why and how the urban poor (mostly rural migrants) constituted such a vital ground for party politics. It also illustrates how urban informality provided a fluid backdrop for the pro-Kurdish party to design and implement programs against the established (state) order. This chapter argues that social networks and NGO programs founded by the municipality—while alleviating poverty—created strong ties between society and the pro-Kurdish party, making communities more accessible for popular support and political mobilization. It illustrates spaces of mobilization where the urban poor were politicized, transforming them into conscious Kurdish urban activists.

Where the previous chapter focuses on the urban poor and rural migrants, chapter 4, "Branding the City," turns to the pro-Kurdish party's ties to the urban upper middle class and rich Kurds. Drawing on fieldwork I conducted in real estate markets, visits to shopping malls and gated communities, and interviews with residents, real estate agents, developers, and urban planners, this chapter examines sites and spaces of bourgeois Kurdish civil society and demonstrates the ways that nationalism and neoliberalism came to mutually resonate in the city. The chapter further posits that networks of pro-Kurdish financiers (mostly former farmers and landowners), who collectively invested billions of dollars in large-scale urban projects, retooled the message of local urban governance, presenting Diyarbakır as a world-class city—the capital of a nascent Kurdistan.

Drawing on participant observations and spatial analysis of specific urban parks and memorial sites as well as interviews with mayors, sculptors, artists, activists, and citizens, chapter 5, "Sculpting Violence, Activating the Street," examines how pro-Kurdish municipal officials appropriated urban space—from the construction of public parks and memorials expressing state violence to the diverse forms of mass demonstrations linked to these sites. Diyarbakır's memorial landscape represents the ongoing struggle for an autonomous Kurdistan. As individual memorials have taken shape on the ground, they have become entwined in the complex realities of political conflict. The chapter studies how appropriations of public space provided an extra-parliamentary channel for disseminating political messages to the rest of the country, mobilized Kurdish society, and established the collective experience of the Kurdish nation.

Where previous chapters demonstrate how urban planning may enhance political articulation for social change, chapter 6, "Dismantling the Kurdish Landscape," shows why—and under what conditions—planning may fail to produce the intended social change. The chapter analyzes the Turkish state's unprecedented urban intervention in the wake of the 2015 armed conflict between the Turkish army and the Kurdish guerrillas in Diyarbakır. Drawing on participant observation, interviews, and spatial analysis, the chapter demonstrates how Turkish state officials deployed a pedagogy of urban development and municipal service premised on the idea of Islamic progress, to disarticulate the Kurdish bloc in Diyarbakır. The chapter is divided into two sections. The first section depicts the simultaneous "destruction" of the built environment, including Kurdish-themed public parks and memorials, and the strategic reconstruction of the city (including new avenues, mosques, and Islamic cultural centers), as part of a campaign to subjugate Kurdish citizens to state power. The second section analyzes the adaptive urban strategies developed by the pro-Kurdish party in the face of new forms of state coercion, examining why the state's spatial interventions may fail to disarticulate the Kurdish bloc in Diyarbakır.

In the concluding chapter, I position evidence from the preceding chapters to summarize my main claims and suggest directions for future research on architecture and urbanism. The Kurdish case may thus open new avenues for rethinking three main issues in urban theory: the slippery slope of party, state, and society relations (rather than the fixed lenses of state or nongovernmental actors) in the city; the shifting relations between local governance and social change; and the creative capacity of planning to shape politics (as an innovative resource to mobilize society, articulate political identity, and endure forces of coercion)—as opposed to politics merely shaping urban space.

1

WHOSE CITY?

In the late nineteenth century, the prominent Ottoman poet, historian, and governor (*mutasarrıf*) Said Paşa Diyarbekirli (from Diyarbakır) was commissioned to write a book on the history of Diyarbakır.[1] In 1884, Said Paşa began his book, *Diyarbekir Vilayetinin Tarihçesi* (The history of Diyarbekir Province), with the following words: "The land of Diyarbekir, to the north of *el-cezire*, found in between two rivers [the Euphrates and Tigris], is located at the western part of the Kurdistan region.... Diyarbekir is sited at the beginning of Kurdistan."[2] Testifying that Diyarbakır is part of Kurdistan, Said Paşa's book narrates the history of the city and its people—Kurds, Armenians, Jews, Chaldeans—from the ancient times up to the Ottoman period. "It is because this land is so fertile and the surrounding mountains of Kurdistan are full with gold and silver mines," writes Said Paşa, "that Diyarbekir was invaded several times."[3]

Only half a century after Said Paşa's book, in 1936, Bedri Günkut described Diyarbakır in a narrative that ran counter to Said Paşa's testimony. At the time, Günkut was one of several authors and bureaucrats commissioned by the new Turkish Republic to rewrite the history of Diyarbakır as a Turkish city. Unlike Said Paşa's account, Günkut's book, *Diyarbekir Tarihi* (History of Diyarbekir), portrays Diyarbakır as an ancient Turkish city. Günkut proclaims, "Whoever says 'I am Kurd' is a nationless [*milliyetsiz*] man who has lost his dignity.... Each traitor should know that the earth of Diyarbakır, every molecule of which came into being from the genuine flesh and bone of Turks, and their soil, which was watered by the very clean blood of Turks, will always remain Turkish just like all other cities of the Turks." Published by

Diyarbekir People's House Press, a press newly founded by the republic, the book argues that Kurds are non-real, a made-up race derived from Turks. As such, the Kurdish language consists of "a perverted version of Turkish under the influence of Iranian today [and those] who are called Kurdish men are the persons who speak with this perverted language."[4] What is more, Günkut emphasizes that "[Kurds] are a collection of deteriorated people from Turks after the invasion of Medes."[5] Günkut proceeds to examine the "accounts about the foundation of this city" and, after dismissing each theory, concludes that Diyarbekir was founded by the Turks from Hittite armies that migrated west from Central Asia even before the 2000s BCE, though the city was invaded by Persian, Romans, and Assyrians several times. He contends that during the period of these invasions, the city never lost its Turkishness or its "national existence" (*milli varlık*) and always remained Turkish.[6] Furthermore, referring to the Kurdish rebellions between 1925 and 1930, Günkut claims, "We can interpret the ends of the Sheikh Said and Ağrı Dağı rebellions as proof that the city will remain Turkish thereafter."[7]

The radical distinction between these two narrations of Diyarbakır marks Turkey's major transition from a pluralistic empire to a unitary nation-state. The difference spells an intense process of Turkification. Indeed, the ideological and cultural foundation of this republican project was Turkish nationalism.[8] The official formulation of this nationalism demanded the assimilation of other ethnic minorities in order to transform a multiethnic, multicultural society into a uniform Turkish society. According to this logic, both the history of Kurds and the history of Diyarbakır were rewritten. The young republic's bureaucrats competed with one another to prove that Diyarbakır was a Turkish city. In fact, Günkut's book was not the only one imposing republican ideology on the city. One of the first comprehensive books on Diyarbakır was the three-volume *Diyarbekir*, authored by the government inspector Basri Konyar. Like Günkut's approach, Konyar's book stresses Diyarbakır as "the large, pervasive, brave land of the Turk," as opposed to "any type of propaganda and distortion of history" suggesting otherwise.[9] These narrations of the city advanced a serious claim: the new republican ideology would not only deny the cultural and political rights of Kurds in Turkey but also, on occasion, go so far as to deny the very existence of Kurds.

Through the years, the Turkish government's position with regard to the Kurdish people—the country's largest minority—has become more sophisticated. But the bedrock assumption that the state cannot abide a separate Kurdish identity within its borders remains largely unchanged. However, Diyarbakır did not "remain" a Turkish city, as Günkut and other republican officials proclaimed; on the contrary, as this book demonstrates, the city and its citizens became even more Kurdified, and Diyarbakır became a central hub for the Kurdish movement.

This chapter aims to set the political context for the chapters to follow. It begins by outlining the processes of Turkification starting in the early decades of the republic. It focuses on institutional and territorial aspects of Turkification efforts in Diyarbakır, then turns to how the Kurdish movement developed historically amid multiple entanglements—including Turkish nationalist modern planning, mass expulsions, waves of forced migration, and urbanization.

Making the Land of a Turk

In Turkey, the end of World War I marked the end of the Ottoman Empire. The year 1923 saw the establishment of the new republic, whose founders strove to make a radical break from the past Ottoman state. Indeed, officials embarked on a project akin to what James Scott calls "authoritarian high-modernism," in which "the builders of the modern nation-state do not merely describe, observe, and map; they strive to shape a people and landscape that will fit their techniques of observation."[10] Establishing the modern Turkish state required assimilating minorities and homogenizing the nation.[11] The republic was founded as a secular modern nation-state within a centralized state power aspiring to a uniform modern Turkish national identity—a model that cast "nations as entirely modern constructions of nationalism."[12] This understanding of Turkishness brought dramatic changes to state and society relationships as well as to citizens' everyday lives. For instance, in December 1925, immediately following the Kurdish rebellions, the Ministry of Education issued a decree banning the use of terms such as "Kurd," "Circassian," and "Laz," "Kurdistan" and "Lazistan."[13] By the 1930s, Turkish newspapers had even begun to replace the word "Kurd" with the term "Mountain Turk."[14]

With this conception of the sovereign nation-state, the power of sovereignty became construed as resting with the nation, while representations of national identity became embedded in that territory.[15] Establishing territorial and spatial power over its homogenized people was one of the state's crucial practices. The territorial and spatial assimilation of Kurds included expulsion, displacement, and resettlement (settling non-Kurds in Kurdish regions), land reform, creating new consolidated villages, changing village names to Turkish names, inscribing signs and symbols of the Turkish nation, and later devising a village guard system.[16] Often the early republican historians ignored the artistic, urban, and architectural culture of past Kurdish dynasties (like Marwanids) and typically credited existing monuments to Turkic dynasties.[17]

As it was critical to eradicate from everyday life any culture or entity that did not represent "Turkishness," local publications and organizations played a great part in enacting the strategies of nationalism that followed Kemalist doctrine. Kemalism, as implemented by Mustafa Kemal Atatürk, exerted control over the public sphere, seeking to suppress alternative ideologies and political dissent, thereby advocating for a standardized Turkish citizenship. Kemalist doctrine, framed through "six arrows," enshrined the bases for the new republic and was constituted from six principles: republicanism, nationalism, populism, statism, secularism, and reformism. In September 1932, the local newspaper, *Diyarbekir*, published Atatürk's address to the citizens:

> Those from Diyarbakır, Van, Erzurum, Istanbul, Thrace, and Macedonia are the children of the same race, the veins of the same one. I am from a heroic Turkish quarter, but sadly this land is called the land of "bekir" [Bekir Diyari].[18] However, we know what our land is. Our land is the refined mansion of Oğuz Turk, and we are the children of this high mansion.... Since we landed here, we tried to explain what we are. And we keep explaining that: the hand of a Turk is great and he is the only greatness on earth. The Turk is the ubiquitous. The face of a Turk shines everywhere.[19]

Atatürk's words reflect the republican ideology—holding claim over both the people and the territory in which they live. This statement not only dispenses with the disparate identities in Turkey but also decrees that Turks are the only owners of the city. The first claim abolishes all notions of diversity, casting the people as "children of the same race, the veins of the same one," and brazenly absorbing non-Turkish elements into Turkish culture. The latter claim asserts ownership of the land by "redefining the roots of the land of Diyarbekir" as Turkish. Together, these claims bind national unity and territorial unity, a benchmark of the nation-state modeled in Turkey.

Certainly, republican efforts to Turkify the Kurdish cities were not limited to publications. This campaign included substantial institutional, territorial, and spatial efforts to mold cities and peoples. Through architecture, culture, and education, the new ideology produced in Ankara would be disseminated with stunning speed to local governments.[20] "Western" architects and urban planners—or those trained in Europe—created new modern planning schemes. New national cities and modern urban life across the country were presented as the physical amalgamation of the new nation.[21] As Berna Turam discusses, the formula of modern Turkish national identity underscored the equation that modernity, civilization, and Westernism were one and the same.[22] Because making modern cities with Western planning models was at the center of forging a new Turkish identity, the modernization of eastern cities in which Kurds were the majority was an explicit part of this aggressive integration project. In this context, Diyarbakır was given top priority.

Diyarbakır's spatial layout manifests this political transformation. Until the early twentieth century, Diyarbakır had been constituted from the historical inner city, Sur (meaning "defensive walls"), bordered by the Tigris, with the Karacadağ Mountains in the distance (figure 3).

For the republicans, Diyarbakır (at the time coextensive with Sur) was an old, cramped city.[23] It represented not only the Kurdish past but also the Ottoman past—and therefore did not qualify as a republican town. In republican eyes, Diyarbakır was a city with "no order in its layout" and represented the "backward" East, always in a medieval state and dominated by the mentality of a "dark era," an Ottoman era.[24] The ideals of high modernism fit with the new republic's Turkification project to civilize and sanitize its backward cities through ambitious authoritarian features.[25] Given these aims, Sur could not represent the new modern republic. Sur, as a grimy, noisy, hazardous city, needed to be modernized—so much so that, in the early 1930s, first the new governor of the republican city demolished a section of the historic city walls on the basis that "the city could not breathe."[26] A second intervention was to open two parallel ring roads within the city walls to facilitate military control. Beyond these direct modifications to Sur, republicans focused on building a new city outside the city walls. Akin to a colonial approach to urban planning in North Africa, the new republic ignored the old city. Right outside Sur, the republic created its own destination called Yenişehir (literally, "New City"). During the planning phase, the governorship depicted the new city as follows: "Next to the Diyarbekir city, between the Mountain Gate and Train station, we will establish a modern city, with all its daily necessities. The entire area allocated for the new city will be taken over by the municipality; after parcels for government buildings and the public space are distributed, the other parts will be sold to the people at a very cheap price and the blueprint will be launched."[27] Hence, the new republic required a new city (Yenişehir); exclusion of the old city from the planning processes was predictable. The initial destruction of a section of the wall opened the connection to the new city. The connection was marked with a boulevard that cuts right through the middle of Sur, Gazi (Veteran) Street, a name commonly attributed to Atatürk. Government officials designated Yenişehir as the new institutional core of the city, where new buildings represented the "modern nation." A little farther away from Yenişehir was a train station that would connect the developing center to the rest of the country. The new nation-state erected its major institutions, one after another: the Government House, with an adjacent memorial park for state ceremonies,

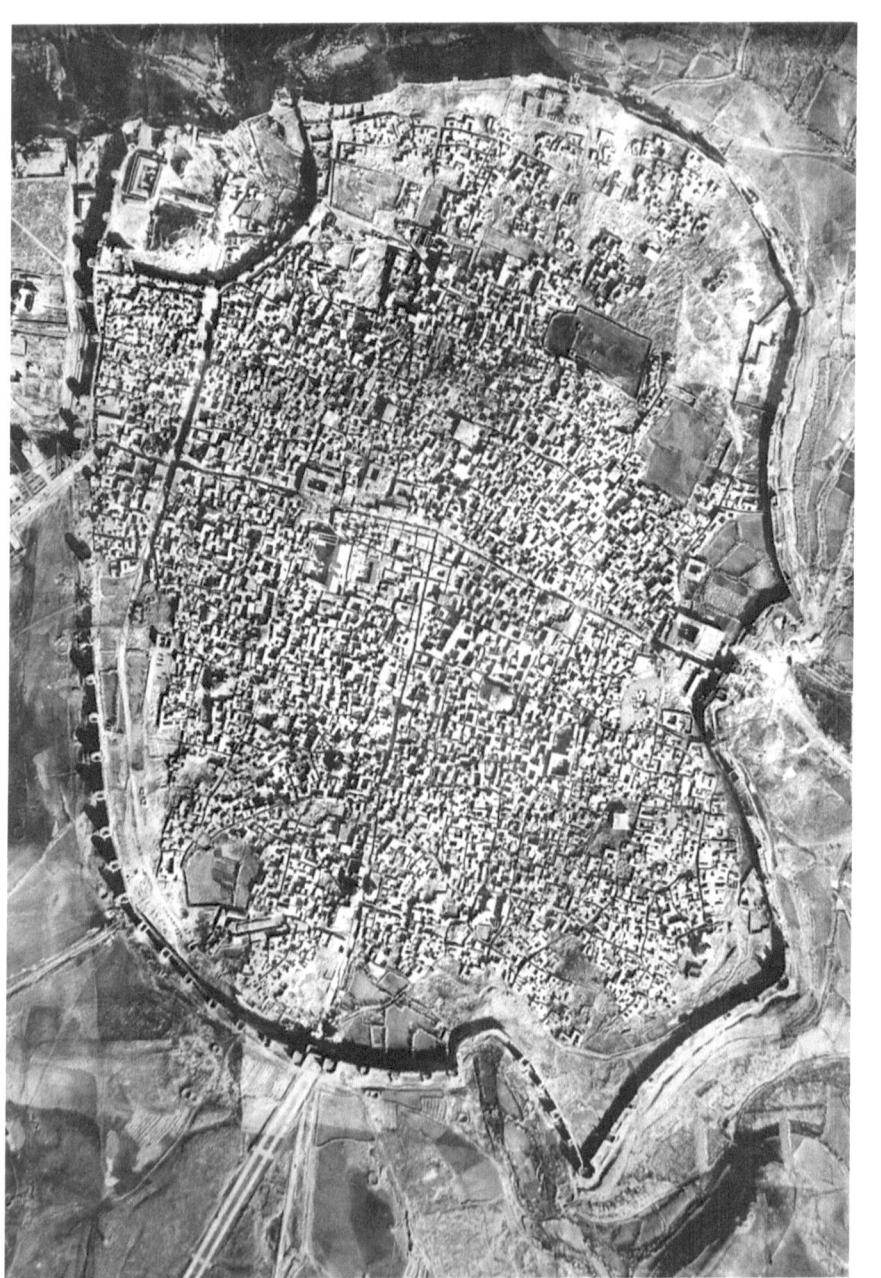

FIGURE 3. Aerial view of Diyarbakır in the 1930s.
Source: Diyarbakır Sur Municipality Planning Office.

followed by the courthouse, and the army and gendarme headquarters, the offices of the First Regional Inspectorate General, and the People's House on the other side of the main road—all representing the new and young republic. This arrangement conspicuously displayed military and bureaucratic buildings side by side.

In fact, this urban planning pattern later became a cookie cutter for a number of Anatolian cities in Turkey. As architectural historian Zeynep Kezer notes, the use of a recurring repertoire of urban design—the application of almost identical design elements—to create new Turkish cities with a uniform character was central to the spatial strategy of the Republican People's Party (CHP) for national integration.[28] For example, in such cities, the name of the main street would frequently hint at either the republic or Atatürk, such as "Gazi Caddesi" or "Mustafa Kemal Caddesi." The main street would usually open onto a main square featuring a statute of Atatürk in the middle. At the head of the square sat a line of governmental buildings—diverse institutions that formed an administrative center created for demographic engineering purposes.[29]

The institutional, territorial, and spatial practices of the new republic all contributed to nation building by enlisting both the imagination of people and the city they shared. The People's Houses exemplify this agenda. The systemic construction of new institutions such as People's Houses in city centers was a vital tool in the production of "ideal," model Turkish citizens.[30]

The Institutionalization of Turkishness: People's Houses

In 1937, during a larger tour in eastern Turkey, Atatürk visited Diyarbakır. In his brief stay, he mostly focused on the new urban developments at Yenişehir, except for a quick trip out to the Urfa Gate and two mansions on the outskirts of the old city. Atatürk addressed Kurdish citizens as follows: "My Diyarbakır fellow citizens: After twenty years I am in Diyarbakır again.[31] Inside the most beautiful and the most modern building of the world, listening to modern, excellent music. . . .[32] In the presence of civilized people of humankind, of course you recognize how great the pleasure and happiness that I feel inside this people's house. I am happy to register this."[33] In his speech at the Diyarbakır's People's House, Atatürk's words marked, once again, how being modern, civilized, and Western were one and the same: an absolute norm that a modernizing country was compelled to adopt.[34] The building Atatürk depicts as "the most beautiful and the most modern building of the world" was the newly constructed Diyarbakır Halkevi (Diyarbakır People's House), founded by the Republican

People's Party. The "excellent music," which was in fact the "Western music," playing in the house was performed by the orchestra of the People's House. Later, in 1937, the People's House moved to a new building designed by Arif Hikmet Holtay, an architect from Diyarbakır who completed his architectural education at the Stuttgart Technical College in Germany. Architects of the new republic described their work as follows: "When we talk about national architecture, there should not be any arches, domes, mosques and caravansaries."[35] Reflecting this view, new buildings embodied a modern architectural style—with the materials concrete, steel, and glass, and the emphasis on geometric transparency, especially at the façades with round and rectangular windows (figure 4). Like several examples of its period, these constructions were bold statements about national pride, progress, and, of course, "being modern." The interior design displayed extensive republican iconography: flags with the CHP emblem of six arrows, Atatürk statues, and inscriptions of Atatürk's words.

For the founders of the republic, pushing this narrative of a secular, Western, modern "nation-state" was especially important. These concrete modern symbols had national resonance in Diyarbakır—the same city in which the rebels of the Sheikh Said Rebellion, one of the most significant Kurdish rebellions of the republican era, were executed by hanging some twelve years previously, in 1925. The new People's House was located a few meters from Dağkapı Square, facing the area where Sheikh Said and his friends were executed. This same square

FIGURE 4. Diyarbakır People's House in the early twentieth century.
Source: Postcard, author's collection.

later featured a large Atatürk sculpture, augmenting the republican presence and display.

In fact, People's Houses were directly founded by, and connected to, the Republican People's Party. Active hubs from the capital to the farthest towns of the country, they were crucial to the modernization and nationalization project. Inspired by Italian Fascist youth clubs and "Dopolavoro" (after-work) recreational centers, the People's Houses were designed for the party's exercise of political power and to propagate the nationalist consciousness and ideals of the Kemalist revolution.[36] The Diyarbakır People's House was one of the first People's Houses among fourteen others founded.[37] It was administered as a unique tool of the republic, serving to connect with, and then Turkify, local Kurdish populations. Every year, the People's House would organize "pure Turkish language competitions" among the peasants in the surrounding districts with "an aim to correct" the tongue and dialect of Diyarbakır peasants and to deliver a "homeland education with pure Turkish."[38]

Each People's House was organized into nine divisions, including diverse social and cultural activities: language literature and history, art, performance, sports, social work, vocational training, library (publications, museum) exhibitions, and village work aimed for adult education. Through these activities, citizens of the new republic were encouraged to engage in modern and Western practices, while simultaneously nurturing a Turkish nationalist consciousness.

The People's House of Diyarbakır, however, was unable to galvanize the locals. Just a couple of years after its founding, the public lost interest in the republican ideology it promoted.[39] Soon, state officials began to criticize the institution, claiming that it was not fulfilling the original objectives of the People's Houses. İsmet İnönü, the second president of Turkey, officially complained that the Diyarbakır People's House was losing sight of its mission.[40] Later, during the rise of Turkey's Democratic Party (DP) in the 1950s, one of the first decrees of the party was to close down the People's Houses as well as other similar institutions. Following this decree, in 1952, the Diyarbakır People's House was shuttered, and the building reopened as a movie theater called "Yenişehir Sineması" (New City cinema). For many years, the theater operated as a family business, until it was demolished in 1994.[41]

The republican plan to sanitize and regularize the city was short-lived. In the span of fifteen years, Yenişehir had begun to take new shape in response to the arrival of peasants who brought their own lifestyles with them. Belying the model republican project, these new, cheap residences initially intended for the working middle class were occupied by freshly arrived rural-to-urban migrants.[42] Visions of a regimented and systematized modern Diyarbakır evaporated amid crowded vegetable bazaars, open meat markets, horse races, and char-grill picnics in public space, welcoming the early arrival of postmodern lifestyles.

Categorizing the "Nation"

During the early years of the republic, in tandem with planning a modern Turkish city, categorizing and mixing diverse ethnicities through strict settlement and resettlement practices served the interest of Turkifying the Kurdish-populated regions. Surprisingly, during this process, while public statements denied the existence of Kurds, internal bureaucratic communications were acknowledging the Kurdish identity and prioritizing an effort to mix them with other populations. After the Kurdish rebellions of 1925, the Grand National Assembly of Turkey, the Ministry of Internal Affairs, and the General Staff prepared reports on the "Kurdish question."[43] The first report, written by the deputy from the city of Çankırı, Abdülhalik Renda, emphasized the density of the Kurdish population to the east of the Euphrates River.[44] The report noted that the number of Kurds exceeded one million, many times more than the size of the Turkish population in the area. The report highlighted that unless the Turkish Republic took precautionary measures, the lands of the eastern Euphrates could be at risk of being lost.[45] In Diyarbakır, following the Sheikh Said Rebellion, the republican settlement policies in the mid-1920s and early 1930s resulted in the evacuation of villages and the exile (*sürgün*) of sheikhs, notable families, and intellectuals from the city. These people were sent to western cities like Izmir, Aydın, Manisa, and Bursa. Sur, once home to prominent families and their mansions, slowly turned into a ghost town. By the 1934 settlement law, the entire region—and particularly Diyarbakır—was reshuffled with the arrival of new Muslim Balkan migrants.[46]

The government's territorial interventions were not limited to resettlement practices. It created regional divisions that eradicated ethnic and cultural diversity across the country. By 1941, following the first Geographical Congress held in Ankara, the country was carved into seven regions and twenty-one sections. Neglecting the variety of cultural and ethnic entities, officials parted the regions along features of climate, flora, and landforms. Further, while the regions on the coast were named after the sea they faced, the rest of the country was called "Anatolia" (Anadolu), divided and named after its physical position with reference to the capital—East Anatolia Region, Southeast Anatolia Region, and so on. Following these divisions, people from these regions would be generally referred to as "Anatolian" regardless of their ethnic identities. In the same manner, cities across the country were promoted through association with different fruits, such as apricot for Malatya and apple for Amasya. For Diyarbakır, the government imposed the watermelon as its promotional symbol. Accordingly, the state later installed watermelon sculptures in different parts of the city, a project of semantic enforcement I return to in chapter 5. In addition to eradicating the distinctions between the myriad ethnicities living across the country, after the 1965 census the Turkish government outlawed altogether the publication of information about ethnicity and language use.

With these territorial, spatial, and institutional interventions, the state had officially dismissed ethnic differences and eschewed any recognition of Kurds as a diverse ethnic group with cultural and political relevance. Furthermore, particularly from the 1930s until the 1990s, the government avoided considering the "Kurdish issue" a political problem. Rather, it opted to conceptualize the issues associated with Kurds as rooted in the social and economic "backwardness" of the region. Even forty years after the foundation of the republic, the state's rejection of Kurdish identity had not changed. Following the 1960 coup d'état, the official book *Doğu İlleri ve Varto Tarihi* (Eastern provinces and the history of Varto), which became mandatory reading in high schools and universities, testifies to this point. The preface, written by Cemal Gürsel, the general and president of the military regime, reads, "This work once more proves that our citizens, those who live in East Anatolia, who imagine themselves non-Turkish just because they speak a language which doesn't resemble Turkish, and who we also once thought to be non-Turkish, are actually plain Turks. There is no such race called 'Kurd' on Earth. . . . Those who lost their way, Eastern Turks, should read this book carefully, it will enlighten them."[47] Since the beginning of the republic, Kurdish demands for recognition of their identity and cultural rights were systematically suppressed on the basis that such requests promoted separatism and contradicted the uniformity of Turkish national identity and the principle of indivisible unity of nation and state. Despite the broad range of institutional, military, territorial, and spatial efforts, however, the state was unable either to fully instill a homogenized Turkish identity or assimilate the Kurds.

The Question of the East

Since the early twentieth century, Kurdish tribes frequently contested the state's homogenization efforts through a series of revolts. Between 1920 and 1938, the young republic witnessed seventeen Kurdish rebellions. Three of them—1925 (Sheikh Said), 1930 (Ağrı), and 1937 (Dersim)—were suppressed by overwhelming state brutality and oppression, which cost thousands of people their lives.[48] After the suppression of these revolts, the period from the late 1930s to the 1960s is known as the "decades of silence."[49] Militarization and systematic depopulation and surveillance of Kurdish territories persisted through this period.[50] Following the coup d'état of 1960, the "decades of silence" ended when Kurdish unrest resumed. Multiple factors—from rural migration to the cities,

Kurdish engagement in leftist political parties, and the emergence of a Kurdish intelligentsia, to positioning Kurdish resistance within a secular and leftist framework—forged a collective movement that challenged tribal structures and state coercion simultaneously.

Beginning in the mid-1950s, the growing inequality between peasants and Kurdish landowners as well as the weakening of tribal ties within Kurdish society led to a significant shift in Kurdish mobilization. Outside of Turkey, the Barzani rebellion in Iraq (1961–1975) had a significant influence on Kurdish intelligentsia in Turkey.[51] During this period, a younger generation of Kurdish elites—led mostly by the intelligentsia, including authors and university students—seized control of the movement from traditional Kurdish leaders and engaged in new types of activism.[52] These Kurdish groups burgeoned as a segment of the rising leftist opposition in Turkey. The relatively liberal constitutional atmosphere that lasted between 1961 and 1980 also allowed Kurdish activism to play a role in bringing the concepts of Kurdish identity, national oppression, and national liberation into the public sphere. Since the beginning of the republic, it was forbidden to use the terms "Kurd," "Kurdish," or "Kurdistan." Even public pronunciation of the word "Kurd" could land someone in court. As a matter of common practice, especially in republican public discourse, the word "Eastern" was a coded way of saying Kurd. In 1979, Şerafettin Elçi, a prominent Kurdish politician, spoke Kurdish in an interview with a Turkish newspaper.[53] "What is the matter with this? There are Kurds in Turkey. I am a Kurd too," he said to Ülkü Arman in the interview for the *Hürriyet* newspaper. Following these remarks, state officials accused Şerafettin Elçi of "separatism."

In tandem with these social transformations, rural migration and urbanization brought the Eastern, or Kurdish, question into the public forum. In the 1950s and 1960s, more than one million people, particularly from Kurdish cities, migrated westward looking for work opportunities in cities such as Istanbul, Izmir, and Ankara. Kurds, for decades pushed to the eastern edge of the country, began to populate western cities—though mostly in informal jobs like construction worker or dishwasher at restaurants. The rise of squatter settlements in major cities occupied by rural migrants working in informal jobs led to new imbalances in the country. In the southeast, the population rose sharply as well. In particular, the population of Diyarbakır almost doubled from 1945 through 1965. The Kurdish author Mehmet Emin Bozarslan described this new urban condition: "Here are five ten-floor luxury apartment buildings in the 'new-city' neighborhoods of certain cities in the East and there are fancy cars wandering on asphalt roads. However, right beside [these neighborhoods] there are numerous shantytowns, their dwellers living in despair and misery."[54]

At the same time, living in urban space led most of the Kurdish population to break out of isolation and to mobilize further.[55] Kurds began to explicitly confront the state's official discourse and policies toward them. They forged their own repertoires of movement through diverse channels of activism and NGOs.[56] The proliferation of Kurdish political and cultural publications, magazines, and books accompanied this new type of activism.

In the following years—with the exchanges among the Kurdish intelligentsia, activists, and politicians—left-wing discourse on Kurdish rights and demands became part of a broader discussion on equality, democracy, and justice in Turkey. Some leftist parties provided a critical platform for Kurdish activists to articulate new demands for justice and equality, developing social and political networks along the way. Among the leftist political parties, perhaps the most important challenger party of the 1960s was the Workers' Party of Turkey (Türkiye İşçi Partisi, TİP).

TİP was the first socialist party in Turkey to gain parliamentary representation. In the national parliamentary elections of 1965, the party received 3.3 percent of the national vote, securing fifteen seats for its members in the Turkish Parliament. Among them, four representatives were from cities with primarily Kurdish populations: Diyarbakır, Kars, Malatya, and Urfa. Following this opportunity, the party made considerable efforts to open branches and organize activities in Diyarbakır. Efforts followed in the cities of Tunceli, Elazığ, Siirt, Bingöl, Muş, and Van.[57] TİP received significant support from members of the Kurdish intelligentsia—Musa Anter, Kemal Burkay, Naci Kutlay, and Mehdi Zana, who served at administrative levels—as well as from workers, peasants, small business owners, the urban poor, and students from the East of Turkey.

For Kurdish activists, the party became an umbrella organization. Activists harnessed TİP's promises of socioeconomic reform in the "East" and its approach to some of the Kurdish demands about justice and inequality. Drawing attention to both the sociological and economic problems of the region, the party's 1964 program included a statement that read, "The provinces of the East and South-East regions are seen as 'zones of deprivation' in the eyes of the majority of the citizens and civil servants. The public services in this region are almost nonexistent. Parallel to the region's economic backwardness is the backward social and cultural conditions faced by our citizens of this region. In particular, those of our citizens who speak Kurdish and Arabic, and those who belong to the Alevi mezhep denomination face discrimination."[58]

While the state pushed Kurds to the periphery, this emerging Kurdish movement placed Kurdistan at the center, pushing the state to its margins—which is why the "East" had a specific place in the territorial claims of Kurdish discourse. Questions of East and Eastern began to be articulated differently in Turkey as Kurdish activists and intelligentsia incorporated "the Kurdish identity" and the issue of "autonomy" into their discussion. The words of the Kurdish activist Ahmet Zeki Okçuoğlu epitomize the movement's territorial claims: "During our first years at the university, putting the map of Turkey in front of us, we would draw a map of Kurdistan, wondering how to delineate the lines of its borders. While discussing if we should include this or that part, considering if we needed a border to the sea, we would include Iskenderun. Further, we would even include Trabzon in order to extend north to the sea. [It was] as if we saw Turkey as an empty canvas."[59] As Zeynep Kaya argues, "Over the time the Kurdistan map became the core symbol of Kurdishness and came to represent a perceived reality in the minds of many Kurds and outsiders."[60] Following this shift, in 1967, a committee composed of Kurdish activists and politicians within the TİP and TKDP (Türkiye Kürdistanı Demokrat Partisi, or Kurdistan Democrat Party of Turkey) began to organize "Eastern Meetings."[61] Initially planned as "protest demonstrations against the backwardness of Eastern Anatolia," these meetings took place in cities throughout the East.[62] They constituted a historic moment in the Kurdish movement, as they mobilized a large number of Kurds in the streets, particularly in Diyarbakır, Silvan, Siverek, and Batman. The Eastern Meetings found a considerable amount of support from mass demonstrations, including labor strikes, sit-ins, and peasant riots in factories. From the end of the 1960s onward, the activism of the Kurdish movement intensified claims to Kurdish rights. The status of Kurds in Turkey began moving from a regional question to a national question.

Following the 1971 military coup, the Kurdish movement began to promote explicitly Kurdish rights, with the establishment of pro-Kurdish organizations. Rather than merely focus on the questions of underdevelopment or justice, the discourse of Kurdish activism began to address the national and cultural oppression of Kurds and started to split from the Turkish socialist movement. Peasants and the working class constituted the majority of the early supporters of the pro-Kurdish movement during this period. A foundational link between the "oppressed Kurdish nation" and the "oppressed classes" of Turkey bound these groups together.[63] The movement thereby posited Kurds' independence as a prerequisite to achieving a socialist society.[64]

While fostering the will to end feudal oppression and exploitation, this foundational link between the oppressed Kurdish nation and the oppressed classes also led to the development of a "revolutionary" strategy against the state. A discourse of national liberation emerged in pro-Kurdish groups. Among these organizations, the Kurdistan Workers' Party (Partîya Karkerên Kurdistanê, or PKK), a Kurdish armed guerrilla organization, has been one of the most influential in the Kurdish movement in Turkey.[65]

During the late 1970s, particularly in the aftermath of the 1980 coup d'état, the PKK took the lead in mobilizing the Kurdish masses and dominated the

Kurdish movement in Turkey.⁶⁶ The ideological formation of the PKK dates to 1974 in Ankara, when Abdullah Öcalan and his friends organized a group known as the "Kurdistan Revolutionaries" (Kürdistan Devrimcileri), which later transformed into the PKK.

Although the Kurdistan Revolutionaries movement was first organized around the student and activist circles of Ankara's urban environment, it quickly began to move toward the rural and urban Kurdish-populated regions in the southeast, which it referred to as "Turkish Kurdistan" and considered the center of the movement and the most appropriate area to start a political and armed struggle for revolutionary change in Turkey.⁶⁷

In PKK's 1978 manifesto, *Kürdistan devriminin yolu* (The roadmap of the Kurdistan revolution), authored by Abdullah Öcalan, the group identified the movement as revolutionary, anti-imperialist, and national-democratic.⁶⁸ Its goal was a broader social and economic emancipation to be achieved by the proletariat fighting all means of exploitation.⁶⁹ According to this manifesto, the creation of an "independent and democratic Kurdistan" would be based on principles that would eliminate all feudal structure and colonial forces in Kurdistan.⁷⁰ In defining the features of this revolutionary roadmap, Öcalan equated this purging process to a "national liberation struggle" in which patriotic youth–intelligentsia groups would play the most crucial roles.⁷¹ By 1984, the PKK was engaged in a guerrilla war against the state.

Initially, having a presence in the region provided the PKK an opportunity to reach out to rural populations and gain support. However, beginning as early as the 1990s, the peasant base—a source of essential support for the PKK—began to erode through village evacuations, ongoing internal displacement, and new migrations from rural to urban areas that intensified after 1980.⁷²

These changes did not necessarily weaken the movement, but they did draw new trajectories. By the early 1990s, while the PKK's guerrilla insurgency grew in strength and size, the PKK's influence started to reach a wider scope of supporters and sympathizers from different parts of Kurdistan as well as from Kurdish communities in Europe. Mass demonstrations and protests—later dubbed as *serhildan* by Kurdish activists—garnered the participation of thousands of Kurds in Diyarbakır and other Kurdish cities. The demonstrations attested to the ample support the Kurdish national movement had earned among local populations.⁷³ Under these circumstances and following a dramatic escalation in the PKK-Turkish military conflict, by the 1990s many more Kurds were obliged to flee their homes. They fled primarily to urban centers like Adana, Diyarbakır, Istanbul, and Mersin, where they sought shelter in chaotic urban shantytowns. Urban residence in itself, while making Kurdishness more visible, politicized Kurdish society, leading to new political landscapes not only in the southeastern region but across the country.

During this period, the Kurdish movement persisted through two interwoven streams. The first stream was the rise of pro-Kurdish politics and the participation of pro-Kurdish politicians in the electoral system.[74] The second was the growth and ideological and organizational change of the PKK. Both developments brought a drastic rise in pro-Kurdish civil society organizations and the mobilization of Kurdish society in urban space. For example, in 1992, for the first time in the republican period, the prime minister of Turkey, Süleyman Demirel, explicitly accepted the Kurdish situation in his address to the crowds in Diyarbakır.[75]

The capture of Abdullah Öcalan and his imprisonment at İmralı Island in 1999 led several scholars and political commentators to argue that the Kurdish national movement's political development would retreat, or that the PKK would dissolve.[76] But neither the destruction of the peasant base nor the imprisonment of Öcalan weakened the rise of Kurdish movement. Particularly in the post-1999 period, the movement managed to yield an even more powerful Kurdish public sphere in Turkey. One of the crucial changes was adopting a more "democratic" and "pluralist" vocabulary. Moreover, the PKK as a popular guerrilla movement survived while further proving itself as a crucial part of urban-based nationalist mobilization. Developments in the PKK went hand in hand with the foundation of pro-Kurdish political parties and their entry into local politics in Turkey. Öcalan's proposal of "democratic autonomy" in the post-1999 period was influential in shaping the Kurdish movement among activist circles in the cities. During the armed conflict between the PKK and the Turkish army, from the early 1990s, the foundation of pro-Kurdish parties and political participation began to form a critical institutional base.

The Pro-Kurdish Political Parties in Turkey and Electoral Participation

Pro-Kurdish parties were not simply founded as parties of Kurdish nationalism; rather, their political agenda always evolved from a dynamic political tendency. From time to time, this tendency overlapped with center-left politics. Throughout the decades, the political agenda of pro-Kurdish parties—initially associated with Marxist-Leninist proposals, and in the post-1999 period parallel to the change in the PKK—evolved into a more democratic pluralist framework. Very roughly, the 1970s "revolutionary" language of "national liberation struggle" against the state and feudal forces in Turkey shifted by the 1990s into a language of "democratic discourse." In so doing, this discourse sought to universalize Kurdish demands—Kurdish-language education, an end to all discriminatory laws in the constitution—into an encompassing language that addressed not only Kurds but all peoples in Turkey demanding more equality and democracy. It is possible to read this change in the creativity of the pro-Kurdish parties as appropriations of the period's popular frameworks, opportunities for new political discourses.[77] Nevertheless, the pro-Kurdish parties and their members have frequently encountered diverse coercive measures that have restricted their political participation in the system. Several times, parties were closed and their properties confiscated, while party members and activists were detained, arrested, or even shot.

In June 1990, the first legally recognized Kurdish political party in Turkey—the People's Labor Party (HEP)—was founded. Emphasizing the promotion of democracy, freedom, and human rights in Turkey, the party explicitly committed itself to the resolution of the Kurdish problem and the advancement of Kurdish rights. The majority of HEP supporters were Kurdish.[78] The foundation of the HEP was groundbreaking for the institutionalization of the Kurdish movement and the incorporation of Kurdish politics into the legal system. At first, the HEP was not granted representation in Parliament. Members of the party yet were able to participate in elections under the umbrella of the Social Democratic Populist Party (SHP). After changing its name to the Democracy Party (DEP), the HEP was closed down by the Turkish constitutional court in 1993. Thirteen of its deputies were imprisoned. In the years that followed, as each successive Kurdish party was outlawed by the Turkish constitutional court, a new party would succeed it. Right after the closure of the DEP in 1994, the People's Democracy Party (HADEP) was founded. HADEP was closed by the court in 2003; but in the interim the Democratic People's Party (DEHAP) had been founded in 1997 and was subsequently replaced by the Democratic Society Party (DTP) in 2005, only to be closed by a court order in 2009. Immediately before its closure, several members of the movement founded the Peace and Democracy Party (BDP). Many members of the DTP transferred to the BDP. The BDP provided the foundation for establishing a new party in 2012, the Peoples' Democratic Party (HDP). Importantly, although these parties–the HEP, DEP, HADEP, DEHAP, DTP, BDP, and HDP—showed some differences in their political agendas, they were not unique groups; in a context hostile to pro-Kurdish parties, each of them was initially founded as a substitute for its immediate predecessor. Despite legal interruptions, and if the leaders were not detained, oftentimes the same leadership would manage the new parties.

The HDP was established as an umbrella party, merging the DTP and smaller-scale parties such as the Revolutionary Workers' Party (Devrimci İşçi Partisi, DİP) and the Green Left Party (Yeşil Sol Parti, YSP). As the HDP officially represented itself as an organization where all segments of the society are represented equally, it became a party that would constitute a new beginning for all segments of society. Initially, while the HDP was emerging, the BDP actively continued its activities. The HDP remained almost like a reserve party, until BDP deputies resigned and became members of the HDP in 2014. In 2021, the Prosecutor's Office of the Supreme Court of Appeals filed a lawsuit demanding the closure of the HDP. By 2022, the pro-Kurdish party revived the YSP to run in the 2023 elections. Subsequently, in 2023, the YSP underwent a name change, rebranding itself as Peoples' Equality and Democracy Party (HEDEP) (see conclusion for further discussion). Initially, with the HDP, the pro-Kurdish movement began to express a more encompassing and inclusive approach for the diverse groups of people in Turkey. In 2013, during a press release, Gültan Kışanak, then cochair of the BDP (in prison after 2016), described the motives of the party with the following words: "Opportunities for self-administration will be created both locally and in the rest of the country. We are in front of the people with a brand-new electoral strategy, where we will bring together the democratic experiences of all Turkey, all its revolutionary forces, all the marginalized, the ignored; everyone who is oppressed and despised."[79] Thus, the party emphasized that it was not a party only for Kurds. It was a party for all who were marginalized, ignored, and treated unjustly. Over the years, while the pro-Kurdish parties adopted a more Kurdist agenda, they also emphasized the urgent need for a more democratic and just environment: sustainable economic development; state investment in health, education, and infrastructure; protection for unions; establishing new laws protecting women's rights in relation to their social and economic status; and LGBTQ rights.

Historically, even though pro-Kurdish parties were able to participate in elections, they were not able to gain seats in the Parliament because of the 10 percent national election threshold, an electoral reform law set in 1983 following the military coup. Parties that did not receive at least 10 percent of the vote could not hold seats in Parliament. The law incentivized coalitions within larger parties that could capture significant portions of the vote. During this time, some conservative pro-Kurdish politicians joined the right-wing ANAP (Motherland Party) and the RP (Welfare Party), while some left-leaning politicians joined the SHP. Because of the 10 percent threshold for parliamentary representation, no official pro-Kurdish party was represented in the Turkish Parliament between 1994 and 2007. To work around the 10 percent threshold restriction, pro-Kurdish parties often participated in elections with independent candidates, which required strong organizational work for the party. In the general elections of 2007 and 2011, for instance, members of the DTP ran as independent candidates and later established their own political bloc in Parliament. Even with the independent candidates, pro-Kurdish party representation in Parliament has always seen low numbers. Exceptionally, in the general elections of June 2015, the pro-Kurdish People's Democratic Party (HDP) achieved its strongest parliamentary representation in its history. Contesting as a party rather than fielding candidates as independents, the HDP surpassed the national threshold and gained 13 percent of the votes across the country, securing eighty seats in Parliament for its members. Despite interruptions to its parliamentary representation, the pro-Kurdish party kept gaining control in municipalities across the Kurdish-populated region. Beginning in 1999, the pro-Kurdish parties repeatedly won sweeping victories in local elections. In the absence of strong parliamentary participation, the question arises as to how the pro-Kurdish party has articulated Kurdish nationhood in Turkey. As this book demonstrates, local power—focused as it was on grassroots community-building toward networks of Kurdish activism and mobilization in the city—allowed the party more independent activity than national politics did.[80]

Toward a Coherent Bloc via Local Politics

Since the early twentieth century, despite serious military, institutional, and territorial efforts, the state was not able to create a modern Turkish republican town out of Diyarbakır. The assimilation and homogenizing processes that played out spatially in Diyarbakır began to erode by the 1960s and especially after 1999, when the pro-Kurdish parties began administering the city. While surviving military regimes and diverse forms of coercion, the Kurdish movement used urban politics to cultivate a sense of Kurdish nationalism that confronted the state's approach to security, violence, and identity. Local power allowed the pro-Kurdish party to prove that Diyarbakır is a Kurdish city. As Nicole Watts writes, "Access to the many different types of resources of local office allowed pro-Kurdish mayors to try to build a kind of 'as-if Kurdistan' that served to convey an impression of authority and to construct a new sociopolitical community."[81] Through this sense of Kurdish nationhood, the party conveyed an "impression of authority" and constructed "a new sociopolitical community."[82] Between 2007 and 2016, in my flights to and from Diyarbakır, many more passengers read pro-Kurdish newspapers and spoke Kurdish to each other than in earlier years. Although in the past speaking Kurdish was mostly practiced among rural migrants in the city, it was clearly becoming the language of choice for the urban elite of Diyarbakır. In cafés and restaurants and on airplanes, typical Westernized professional types in power suits and clean-shaven faces, and women in modern daily attire, spoke Kurdish.

In every successive visit over the span of just three years, in 2007, 2008, and 2009, for example, I encountered more Kurdish-speaking people in the city, and many more restaurants and coffeehouses displayed Kurdish names, decorating their walls with the colors of the Kurdistan flag. Displays featuring the Kurdish past increased in public squares; monuments, engravings, and drawings filled the streets;[83] while protests and street action emphasizing Kurdishness demonstrated more elaborate organization. Each time I returned to the city, I witnessed bolder claims about the existence of Kurdistan in Turkey, not only among the party members but also among ordinary people talking in the streets. During this period, the central government's response to these developments arrived swiftly. In 2009, Ankara introduced the "Democratic Initiative" project, providing limited freedom in public space, for a short period of time.[84] A key element in the achievements of pro-Kurdish parties was their adept utilization of urban resources, uniting various local elements such as youth and women's organizations, unions, political associations, traders, and business leaders within the urban landscape. By mobilizing NGOs, civil society groups, ordinary citizens, and political organizations, the party united different segments of society through a fresh narrative of Kurdish nationhood in the city. Through municipal administrations, the pro-Kurdish party was able to pull together different strands in civil society (such as schools, associations, neighborhood networks), even to create new civil society organizations that animated everyday life in the city.[85] Notably, these organizations—both formal (associations, unions, political schools and workshops) and informal (neighborhood networks)—helped the party mobilize the population and integrate "diverse interests and identities among the society into [a] coherent bloc."[86] This bloc, in turn, congealed around a politicized Kurdish identity.

Certainly the Kurdish identity did not develop in an elegant arc. Over the course of this history, the pro-Kurdish party and local mayors faced severe juridical and bureaucratic pressure. Several times, administrators from the pro-Kurdish parties and activists were taken to court, fined, and even jailed for their actions. The governors, appointed by the central government, constituted a major challenge for the elected pro-Kurdish mayors in the city.[87] In response, the party devised unique strategies and urban maneuvers—what I refer to as "wiggle room."[88] The following chapters discuss the ways in which the pro-Kurdish municipalities found loopholes in urban law and managed to contrive wiggle room through distinct urban planning strategies at various levels, from housing to urban infrastructure and public spaces.

In the next chapter, while investigating cases of urban renewal and housing, I demonstrate how the succession of pro-Kurdish parties, using strategic urban action, creatively turned state coercion into opportunities to generate Kurdish collectivity and thereby mobilize the urban population.

2

BUILDING THE FRONTIER
"We Will Not Surrender"

On November 3, 2012, the mayor of Diyarbakır and a group of pro-Kurdish Peace and Democracy Party (BDP) Parliament members jumped over a police barricade and broke into the garden of the governor's office. The governor of Diyarbakır had locked himself in his office. Chased by the police, the mayor and Parliament members reached the gates of the building. Despite their pressing demands to speak with the governor, they were turned down on the grounds that they had failed to make an appointment. The gates of the governor's office remained locked. Pounding on the large doors of the building, Parliament member Altan Tan exclaimed, "If he [the governor] does not open the door, we will break down this door. He should open and confront us. Only elected representatives are here. There is no need for an appointment; here are the Parliament members of Diyarbakır."[1]

What brought BDP officials to the governor's gates was the latter's veto of a BDP rally. With the rally banned, the city turned into a battlefield. Violence between protesters and police spread across the city. The mayor and the BDP's Parliament members came to the governor's office hoping to lift the ban in the city. It was perhaps the first time a governor had locked himself in the office in a blatant attempt to avoid BDP officials. This incident, however, was neither the first nor the last in which mayors and governors confronted each other over controlling the city.

As the gates remained locked, tension between the police force and the Parliament members intensified. Along with the Parliament members and the mayor, journalists were cornered by the police and awaiting a resolution. After a short while, standing in front of the locked gates of the governor's office, the chairman of the BDP, Selahattin Demirtaş (imprisoned since 2016), remarked, "He is not the governor of Diyarbakır, nor the governor of its people. We are elected, we have 65 percent of the votes of this city." Echoing Demirtaş's sentiment, Altan Tan stated, "One day this governor will be gone—" Turning his face to the cameras, he added, "but I am the owner of this city." Both statements, Demirtaş's and Tan's, underscored the temporary nature of the tenure of the governor—a figure who is not locally elected in Diyarbakır but rather appointed by the central government in Ankara. Nevertheless, their statements go beyond stressing the appointment of the governor. This confrontation not only betrayed the unique administrative system that convenes multiple—and often competing—levels of governance in an apparatus of local administration, but also highlighted the party's claims over Diyarbakır, the informal capital of Kurdistan.

Although, historically, pro-Kurdish parties accessed great opportunities through municipalities, merely holding municipal power was not enough to expand and articulate a Kurdish bloc. Since the early moments they came to power, the pro-Kurdish municipalities were exposed to state coercion particularly through the institution of the governorship. Consequently, the political conflict between the Kurdish movement and the central government took shape through urban contestation in Diyarbakır. As this chapter demonstrates, interlocking power struggles between the mayors and the governors—frequently surfacing over projects of urban renewal, zoning, and housing—shaped that urban contestation and, by extension, the city.

Recent scholarly work on urban renewal and housing has examined these urban processes within the city's neoliberal turn. My analysis takes stock of this tradition but expands it, arguing that neoliberal urbanism can be used as a strong political instrument through contingent struggles over attempts to gain control of urban space.[2] Since the late 1990s, Diyarbakır has been constantly reshaped not by rules of modern planning and urban development ideals, but by disputes over urban development projects, multiple strategies of zoning, and political maneuvers over urban law. With over 1.8 million residents, Diyarbakır is a city in which urban planning schemes are set and reset amid political conflict between the central government and the pro-Kurdish party.

In Diyarbakır, as in other cities across the world, the government's attempts at displacement and relocation have been couched in urban projects—interchangeably labeled as urban renewal, urban development, or regeneration—infused with rhetoric about improving life standards for squatter settlers or, appositely, with images conjuring a modern city. Oren Yiftachel calls this system the "dark side of planning"—urban planning as a mechanism for imposing state control over minorities.³ In its analysis of neoliberal urbanism, this chapter delves into the dark side of planning. Using the case of urban renewal—the state's urban projections over Kurds—I demonstrate how the Turkish government sought to employ urban development as a tool to demobilize the Kurdish movement. I also show how, in response, the pro-Kurdish municipalities creatively opened up some wiggle room and turned this coercion into another opportunity for mobilization, building a Kurdish frontier in the city. I first examine the dual-status administrative system (between governors and municipality) in cities and specify the correlation between urban renewal and contestation. Next, I depict how urban renewal emerged as an arena of contestation and rivalry between the pro-Kurdish municipalities and the central state. I discuss the urban maneuvers of the pro-Kurdish party amid the state's fast-changing urban development laws and acts, and demonstrate how the party's strategic urban actions generated conditions of collectivity and manifestations of Kurdish community. In analyzing the contestation over urban renewal projects in Diyarbakır, this chapter shows how these conditions (such as urban renewal practices affecting urban poor) may be characterized not only by dispute and disillusionment but also by contradiction and creativity.

Control over Cities: Central versus Local

Unlike many other cases across the world, in Diyarbakır, urban contestation over squatter settlements did not develop around the common dichotomy of municipality-led razing of squatter settlements countered by the resistance of squatter settlers. In Diyarbakır, urban contestation erupted between two state organs: the governor, who enforced urban renewal and demolitions, and the municipality, which battled against such politically motivated urban regeneration. This unique struggle for control over the city between two state apparatuses is partially tied to Turkey's complex local governance system.

Turkey is divided into eighty-one provinces, each with its central administrative city. Each province is further divided into a number of districts (*ilçe*) and towns (*belde*). The provinces operate under two parallel administrative systems: eighty-one governors (*vali*), each appointed by the central government in the capital, Ankara, and eighty-one mayors (*belediye başkanı*) elected by popular vote for five-year terms. This arrangement encompasses thirty metropolitan municipalities, determined by their greater size and population, along with fifty-one mayors.⁴ In addition to this larger organization, each district and town has its own smaller municipalities, for a total of 1,393 municipalities across the country. Operating in tandem with this structure, each district has its own district governor (*kaymakam*) appointed by the state and aligned with the politics and policies of the province governor.

City governors, appointed with the president's approval, serve as the main representatives of the central government. They oversee district governors and ministerial functions, enforcing administrative and political law while supervising various sectors, including health, social assistance, education, and security.[5] Meanwhile, municipalities, headed by officials elected through popular vote, address common local needs. They focus on urban planning and development, housing, water, transport, and environmental services. Additionally, they cater to the cultural and artistic resources for city residents.[6]

Despite this distinction—from the early years of the republic to today—the state sees local administrations as extensions of the central government. In cities where elected municipal officials belong to the same party as that in charge in Ankara (currently the Justice and Development Party, AKP), political life tends to function smoothly. In cities like Diyarbakır, where municipalities are held by an opposition party, the city can become an arena of antagonism and rivalry between two opposing ideologies at the municipal and governorship levels.

The founding of such municipalities began in the early 1930s; but it took longer for the mayorship to come under the electoral system in which mayors were accepted as administrators of the city, sharing responsibilities with the governors.[7] Until the early 1960s, mayors were still appointed by the central government. With the rapid rise of migration from rural to urban centers, local administration in large cities encountered growing problems in terms of infrastructure, transportation, and housing. In 1963, the new Municipality Law introduced regulations regarding the election of the local administration—that is, the mayors.[8] Following this act, several urban and economic laws extended the status and the role of mayors in the cities amid swift urbanization. Beginning in the 1970s, municipalities began to emerge as distinct political mechanisms in the country's political environment.[9] The tensions between central and local power in municipal governance became increasingly pronounced in Turkey after the 1970s, spurred by the accelerated pace of urbanization.[10] For instance, in 1973, when the Social Democrats managed to control Turkey's largest cities (Istanbul, Ankara, and Izmir), the distinction between the central and local governments became visible in the country's agenda.[11] Rising neoliberalization within the country in the early 1980s—as well as the increasing salience of new international concerns favoring local empowerment and governance—swept in another major reform to the municipalities.[12] In 1984, one of the main objectives of municipality reform was to enhance the financial resources of the municipal administrations and broaden the scope of their activities. This aimed to strengthen local governments and to foster greater independence for municipalities from the central government, thereby accelerating decision-making within cities.[13] This reform also elevated cities with populations exceeding 750,000 to "metropolitan" municipality status. Consequently, metropolises like Istanbul, Ankara, Izmir, and Diyarbakır underwent significant structural alterations, adopting a two-tier system through the establishment of metropolitan municipalities.[14] The first tier consisted of district municipalities, each with its own mayor responsible for basic municipal services, whereas metropolitan municipalities, encompassing the entire city (with its own mayor as well), were charged with implementing larger urban projects. Diyarbakır attained the status of a metropolitan municipality in 1993. It comprises one governor, one metropolitan mayor, seventeen district governors, and seventeen district mayors.

Across the country, the establishment of metropolitan municipalities not only rendered them eligible for additional governmental funding but also significantly elevated the political status and authority wielded by mayors. With the large concentration of voters in urban centers, political parties have increasingly viewed local governments—and, therefore, local elections—as crucial to expanding their electoral popularity. In fact, over the last few decades, holding power in municipalities, particularly in large metropolitan cities, has come to be interpreted as a significant consolidation of political power.[15] In the 1990s, the Islamist movement used its success in municipal elections to embark on a wider project of "Islamizing" society. Parties such as RP (the Welfare Party) used their control of local administration to build connections to civil society, lending special support to groups that were aligned with their political objectives and ideology. In doing so, they effectively created Islamist municipalities that sociologist Cihan Tuğal has described as institutional vanguards of a sociopolitical project which attack[ed] the established order.[16] Much like these 1990s Islamists who employed municipal power to form pro-Islamist blocs that stood against the central government, in the early 2000s Kurdish municipal administrations employed similar strategies to strengthen Kurdish identity and political mobilization.

Early Paths of Local Administrations in Diyarbakır

Since the early republican period, the trajectories of local administration in Kurdish cities have been entirely different from those in the rest of the country. From the republican era until the 1990s, Diyarbakır municipalities were oftentimes administered by local elites (prominent families of the city, with feudal backgrounds), governors, or other state bureaucrats appointed by the central government. Exceptionally, in December 1977, an independent candidate, prominent Kurdish activist Mehdi Zana, was elected mayor of Diyarbakır. In the same period, another pro-Kurdish candidate, Edip Solmaz, was elected from another Kurdish-populated city near Diyarbakır, Batman; however, two years later, Solmaz was assassinated.

Mehdi Zana's election disrupted the state's control over Diyarbakır, which had been maintained almost since the beginning of the republican period. Coming from a working-class family with an elementary school education, Zana had long been a local leader and a prominent left-wing pro-Kurdish figure in Diyarbakır. Prior to his election, he was a member of the Workers Party of Turkey (Türkiye İşçi Partisi, TİP). He had served in different administrative positions in the party and organized the Eastern Meetings of 1967.[17] Although Zana ran as an independent candidate without any direct political party support, he won approximately 35 percent of the votes and became Diyarbakır's mayor. What made Zana's case exceptional was not only his independent status; it was the first time a prominent pro-Kurdish activist explicitly struggling for Kurdish rights was elected. Years after his mayorship, in an interview, Zana explained how he won the elections not necessarily through his promises to serve the city, but through his emphasis on the Kurdish struggle: "When I declared my candidacy, I was not talking about the service to the city. I was only speaking in Kurdish, and the people who saw this were cheering up [zılgıt çekiyorlardı]. The issue was the Kurdish issue, and this issue was no small issue. No people in the world have been exposed to as much cruelty and hardship as the Kurds."[18] In the mayoral office, Zana continued to explicitly emphasize the struggle for Kurdish rights, culture, and identity, and mobilized support from a number of pro-Kurdish civil society organizations, grassroot networks, unions, and student networks that helped him "break the traditional hold of the national parties and local notables over local politics."[19] Even though speaking Kurdish was banned, particularly during official and municipal meetings, he and his staff members deliberately used the Kurdish language (although they were later charged for doing so) to express Kurdishness. But Zana's mayorship did not last long. Shortly after he was elected, the 1980 coup d'état sent him to military prison, where he was tortured and spent eleven years (and was imprisoned again from 1994 to 1995). During his short time in office, Zana built and strengthened both local and international support with pro-Kurdish network organization. To some extent, through his links with Kurdish activists and organizations in Europe, Zana established transnational ties, as well as an aid network in Kurdish politics.[20] Zana's campaign and his mayorship were milestones for developing the local administration approach to the Kurdish movement. First, Zana's mayorship initiated the local governing tradition in pro-Kurdish politics of using municipal power to promote Kurdish culture and rights. Second, his campaign brought new prominence to pro-Kurdish politics in the context of the crucial role of mobilizing local networks (students, some union activists, and local tribes) in support of pro-Kurdish activism. Particularly by establishing strong links with civil society organizations and attracting votes from different backgrounds, Zana not only broke the state's hold on Diyarbakır but also forged a new path in promoting a sense of Kurdish identity through mayorship.[21]

Between 1980 and 1987, many Kurdish cities were under martial law. When martial law was lifted in the summer of 1987, a State of Emergency (Olağanüstü Hal, OHAL) directly replaced it in Bingöl, Diyarbakır, Şırnak, Hakkari, Mardin, Siirt, Tunceli, Van, Adıyaman, Bitlis, Batman, and Muş. In the following years, even as governments in some of these cities revoked it, OHAL lasted in Tunceli, Hakkari, Diyarbakır, and Şırnak until 2002.[22] OHAL brought these cities under the jurisdiction of a regional governor with extraordinary powers. Without the need of a warrant, the governor could authorize security forces to enter and search homes and party offices, order evacuations of entire villages effective immediately, ban meetings, and fine publications. Governors also possessed several mayoral duties, functioning as though they held the main authority over a city's municipalities. These practices included making all decisions about urban planning and empowering security forces. Furthermore, governors were granted immunity from any legal prosecution related to actions they took while exercising their powers. Not until 1999 were municipalities won by one single pro-Kurdish party in Diyarbakır. In the early 1990s, the pro-Kurdish DEP (Democracy Party) was not allowed to participate in local elections.[23] Local elections in April 1999 were remarkable for the pro-Kurdish party in terms movement expansion. During local elections, the People's Democracy Party (HADEP) had sweeping victories and won thirty-seven mayoral races as well as several city councils across the southeast, including Diyarbakır, Van, Batman, Mardin, and Hakkari. In Diyarbakır, with 62.5 percent of the votes, HADEP took over the metropolitan municipality office as well as several subdistricts in the city, including Sur, Yenişehir, and Bağlar. The local election in 1999 was the first time a Kurdish political party expressly committed to Kurdish rights and justice had gained municipal power. HADEP's election slogan was "We [Kurds] will administer ourselves and our cities on our own" (Kendimizi de kentimizi de biz yöneteceğiz).[24] Subsequently, politicians and activists of the pro-Kurdish party often used and repeated the slogan in their electoral campaigns. Beginning in 1999, the pro-Kurdish politicians who obtained control of municipalities increased the opportunity to govern themselves and "expanded their capacity to administer"—privileges they would not be able to secure through the parliamentary system.[25] In other words, taking over municipalities gave pro-Kurdish parties an important platform from which to exercise formal state power through municipal administrations. Under circumstances of limited political representation and state coercion, Kurdish leaders saw this achievement as an opportunity to cultivate the movement via urban politics and activism. Feridun Çelik's victory in 1999 in Diyarbakır was followed by Osman Baydemir's mayorship between 2004 and 2014, then by co-mayors Gültan Kışanak and Fırat Anlı, until the Turkish government's intervention in 2016; and later again, in 2019, mayor Adnan Selçuk Mızraklı (imprisoned after 2019) won election but stayed in office only for a couple of months before he was dismissed by the government.[26]

The pro-Kurdish politicians who held mayoral office in Kurdish-populated cities secured several resources that pro-Kurdish parties were unable to acquire through their parliamentary seats. Diverse resources in administering the cities—designing and implementing master plans; building and naming public spaces such as squares, parks, and streets; providing public services such as water, sewage, and mass transit; collecting garbage; supplying social and cultural services; organizing cultural festivals; and administering women's support programs—were successfully transformed into sources of strength for Kurdish mobilization.[27] As discussed in chapter 1, local administration allowed more independent activity than national politics did, and because of the concentration of Kurds in the southeast, role-related resources allowed pro-Kurdish parties to disaggregate local concerns from national-level political debates and focus on grassroots community building.[28] However, municipal power was not limitless. First, because of the bureaucratic structure, municipality budgets were still tied to the central government. Almost all projects, budgets, and international funds needed to be approved by the central government in Ankara. These bureaucratic, particularly economic, constraints introduced several complications to the municipality, particularly in establishing and realizing large-scale projects in the city. Second, the presence of a governorship was a challenging factor for the municipality. The lifting of emergency law (in some cities in the late 1990s; in Diyarbakır and Şırnak in 2002) afforded relative freedom to the municipal capacity; however, as this chapter shows, this lifting never eradicated state coercion from Diyarbakır.

As noted earlier, in pro-Kurdish cities, while pro-Kurdish mayors, NGOs, and civil society organizations occupy one end of the political spectrum, the state-appointed governorship—with the chief officers tied to the governorship and a large military presence—resides at the other. For many gatherings—a festival or a demonstration, for instance—the municipality needs the governor's permission. As these two legal authorities have overlapping (yet competitive) agendas, the city becomes a site of contestation. Thus, even the most routine urban practices, from large-scale urban development projects to small-scale projects (e.g., giving a park a Kurdish name, or erecting a monument in a neighborhood), often involve political struggles between the governorship and the municipalities. The state thereby exerts its influence over local politics through the seat of governorship, extending its activities to include a large variety of urban renewal projects.

AKP's New Urban Development: "We Are Building the Cities of the Future for the Future of Turkey"

Turkey was introduced to a major urban renewal campaign in 2002, when the AKP won the national elections in the aftermath of an economic crisis and a major earthquake in 1999.[29] With the promise of urban redevelopment, improving housing standards, infrastructure, and city economies, the AKP embarked on an effort to become the builder of a "new Turkey." In a span of twenty years, this massive nationwide project not only transformed the cities but also restructured state and society relations and more radically altered the future of urban institutions and urban planning across the country.

In the first decade of the 2000s, one of the primary goals of this "new Turkey" was to eliminate *gecekondus*—literally meaning "settled overnight" (squatter settlements)—in major cities, partly because squatter settlements were sitting on some of the most valuable land in and around the cities.[30] *Gecekondus* are not a new phenomenon in Turkey.

The *gecekondus* dated to the early 1950s with the influx of migrants from rural to urban areas for various economic and political reasons. In the early 1960s, the general public accepted *gecekondu* settlements as an alternative solution to the problem of housing in cities where the supply of government-initiated models of housing failed to meet the demands of the migrant influx.[31] Later, governments in Turkey typically dealt with the housing problem by not enforcing the law against the informally built settlements, thereby contributing to the expansion of squatter settlements within the cities. When demolitions did occur, new *gecekondus* would often be rebuilt on nearby land, sometimes even on the same spot. During this period, especially by the 1980s, squatter settlements became potential voting hubs for political parties, which responded to the lack of infrastructure in these communities by promoting the provision of basic infrastructural elements like electricity and water, as well as land titles for residents. Beginning in the mid-1990s, however, with the unrestrained liberalization of the housing economy, rising land values, urban sprawl, and the emergence of new housing markets, the state's previous attitude toward the urban poor came to an end. In the first decade of the twenty-first century, the government began transforming *gecekondu* areas by relocating residents and incorporating the land into urban development plans.[32]

Early in 2005, following consolidation of municipal powers around the country, the AKP renewed the local administration law in undertaking massive urban regeneration projects nationwide. By increasing the revenue and authority of the local municipality, the new law introduced more independence to municipalities.[33] That same year, the AKP reinvented several housing institutions, such as Kiptaş (Housing Development and Development Corporation of Istanbul Metropolitan Municipality), Emlak Konut (a real estate investment trust, established by the state in the 1950s), and TOKİ (Housing Development Administration of Turkey). Among these institutions, TOKİ emerged as the most active nationwide institution while embodying its new institutional identity with the motto "We Are Building the Cities of the Future for the Future of Turkey."[34]

TOKİ was initially founded in 1984 as a governmental institution for an affordable public housing program targeting low- and middle-income people who, in its words, "cannot own a housing unit under the existing market conditions." Under the AKP government, TOKİ became a major tool in Turkey, leading massive urban renewal projects equipped with extensive planning and zoning authority as well as building rights in regeneration areas.[35] Following its reorganization by the AKP government, TOKİ, as a public housing agency, radically increased its housing production rates under the Planned Urbanization and Housing Production Program. Authority was granted to TOKİ for approval of the boundaries of *gecekondu* rehabilitation zones, *gecekondu* refinement areas, and *gecekondu* prevention areas within the limits of local administrations. Although plans for development and rehabilitation zones were prepared by local administrations, only TOKİ was authorized to reject or approve the urban plan proposals within this context of urban renewal.

Despite holding all this power, in terms of architectural design TOKİ did not have much to offer. TOKİ housing projects adopted a prototype of high-rise or mid-rise apartments (from about five to ten stories) each with a balcony and a large pitched roof. Typically, the housing projects would be located at city fringes, where land was cheaper. Little or no recreational areas were provided for their residents. The apartment blocks were built in clusters of at least five, with similar if not identical repetitive layouts and façades. With such a cookie-cutter style imposed across the country, one could not differentiate these apartment blocks one city to the next.[36]

Despite this monotonous architectural style, in a span of just five years, by 2007, TOKİ had become the principal owner, planner, and builder of the country and began to dominate the real estate sector.[37] TOKİ increased its revenue and capacity to such an extent that urban activities and interventions went beyond programs of public housing into the realm of urban projects. In the first decade of the twenty-first century, with the help of private partnerships, TOKİ gradually became the largest construction agent and chief actor of urban renewal projects. TOKİ's building agenda went beyond housing to cover a variety of small- and large-scale social facilities, including schools, gymnasiums, dormitories and guest houses, health clinics, hospitals, mosques, libraries, commercial centers, and stadiums.

Since 2010 or so, the policies of the Turkish government in part facilitated this expanded role. Under AKP's regime, the Turkish state significantly changed its approach to housing, urban renewal, and urban planning. Particularly, legal changes beginning early in 2005 gave TOKİ near-unlimited power in urban governance, empowering it to regulate and dominate real estate markets around the country. With the backing of the state, TOKİ became the main actor in Turkey's booming real estate market. Serving as a catalyst for the construction sector, TOKİ's welfarist attitude, in fact, was reinvented under the neoliberal practices of the AKP government. By 2010, an estimated 72 percent of the Turkish population lived in urban areas or within municipal boundaries, a statistic that underscores the crucial role of TOKİ and local administrations in the cities.[38] For instance, by 2011, TOKİ was meeting 5 to 10 percent of the housing needs of Turkey, with its building numbering approximately twenty million at that time. What came to be defined as a neoliberal city was often characterized by projects that aimed to generate a steady revenue flow to private investors and a higher tax base for local administrations.[39] In Turkey's case, the government's construction firm dominated the production of this revenue. The massive wave of housing construction set off by TOKİ expanded tremendously and opened up channels for new construction companies (most regime-friendly) to build housing at record numbers.[40] In about twenty years, between 2002 and 2022, close to nine million dwelling permits for new homes were issued, which inevitably led to gentrification and commodification of land across the country.[41]

In early 2023, a catastrophic earthquake hit the south of Turkey. Despite the AKP's twenty-year-long urban development campaign, and the exceptional powers exercised by TOKİ and the Ministry of Urban Planning, the earthquake disaster left more than fifty thousand people dead and hundreds of thousands homeless. While none of TOKİ's apartment units were destroyed during the earthquake, the disaster made clear that the runaway train of Turkey's real estate boom had gone off the rails. It was not the lack of public housing or urban planning but rather the centralization of urban planning and the construction frenzy that made the Turkish cities vulnerable to earthquakes. Such slipshod approach to centralized urban planning, merged with neoliberal politics, made the cities even more susceptible to disasters.

Over the past two decades, the massive urban renewal projects that constituted a large part of the AKP's agenda of "creating a new Turkey" spiraled into rhetoric of urban development and progress. The "new Turkey," as the AKP once put it, would be rebuilt via these massive urban development projects, some of which the party later called "crazy projects," with billions of dollars in budget cost. These projects included a third bridge on the Bosporus Strait; a new airport to be the largest in the world; the Istanbul Canal, connecting the Black Sea to the Sea of Marmara; and Galataport, a mega-size mixed-use development featuring an underground cruise-ship port.[42] They were not "crazy" just because they were mega; they were also spectacular and glamorous, broadcasting a message that the AKP could achieve the impossible. While illustrating the image of a powerful global Turkey, these mega projects were the consolidation of President Recep Tayyip Erdoğan's power and markers of "Turkey's neoliberal statism."[43] The AKP was not the first political party to utilize urban development as a form of populist practice, but it was distinguished by its careful calculation of political benefits, highly supplemented and facilitated by a very strong neoliberal stance.[44]

The AKP's rule shaped the country through constantly changing zoning laws—in major western cities through privatizing the land or making previously industrial zones available for housing and construction. The main axes of urban development and the construction industry were dominated by the AKP's government and its bureaucratic and business network. In creating the axes of neoliberal urbanization, the AKP government created new urban institutions and reconstituted the relationship between society and space along market lines.[45]

In earlier phases, collaboration with local administrations was central to TOKİ's work in implementing these projects, which would be launched upon submission of a request by municipalities. As the majority of municipal administration was under the control of the AKP, with the assistance of local municipalities residents were relocated into public housing projects built on land designated and owned by TOKİ. However, in Diyarbakır, the story was different. Unlike in the rest of the country, in the early 2000s AKP couldn't secure municipal power in Diyarbakır. Thus, the central government's intervention into urban development was not going to be smooth. For Diyarbakır, urban regeneration would mean yet more rough waters for the pro-Kurdish municipality and the Turkish state to navigate.

Testing the Waters: Housing Crisis

My arrival in Diyarbakır back in the hot summer of 2009 was an introduction to the charged urban politics of the city. From the governor to the mayors, from civil society organizations to unions, all the stakeholders in the city were divided over the urban renewal and development projects. Earlier, in March 2009, urban development projects and the construction of new public housing had been part of the AKP's election campaign. Particularly for the local elections for each city, the number of housing units built, the number of new "homeowners," the length of roads built for the city, and so on—all work performed by TOKİ—were touted as a measure of progress. Housing projects, dams built, or airports constructed were the first images to appear on large campaign screens and billboards. The equation of urban renewal with development and progress generally worked relatively smoothly for the majority of cities across Turkey and increased the AKP's popularity. However, that equation was clearly not working in Diyarbakır, where the AKP's urban interventions were backfiring. At the peak of the development debates, in the March 2009 local elections, the AKP got only 31.3 percent of the votes, while the pro-Kurdish DTP (Democratic Society Party) swept almost all the Kurdish-populated cities in southeastern Turkey. The election was seen as a consolidation of political power for the pro-Kurdish party. Gaining 66.5 percent of the votes, Osman Baydemir, the mayor of Diyarbakır between 2004 and 2014, dubbed the city the "castle" of pro-Kurdish politics.[46] Following the election, the polemic of urban renewal got even more heated. The city was awash with rumors of development projects to come. Every other day a demonstration was organized in the city, with the participation of residents not only from Sur but also from the entire city—party and municipality members, architects and planner unions in solidarity. The political conflict between the governor and the municipalities was, at the moment, over the intended demolition of squatter settlements and relocation of settlers in Sur.[47] Meetings upon meetings, public statements by the governors and the mayors, urban workshops, rallies, and demonstrations were organized over and over again. From women to youth, from public officials to real estate developers, rumors spread about the new urban development projects—particularly the forced evictions to come. In July 2009, I went to the source of these rumors, Sur, the oldest district and historic core of Diyarbakır, located on the banks of the Tigris River.[48] Covering some ninety-five hectares (about a third of a square mile), Sur is surrounded by historic walls, which from the air appear to outline the shape of a flatfish. Divided into four nearly equal sections by intersecting arteries, the urban fabric of Sur represented a traditional Middle Eastern city. It consisted of two-story traditional stone houses with interior courtyards attached within an organic growth of narrow labyrinths of serpentine alleys, often with dead ends. As discussed earlier, until the republican period Diyarbakır included only the walled city of Sur. As the historical center of the city, Sur was the hub of Diyarbakır's most prominent families.[49] With the influx of thousands of rural immigrants, the city began to expand beyond its walls toward the northwest; and later, in the 1980s and 1990s, Sur was left to rural migrants and thousands of displaced persons who lost their homes during the fiercest years of armed conflict between the Turkish military and the PKK. Over the years, particularly between 1984 and 2000, the Kurdish-populated regions in the eastern part of Turkey were devastated by the conflict between the PKK and the state of Turkey. Around the 1990s, roughly over one million Kurdish villagers fled their homes and land, either forced to or by choice, and resettled elsewhere in Turkey.[50] During this period, most of Sur began to develop into an area of squatter settlements, or *gecekondus* (figure 5).

While the commercial part of the district aligning with the main arteries consisted of illegal low-scale apartment buildings, the rest of Sur was largely characterized by thousands of squatter settlements. Oftentimes, these communities developed through occupation of abandoned houses still owned by former residents or through the illegal reconstruction of houses on abandoned land that, at one point, had had a house on it. Numerous decaying houses abandoned by previous residents had been precariously rebuilt by the new Kurdish forced-migrants seeking shelter. Over time, the alteration and remodeling of these houses by the new residents resulted in the transformation of traditional

FIGURE 5. A view of squatter settlements in Sur, Diyarbakır. The area is characterized by unfinished, low-quality construction and a lack of street infrastructure. Historic city walls can be seen at the top left of the photograph.
Source: Author, 2008.

courtyard-centered designs through the addition of rooms or appropriations of courtyard space for new functions—for instance, to grow crops. Most of the housing in Sur, if not illegal, was at least informal and lacked proper infrastructure and building codes.

My first interview was with Abdullah Demirbaş, then-mayor of Sur under the DTP. I met with him many more times, both in Diyarbakır and in the following years in Istanbul. During this period he was jailed off and on, in 2009 and released for medical reasons in 2010, then arrested again in 2015 and released months later, again for medical reasons. A former schoolteacher, Demirbaş is known for his strong pro-Kurdish activism and enthusiasm for Kurdish-language projects. The mayor's office was on the top floor of a six-story Sur municipality building on the İnönü Boulevard, named after İsmet İnönü, a Turkish general and the second president of Turkey, a man acknowledged as Atatürk's right hand. The building represents a postmodern taste. The main façade is supported by four round aluminum-clad columns that form an arcade in front of the entrance. The first two stories behind the arcade feature gray basalt stone, while the rest of the floors above are sheathed in aluminum—the choice of gray signals an effort to blend in with the walls of Sur. Wooden window frames form a pointed arch—a reference to Artuqids architecture. I climbed the stairs and arrived in a large hallway. The top floor consisted of a small kitchen for tea, a meeting room for the municipal council, and the mayor's office. In front of Demirbaş's office the hallway was full of visitors, both young and old, waiting to talk with their mayor. In his large office, he would listen to them, one by one, without any hesitation. Demirbaş was proud to have established "a transparent municipality practice"—what he called his frequent engagement with Sur residents in his office or even on the streets. When I arrived, he was wrapping up a meeting with local press about the restoration of the Armenian church in Sur. Demirbaş was a tall man with dark hair. He wore a light blue shirt without a tie, paired with gray pants. His voice and speech mirrored the energy of his appearance. Before I could even start asking questions, he began to excitedly talk about the projects he had overseen for Sur: promoting a multilingual and multicultural municipality, opening parks, organizing a Kurdish-language campaign, restoring an Armenian church, and more. After summarizing his municipality's achievements, he noted that the state and governorship always threw obstacles in his path; he emphasized that he would never give up.

Since taking office in 2004, Mayor Demirbaş had faced dozens of investigations on the grounds that he had violated the equality principle of the constitution. In 2007, a Council of State charged him with malfeasance and dismissed him from office, ruling that he was attempting to provide multilingual municipality services—in Kurdish, English, and Turkish—to residents. The court acquitted him. He wore a very driven and undaunted expression and spoke clearly. Even as I was recording, I took quick notes on all these details. Later, when asking about the obstacles the municipality faced, I encountered a sentiment of urban contestation. "Let me give you an example," he said:

> In order to test the "state" [the central government in Ankara, ruled by the AKP], I applied a very interesting method. I prepared a very small-scale project, a children's park for Sur that cost no more than 10,000 TL [Turkish lira].[51] Then I sent this project to the Ministry of Environment, asking for a budget to support our municipality in making the children's park. Our project was rejected by the ministry, which asked that we refrain from further requests for funding such a project. However, the same ministry sent a grant of 10 million euros to the Urfa municipality [administered by the AKP] for the project of a solid-waste plant.[52] Our own Diyarbakır Metropolitan Municipality demanded the same support for our own solid waste plan project, but unfortunately again, this request was rejected.

Emphasizing how his test revealed political and economic discrimination by the government toward pro-Kurdish municipalities, Demirbaş concluded, "See how they support the Urfa municipality, because the municipality of Urfa is theirs?" Indeed, the Urfa municipality was administered by the AKP. I was swiftly introduced to the city's contentious politics. Demirbaş continued, "Let me give you another very interesting example: the state's intervention in cultural inheritance and how the state manipulates the city." What Demirbaş called the "state's intervention in cultural inheritance" was actually the government's urban development project proposed for the area of the squatter settlements of Lalebey and Ali Paşa in the Sur district. Administered by TOKİ via the governorship of Diyarbakır, the project aimed to relocate residents of Lalebey and Ali Paşa to new public housing projects planned for construction on the outskirts of the city. Like the majority of Sur, the Lalebey and Ali Paşa neighborhoods consisted of two- to three-story *gecekondus* occupied by rural migrants, as well as people displaced by the conflict between the PKK guerrillas and the Turkish army in the 1990s.

In these areas, *gecekondus* were typically developed by squatting on the ruins of former buildings or by reappropriating former buildings and making alterations and expansions as needed to house additional family members. The majority of people in these neighborhoods lived in poverty—men worked in informal job sectors, as temporary workers in construction or street vendors in the city center; most women were housewives.

Shortly before the local elections in 2009, the governorship invited mayors, civil society organizations, representatives, and public officials to the official announcement of TOKİ's "urban renewal project" for the Lalebey and Ali Paşa neighborhoods. During the interview, alluding to the government's proactive approach to project implementation, Demirbaş leaned toward me and, in an angry yet confident tone, remarked: "This government made such a law that TOKİ [first] designates the areas for urban regeneration, and [then] without consulting with or asking any local administration, it directly implements [its own] projects by law. They cannot do whatever they want to our city, our Diyarbakır!" The project drew a heated response not only from the party but also from the civil society organization and unions aligned with the party—many of which explicitly voiced their rejection of the project. The initial response from the municipality was, how could it be possible for the governorship to handle urban development when this duty usually fell under the legislation of the municipality? To learn more about the story, I wanted to speak with the governor. Though it took me longer (and was more difficult) to schedule an interview with the governor of Diyarbakır, almost a week following my interview with Mayor Demirbaş I was at the office of Governor H, a Turkish bureaucrat. Before he was appointed to Diyarbakır in 2007, Governor H, a graduate of law school, had served as a governor in several cities, including Siirt and Şırnak. The meeting carried a distinct formality. Initially, his demeanor remained calm and reserved, as he responded to my questions with concise answers. However, as our conversation progressed, he gradually opened up and became more expressive. I began to pose my questions directly. I asked about the "urban renewal" project the governorship had initiated for Sur.

"This [Lalebey and Ali Paşa] urban renewal project is a test for these [Kurdish] people," he stated. I was startled to hear the word "test" again, this time coming from the governor. In fact, for both the pro-Kurdish party and the government, the urban projects they mentioned were seen as a trial—an assessment tool to reveal the "true politics" of the other. In these claims of testing each other, the mayor and the governor revealed the exclusionary tendencies of each party toward the other, stressing the division between the state, on one side, and the pro-Kurdish party and its municipalities and civic organizations on the other side. In this contestation, the division of us and them delineated the political frontier that defined the opposed other. Therefore, as governors and mayors performed these urban trials with the hope of uncovering the genuine motivations and stances of their counterparts, distrust between the state and the pro-Kurdish party and its civic organizations was deepening. Governor H continued, reiterating his position on the "test": "I presented this urban renewal project in order to test all the dynamics of the city. In order to disclose their approach and response to the city, I invited all civil society organizations, unions, activist groups, and mayors of Diyarbakır and presented this project. However, it looked like they [the pro-Kurdish party] had another agenda." The governor was already revealing the results of his test. When I asked him what he meant by "another agenda," he continued:

> Look, the compensation and the subsidies we offered to squatter settlers to relocate in public housing projects are extraordinary. It is way higher than what TOKİ offers to the rest of the country. We even offered to postpone the payments they may need to make for two years. But I don't understand how it is possible that despite all the compensation we offer these people [squatter settlers], they don't want to relocate. And I don't understand why municipalities put up obstacles against our plan.

The alignment was clear in the governor's words—what he meant by "we" was the central government, the governorship, and TOKİ, who were on one side, with the residents and pro-Kurdish party on the other. However, TOKİ's housing development for Diyarbakır was not new. In the western part of the city, in the Kayapınar and Üç Kuyular districts, TOKİ had built public housing developments during the late 1990s. These projects, inhabited by the working class, were not intended for the relocation of squatter settlers. TOKİ proposed relocating Lalebey's and Ali Paşa's squatter settlers to public housing projects at the outskirts of the city at Çölgüzeli—miles away from Sur (figure 6). Subsequently, they aimed to redevelop the Sur area for tourist attractions, hotels, restaurants, commercial centers, and various recreational uses. By making squatter settlers homeowners, the project, at first glance, seemed advantageous to this population. However, like several other TOKİ projects, the plans for Lalebey and Ali Paşa raised questions about the consequences of state-led gentrification endured by the residents.

Nevertheless, TOKİ encountered rejection and dispute from the municipalities, as well as from NGOs and other civil society organizations that sided with the residents. Because of the distinct dual-power relations inherent in the state's regulatory system at the local level, the city's informal settlement problem pitted the governorship against the municipality.

In this vein, Sur presents another case of what urban theorists Neil Brenner, Peter Marcuse, and Margit Mayer describe as "the transformation of the city under neoliberalism where the state is operator in chief of those transformations."[53] Moreover, it was not the first time that TOKİ urban renewal and housing projects across the country would relocate local residents to the outskirts of the city. Like the Sulukule-Tarlabaşı project that disrupted the social and economic networks of its residents in Istanbul, TOKİ's plans for Diyarbakır pushed the residents to an unwelcoming and sometimes impoverishing life.[54] While

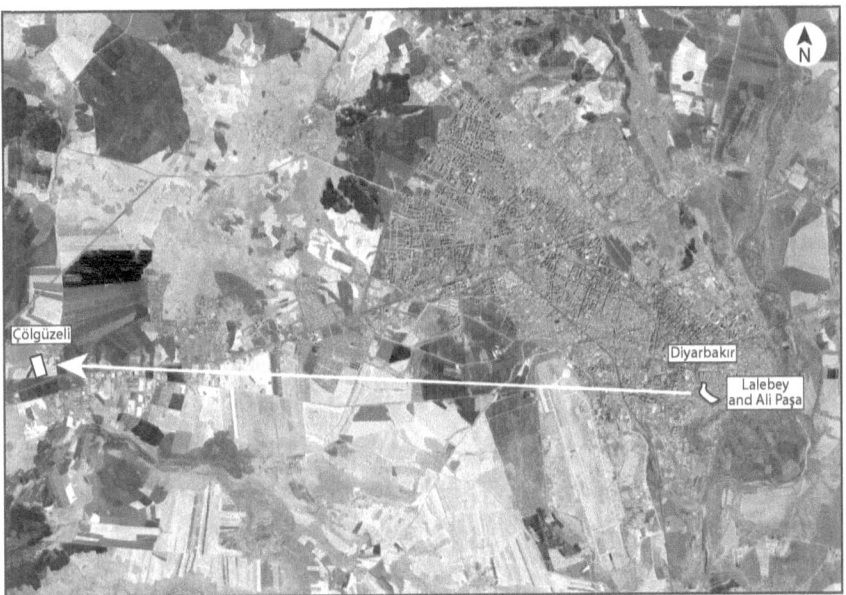

FIGURE 6. Proposed relocation of the residents from Lalebey and Ali Paşa in Sur to Çölgüzeli, on the outskirts of the city.
Source: Image created from Google Earth.

former "informal" settlers often have an unstable or informal income, new TOKİ settlers must carry a debt of monthly installments to become "new" homeowners. Furthermore, in infrastructural, social, and economic terms, Çölgüzeli, the proposed location of the housing projects, was virtually a small town without much business development, drastically cut off from rest of the city. Settlers who worked temporary jobs in the city would have long commutes to the city center, having to use at least two or three different forms of transportation at great personal expense. In addition, moving from one- or two-story housing with a courtyard to a small apartment building would have sweeping impacts on the everyday life of residents. It meant an end to neighborhood relations and networks of help and the loss of courtyard use for storage, growing crops, or production of goods (like dried vegetables and pickles), as well as the loss of opportunities to sell goods in the informal market as an additional household income.[55] Still, the government was zealous about relocating the squatter settlers in Sur. In this case, in order to encourage citizens to relocate to the proposed sites, TOKİ offered 30 percent less than its optimal housing rates nationwide. Moreover, with subsidies, the discount reached up to 40 percent, drastically higher than its typical offerings.

Urban renewal in Diyarbakır was grounded in a political conflict between the state and the pro-Kurdish party, intermingled with a complex form of identity politics. The condition of the squatter settlements the governor described during our interviews was typical across the country, but why would the state create such extraordinary subsidies and conditions to relocate the residents of Sur? When asked about the conditions of the project, Governor H offered a clue to the state's motive—in effect the rupturing of settler ties with the pro-Kurdish party. "We need to regulate their [the settlers'] lives. They [pro-Kurdish mayors] keep talking about the 'disturbance of our cultural inheritance.' . . . But those people are living in houses in miserable conditions. . . . There [in Sur] a family of eight live in one single room. What culture are they talking about? How can you talk about culture when you live in such miserable conditions?" In the eyes of the state, the squatter residents of Sur who would be relocated to the urban periphery needed to be "regulated." Such relocation would effectively extinguish their network for mobilization and stymie the pro-Kurdish party's efforts to recruit and galvanize residents. According to the AKP's government, outside the city the squatter settlers' living standards would be "improved" and the people would be away from the influence of the pro-Kurdish party.[56] This echoes the colonialist idea of "regulation" reminiscent of the new republic's ambitions a century earlier, when establishing a new city outside Sur with People's Houses, as discussed in the first chapter.[57]

Notably, at the beginning of this urban renewal undertaking, the pro-Kurdish party was the Democratic Society Party, the DTP; however, in December 2009, the Constitutional Court of Turkey banned the DTP, ruling that it had become a "center of activities against the indivisible unity of the state, the country and the nation." After the ban, the pro-Kurdish party was reestablished as the Peace and Democracy Party, the BDP.

Finding Loopholes

In 2009, following the governor's press release regarding the eviction of the Lalebey and Ali Paşa neighborhoods, the metropolitan municipality, in an effort to prevent the immediate relocation of informal settlers from Sur, proposed two actions against the state order. The first action was to find the loopholes in existing urban law. Using its municipal power, the DTP claimed that Sur was a historical preservation site and that no intervention could be done without a "preservation plan." Any changes or interventions to the region had to follow the preservation plan, to be prepared by the municipality. The pro-Kurdish municipality was able to open up wiggle room by using to its own advantage existing municipal laws initially created by the AKP. Following a survey of the entire built environment inside the city walls, the urban texture of Sur was categorized according its status as private property, registered historical landmarks, public enterprise, public roads, or ruins to be demolished.

According to this plan, if TOKİ applied its project in the Lalebey and Ali Paşa neighborhoods, it had to purchase the properties from their owners. Further, there would not be any intervention concerning "registered historical landmarks," as determined by the municipality. In fact, preparing the "preservation plan" for Sur was one of the very few strategies that the pro-Kurdish municipalities could undertake to prevent the immediate demolition of informal settlements. This time, through urban maneuvering, the municipality was exploiting a 2005 municipal law that the AKP had implemented initially to empower its own local authority. The party's aim was to gain time and, later, prevent as many evictions as it could. Sur was indeed a historical district, with historical registered buildings, so any urban development intervention had to follow the preservation plan. Also, by law, any urban development had to halt at protected areas until a preservation plan could be formed. And urban development plans in the protected areas had to comply with zoning decisions, as determined by preservation plans. Therefore, the "preservation plan" for Sur was a golden weapon the municipality wielded against the governor's intervention.

With this action, the municipality bought two years to prevent TOKİ from taking any action in the city. By 2011, the preservation plan was ready to be presented to the city. The Diyarbakır Metropolitan Municipality organized "Sur preservation meetings" with local participants, including the mayor of Sur (Abdullah Demirbaş), the Diyarbakır mayor (Osman Baydemir), the head of urban planning and the zoning office of the municipality, the union of architecture in Diyarbakır, local architects and city planners, and academics from Dicle University in Diyarbakır. In these daylong meetings, which I attended, the contracted planning offices would come to the city and make presentations, allowing comments from participants. The main question was how to prevent TOKİ from demolishing the housing in Sur.

Although it appeared that TOKİ and the municipality agreed on the proposal to draft and review a preservation plan, the possibility of TOKİ enacting eminent domain was generating resentment and anxiety among party members. Frequently, discussions would be dominated by the subject of ownership of the city, the intervention of TOKİ as an outside agent, and the perceived lack of authority over decision-making processes in the city.

The conversation between Diyarbakır's mayor Osman Baydemir and the archaeologist Nevin Soyukaya—then the director of the Diyarbakır Museum—exemplifies these anxieties. Mayor Baydemir stated, "I don't feel uncomfortable about the point that TOKİ, the governorship, and the municipality reached because TOKİ has the money. In order to evacuate İç Kale [a historical part of Sur occupied by informal settlements], we didn't have any other choice but TOKİ. Yes, in it there is politics! When we finalized the preservation plan, there might be a decision prohibiting the destruction [of informal settlements]. However, just the cost of evacuation of these areas is 76 trillion lira." Soyukaya replied, "Yes, indeed, we cannot stop TOKİ's intervention. Yes to its money, but—" Mayor Baydemir continued, "We are involved in this process in order not to surrender to TOKİ, and we will not surrender [*teslim olmayacağız*]!" Perhaps Baydemir's choice of the word *surrender* was not accidental. His words, while assuring the Kurdish movement's ownership of the city, underscored once more the larger political battle between his party and the state. Yet, for the municipality, being involved in the process of urban development was an opportunity to influence the state's intervention in the city.

Strikingly, during these meetings, the pro-Kurdish municipality and its urban planners did not reject the project by insisting on the inability of the urban poor to afford to live in these housing projects or on the grounds of the accessibility problem presented by the new projects' proposed location on the far outskirts of the city. There were almost no mentions of urban poverty or any concerns about loss or despair. Very few of my interviewees—one local architect and one planner outside the municipal office—raised the concerns of residents: How would previously informal settlers strictly tied to an informal job market in the city center survive outside the city without even their unstable income?

Instead, during the meetings, most of the criticism of urban development plans focused solely on claims about the state's political authority over land use and the fact that TOKİ's urban renewal would "depopulate" the city, leading to the "eradication of Kurdish culture from the town." As Mayor Demirbaş explained, "Look, what we are thinking about here is not an urban renewal, but rather a way to show the identity of the city and its cultural and spiritual values. . . . The state aims to prevent the livelihood of these people; with this preservation plan it will be a project of revival for those that have been at risk of eradication." Echoing Mayor Demirbaş, several opinions concurred that TOKİ's program was not a simple urban renewal plan but an urban eradication plan. Debates between the governor and the pro-Kurdish party and mayoral administration were interwoven with assertions regarding ownership and identity politics in Diyarbakır.

In Search of International Support

To curb the state's intervention in Sur, the municipality's second urban maneuver involved seeking alternative planning strategies from the international community. On several occasions, from 2009 to 2011, the Diyarbakır Metropolitan Municipality invited representatives of internationally renowned architecture and urban design institutes, mainly from Europe, to organize workshops and develop new planning strategies for Sur. With these workshops and the reports they would generate, the party created wiggle room to sideline the state's plan and demonstrate possible urban solutions to the larger public without destroying squatter settlements and displacing residents.

Typically, these on-site workshops were organized for a period of two weeks. The foreign participants, mainly European architects, planners, and sometimes political scientists (ten to fifteen participants in total), would first receive a presentation from local officials describing the existing conditions of informal settlements. The formal presentation would be followed by site visits, accompanied by architects and urban planners of the municipality; then the groups would begin working on "alternative renewal solutions" without displacement. In these workshops, emphasis was generally placed on the fact that the population was already displaced and disadvantaged, and that TOKİ's plan of relocating the settlers would traumatize them even more. With these workshops, the municipality aimed at finding another stakeholder to legitimize its stance with the settlers. From the start, these workshops were planned to envision a set of concrete design strategies and typological solutions that would later easily translate into the regulations and policies of the preservation plan.

One of the first international proposals was the study of the Berlage Institute, an international postgraduate laboratory for research and development in the fields of architecture, urban planning, and landscape design with the support of the Matra Social Transformation Program of the Dutch Foreign Ministry. The Diyarbakır Metropolitan Municipality had asked the Berlage Institute to develop possible design strategies to be integrated into the forthcoming preservation plans. As a result of a summer workshop conducted in Diyarbakır in 2010, the Berlage Institute published a ninety-three-page report, *Accommodating the Displaced: A New Municipal Housing Service in Diyarbakır*. The report presented a large scope of analysis of the city's existing urban fabric, reasons for its decay, and a set of rehabilitation strategies and precedents at the end.

In the span of one year, the Berlage Institute published another report, *After Displacement: Ideas Toward the Preservation of Sur, Diyarbakır*, which suggested adopting a preservation logic based on the earliest photograph of Sur—dating back to 1939—and corresponded almost completely to the municipalities' approach to the squatter settlements. The proposal (also referred to as the Matra Project), while investigating the possible role of municipal housing schemes able to meet the desires and demands of an urban population with a rural background and agricultural livelihood, also explicitly criticized TOKİ's failure to serve these needs of the local population.⁵⁸ Further, the goals the report set were broader than just preserving squatter settlements but rather sought to inaugurate an innovative model for municipal social housing for the region. In the preface to the project's report, Mayor Baydemir stated that the Matra Project "is the first ever comprehensive international collaboration turning Diyarbakır's dream of creating a democratic, socially inclusive, egalitarian and peaceful public space into an urban reality that can be felt, seen, and lived by its local citizens. . . . Our eventual objective in the Matra Project is to establish a pioneering model for municipal social housing for Diyarbakır in particular, and for the region to which it belongs more broadly."⁵⁹ Following Berlage's work, in the fall of 2011, the Diyarbakır Municipality organized another workshop on international planning and urban design. This time they collaborated with Les Ateliers, a nonprofit organization that worked on city planning questions by organizing international workshops.

Les Ateliers stayed in Diyarbakır for about two weeks, working on alternative solutions for the residents of the *gecekondus* in the Ben-u-Sen neighborhood, one of the largest informal settlements of the city, located at the fringes of Sur. Around fifteen participants of Les Ateliers, including architects and urban planners from around the world, first received guided tours and briefings on the cultural and political history of the city, the urban fabric, and the Ben-u Sen neighborhood from local guides, authors, and planners. Later, participants were divided into three teams. Each team included one or two local architects or urban planners. At the end of two weeks, the teams presented their findings to an international jury, "to identify the most reliable analysis that can be used by the local authorities and to provide guidelines for TOKİ's regeneration plan," as they stated in their reports.⁶⁰ Generally, the teams presented detailed and colorful analysis through schemes, renderings, and photographs, and proposed to rehabilitate the streets, renovate or even rebuild existing housing for its current residents, and repurpose vacant lots with community centers and social facilities to respond to the disadvantaged populations' specific needs. They also emphasized making community use of historic structures and providing more accessibility, such as opening a ring road surrounding Sur and reconstructing avenues for more commerce—all without changing the traditional urban fabric. They provided rough guidelines with budget estimates and suggested including residents in participatory planning and architecture. The overall goal was to rehabilitate the residents' social and physical conditions without displacing them to public housing projects on the city's outskirts. At the same time, for Les Atelier, there was an important aspect of learning from the squatter settlements of Ben-u Sen, as they presented in their reports. In a twenty-four-page report titled *Ben U Sen in Diyarbakir: Potentials of Evolution of a Self-Made District*, the squatter settlements of Ben-u Sen were tagged as "a source of inspiration for a new urbanity," where one can develop learning tools "for a more sustainable urban way of life."[61]

In the end, however, none of the ideas offered in these workshops was implemented. TOKİ rejected these alternative methods of housing. And the municipality did not have the budget to realize them. When I returned to the city in 2012, I had the opportunity to inquire about those alternative projects and previous workshops at the Diyarbakır Metropolitan Municipality. I was given a simple answer: "We are done with those projects; they are completed." It was surprising to learn that the urban workshops of the past two years, months of studies, and pages of reports had all been shelved. The municipality planners also appeared to be frustrated by it as well. These international workshops did work in one sense, however: they created an extended debate in the city that literally paused the governor's urban intervention. All the projects were advertised on billboards throughout the city and on municipality websites. Each workshop concluded with a spectacular presentation and a gathering organized in Sümerpark, the municipality's cultural center. The municipality would publicly announce these event days before the workshop were held. Unions, civil society organizations, university professors, mayors, and—in particular—the press were invited. The alternative plans and suggestions were published and distributed among civil society organizations. Local newspapers wrote about the work of the municipality before and after the events. The mayors delivered talks about the importance of these workshops, emphasizing Kurdish identity in the city, the preservation of "Kurdish life," and solutions for the government's relocation plans.

For the BDP, the project's international as well as European dimension generated important wiggle room for translating and justifying the municipality's approach concerning city administration. Bringing this international scale down to housing problems at the local level was crucial to the municipality for at least two reasons. First, by organizing workshops with renowned European urban design institutions, the municipality would legitimize its approach while consolidating its power over urban development. Second, by establishing links with organizations outside the country, Diyarbakır would be linked to the world—without the government's patronage. For example, in an attempt to further protect the area, the Diyarbakır municipality sought to have Sur's fortress and Hevsel Gardens considered for UNESCO's World Heritage List. The gardens were added to UNESCO's tentative list in 2013 and became a World Heritage Site in 2015, as were the walls of the Diyarbakır fortress. Indeed, these projects, embraced by the pro-Kurdish mayors, spelled the transnationalization of Kurdish culture and rights. They also exemplify how pro-Kurdish party elites tried to bolster recognition of Kurdish identity in a time of globalization. In such transnational urban projects, several other pro-Kurdish party officials saw themselves as representatives of an autonomous nation.

When the Rhetoric of "Urban Development" Does Not Work

By the end of 2011, after years of the AKP's rhetoric of "urban development," TOKİ's urban renewal plans were still not working in Diyarbakır. The AKP was not able to get control of the city. What is more, despite all the laws favoring TOKİ, it was not able to begin demolition of the Lalebey and Ali Paşa neighborhoods. The urban and municipal laws once created by the AKP's government to increase the financial and administrative capacities of municipalities were creating obligations for the AKP in Kurdish cities.

Beginning as early as 2010, the AKP government had passed numerous urban laws that vastly increased the power of the central government. Later, in 2012, with a series of actions and law enforcement, the AKP government took major steps to limit the role of municipalities and local administrations, in order to bring urban development completely under its own purview. The government first created a new ministry, the Ministry of Environment and Urban Planning, and equipped it with wide-ranging zoning authority in transforming land. The same year, it established a new urban law, the "Disaster Law," which arrogated even more power from the municipalities. This law was initially created to prepare cities for the probable damage of natural disasters such as floods and earthquakes. According to the law, following risk determination, residential areas are classified according to disaster risk level, and high-risk areas are determined by TOKİ. In fact, once local administrations designated an area a "transformation zone," TOKİ carried out most of the law's implementation, such as preparing land-use plans for the area, constructing the new buildings, and rehousing the inhabitants in subsidized housing elsewhere.[62]

This change further empowered new large-scale developers and state actors (ministries, governors, TOKİ), who dominated urban development in the city centers. In addition to laws amended in 2005, 2007, 2012, and finally in 2013, the authority of TOKİ over squatter settlements (*gecekondus*) was expanded so that the authorities and tasks of the Ministry of Public Works and Settlement,[63] as well as those of the Department of Dwelling Affairs within the ministry, were assigned to TOKİ.[64] In other words, when the rhetoric of "urban development" did not work, the state adopted an even more authoritative and central model of urban planning. Within these changes, the authority of municipalities over housing was deactivated, and TOKİ was fully entitled to make any urban renewal plans in all types and scales on lots and lands under its possession or on areas determined as public housing sites by governorships. These new changes in urban law afforded extraordinary, immediate powers to both TOKİ and the Ministry of Urban Planning while stripping all powers from municipalities. TOKİ was authorized to implement its own urban renewal projects exempt from almost all outside control—meaning that any lot of land belonging to the state treasury could be allocated to TOKİ projects or left to the initiative of TOKİ to be sold to private construction contractors. As expected, mere days after this new law passed, the Lalebey and Ali Paşa neighborhoods of Sur were declared "high-risk zones." TOKİ could therefore implement the evictions quickly. By 2013 the Ali Paşa and Lalebey neighborhoods were expropriated (figure 7).[65]

A couple of months later, news began to appear in local newspapers: TOKİ was proceeding with its relocation plan. The municipality was assigned to vacate and demolish the *gecekondus* by paying the cost of the houses in the Ali Paşa

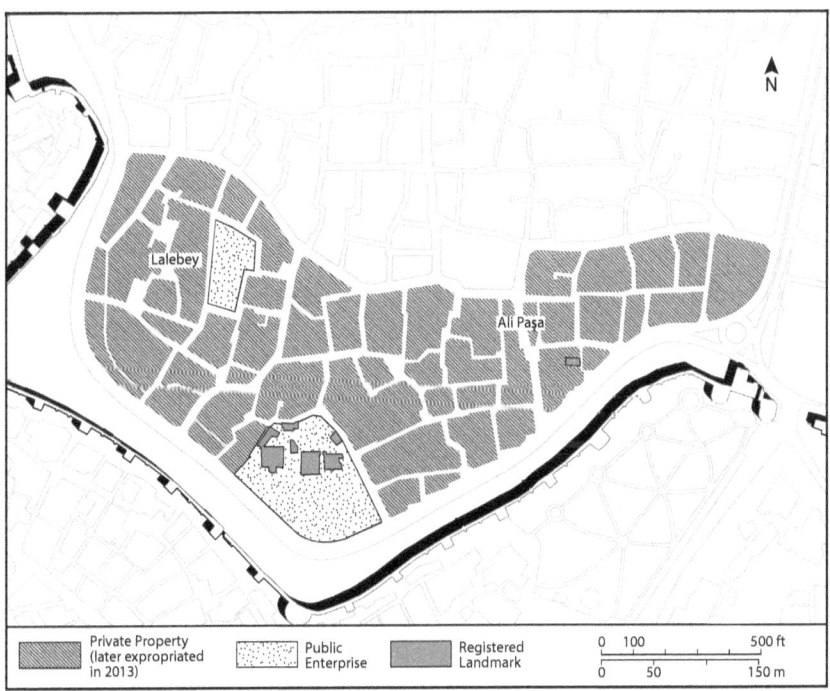

FIGURE 7. Map showing the expropriated properties of Lalebey and Ali Paşa neighborhoods in Sur, 2013.
Source: Based on plan provided by the Sur municipality.

and Lalebey neighborhoods, while TOKİ would relocate the residents to public houses in Çölgüzeli, outside the city. According to the protocol between TOKİ and the prospective owners, one option was for those displaced to take the cost of the *gecekondu* as an advanced payment for the house they would own, after approximately fifteen to twenty years of additional payments. Another option given to *gecekondu* owners was for TOKİ to simply buy their houses in Sur by paying costs. Several of those who agreed to leave chose the latter option, preferring to move into another *gecekondu* in the same area, close to their previous neighborhoods. The majority of Lalebey and Ali Paşa settlers refused to move out. Despite the years-long urban conflict between the governor and the municipality, TOKİ was able to evacuate only around 15 percent of the residents.[66] Amid the preservation meetings, international workshops, and public protests, TOKİ's intervention in the urban renewal project of Lalebey and Ali Paşa was effectively paused for about six years. As I discuss in chapter 6, only after the armed conflict in Sur in 2015 between the PKK guerrillas and the Turkish army was TOKİ able to intervene again in the neighborhood—this time in the wake of military power.[67]

From Urban Contestation to Articulating the Kurdish Bloc

A massive body of literature on urban renewal and development has accumulated over the past decade. Scholarship with a particular focus on the displacement of squatter settlers across the Global South has generally conceptualized these dramatic land transformations in terms of neoliberal changes to the city shaped by state actors, urban elites, and large developers, and characterized these changes by a loss of sociability, despair, and increasing inequality among the settlers.[68] Within this realm, scholars have paid substantial attention to urban contestations between the squatter settlers and the state. These urban development projects came to be understood within changes to the neoliberal regime or global economic development in which the commodification of land and urban dislocation developed through lucrative relations among private capital, urban elites, and the state.

In fact, the Lalebey and Ali Paşa cases illustrate a neoliberal turn in the city wherein several urban policies sought to displace the urban poor in the name of promoting urban revitalization—yet another case of gentrification.[69] However, urban renewal in Diyarbakır was not only about capitalist accumulation, as several urban scholars would maintain; it was, I argue, more about maintaining control over urban space. By moving residents from their informal houses in

Sur to high-rise apartment buildings on the fringes of the city, the government attempted to dismantle the network of mobilized citizens, both physically and socially. In fact, government officials would, from time to time, make statements like, "If we cannot complete urban renewal and resolve the *gecekondu* problem, we cannot end terrorism."[70] However, urban renewal attempts by the AKP were not able to break the ties between the residents and the party.[71]

Perhaps not the governorship but the pro-Kurdish party creatively turned this existing contestation into an opportunity to strengthen its popular base in the city. During this process, Diyarbakır witnessed several Sur preservation plan meetings, meetings with the governor and the residents, international workshops, and organized protests by Sur residents resisting eviction. Between 2009 and 2015 in Diyarbakır, I encountered many furious voices when I attempted to ask about TOKİ's eviction and relocation plans. In 2011, I attended an informal neighborhood meeting in Sur in the courtyard of one of the residents' houses, organized by the neighborhood council. I was not allowed to record the conversation, but I took notes. When the neighbors learned that I was an architect conducting urban planning research in Diyarbakır, they begun to address me as "Ms. Architect" (*Mimar Hanım*). One resident, Rasim, a cook in a local restaurant in Sur who was waiting to be evicted, turned to me and said, "Yes, we will be given a house, but we will be still jobless. How am I going to pay my bills there? We will be so far away from the city. How are we going to commute to the city to look for a job? You tell me, *Mimar Hanım*," looking for confirmation from me. Another resident, Ahmet, a construction worker in his mid-thirties, interrupted Rasim's words: "There is no point for us to move to those state houses; we cannot leave Sur. Our life is here. We will move to another house—this time again it will be *gecekondu*, in this area. The state once took away our houses, we moved here. Now they are taking our home away from us again. By forcing us out, the state is taking our Kurdish rights away from us. As you are an architect, you know how much it would cost us to rebuild our house."

Strikingly, in their daily conversations, residents never used the term "social housing" or "public housing," as the projects had been promoted. In the eyes of Diyarbakırians, these housing units were a "state project"—yet another imposition from the Turkish state. The distinction between "us" and "them," drawn between the party and the state, was also evident among the residents. As Laclau and Mouffe suggest, for articulatory practice to be considered hegemonic practice, "articulation should take place through a confrontation with antagonistic articulatory practices—in other words, that hegemony should emerge in a field crisscrossed by antagonisms and therefore suppose phenomena of equivalence and frontier effects."[72] In this sense, within the housing debate, the party successfully cultivated a sense of unity and coherence among diverse residents. The conflict between the state and the party, in this instance, was pursued over urban development. By leveraging municipal power, the pro-Kurdish party managed to turn this contestation in its favor. Any talk about urban renewal or housing would easily lead to talk of state intervention and state politics. My interviews exemplify this point. Nidar, a fifty-year-old street vendor with a family of six, was a migrant who came to Sur from Cizre in 1996. I met Nidar accidentally, in 2011, while I was in the Ali Paşa neighborhood photographing squatter settlements. That afternoon, when I stopped at a little grocery to buy water, Nidar, sitting on the stairs by the shop, was smoking a cigarette and resting in the shade by the store. When I learned that he was a resident of the squatter settlements in Lalebey, I asked him if he was planning to take the compensation and move out. He did not tell me directly if he was actually going to move out, but he expressed his frustration: "The soldier [meaning military forces] burnt our village. We came here to set up a new life, and we will not let the state do this [evict us] one more time. What is service? What is state? We don't expect any service, but we want to live like humans, you know, like humans. We are Kurds."

Nidar reminded me of Havin, who had told me a couple of years previously with almost same words, "We want our Kurdish identity back." I was struck by the fact that, from a university student like Havin to a street vendor, frequent emphasis was placed on "Kurdishness" and "Kurdish identity," even during ordinary conversations—such as, in this case, about housing. Nidar's narrative further exemplifies how residents made sense of the role of a pro-Kurdish municipality. The municipality, once again, more than service provider, was a defender of Kurdish rights and identity. For Diyarbakırians, TOKİ's relocation plan went beyond simply being an urban development plan disfavoring urban poor; it was viewed as an attack on Kurdish culture and rights. This sentiment was expressed by mayors, in the newspapers, in workshops, and echoed through Diyarbakırians' everyday life.

The BDP was able to spark mobilization against state coercion around housing. When anti-TOKİ housing protests took place, not only Sur residents but also residents from other districts would participate. In Diyarbakır, mobilization against the AKP's urban interventions was able to "galvanize group feeling and articulate pre-existing levels of groupness."[73] What gave residents a sense of their shared experience was not only their common past or the common practice of conversing about housing plans, but also the political party creating articulation through consent, connection, and recognition across the city.

Debates in newspapers, demonstrations, daily conversations in the streets, coffee meetings critiquing the TOKİ houses and the state's plan for squatter settlements, discussions in urban workshops, chants during rallies—all were marking the "state acting against Kurds and Kurdish culture."[74] At the same time, these daily debates and conversations characterized the practice of "nationness"—what Rogers Brubaker calls "a contingent event that crystallize[s] and spread[s] through the warp and woof of everyday political experience."[75] Here the party's significance, I argue, resides in its ability to reproduce this "contingent event" and the vocabularies of imagined community. Housing cases examined in this chapter suggest that national belonging can be generated by "transient events of collective vulnerability."[76] People associating the municipality with the "defender of Kurdish rights" and with their anti–urban renewal demonstrations, and interpreting relocation plans as attacks on Kurdish culture—all this coming together was not accidental, nor did it occur in a vacuum. In building a Kurdish frontier, the pro-Kurdish party influenced how people came together and how they thought about the "state" and about "Kurdishness."

The urban contestation over squatter settlements discussed in these pages raises another essential question. Unlike in several other cases around the world in which state authorities have worked on ending urban informality, the municipality of Diyarbakır was, in fact, advocating urban informality. Simultaneously, despite extraordinary conditions of compensation and subsidies, most of the residents of Sur insisted on staying in their squatter settlements. Why did the municipality want to sustain squatter settlements in the midst of the city? Was it simply a matter of claiming ownership, or concerns about voting power? In the next chapter, I explore why and how urban informality constituted such a vital ground for the Kurdish movement. I reveal the creation of networks among the squatter settlers and how they provided a fluid backdrop for the pro-Kurdish party to design and implement programs against the established (state) order.

3

SEEING LIKE A MOVEMENT, ACTING LIKE A STATE

"We Will Administer Ourselves"

Why have pro-Kurdish municipalities sought to keep squatter settlements (*gecekondus*) in the midst of the city? The approach of pro-Kurdish municipalities to squatter settlements presents a puzzle. Unlike several other cases around the world in which municipalities work to end urban informality in the city, the municipality of Diyarbakır, in fact, wanted to sustain just such conditions. Moreover, why did settlers resist leaving their informal settlements for public housing units despite relatively generous subsidization efforts from the central government in Ankara?

In such situations, some urban scholars would reason that a municipality's attempts are tied to its electoral concerns with sustaining popular votes. Others would ascribe the resistance of squatter settlers to leave informal settlements and city centers to job-related concerns as well as accessibility. While these reasons are relevant, the political engagement of the municipality vis-à-vis urban informality should compel us to dig deeper. What, we might ask, explains the desire to keep squatter settlements in the midst of the city other than voting or relocation concerns? How are we to understand these urban processes of squatter settlements when an oppositional political party performs like a social movement at the same time that it acts like a state? In this chapter, I aim to explore the link between urban informality and political articulation.[1]

As early as the 1970s, several urbanists rightly moved away from framing squatter settlers as "marginals" and squatter settlements as "sick cells" in need of removal.[2] Instead, they looked at how "urban informality," as they called it, may provide venues for participation, recourse, and accountability.[3] As Nezar

AlSayyad and Ananya Roy once argued, urban informality does not consist solely of illegal settlements and the activities of the urban poor, or of a particular status of labor or marginality.[4] Rather, urban informality is an "organizing urban logic that constitutes the rules of the game, determining the nature of transactions between individuals and institutions, and within institutions."[5] It is the organizing logic, I argue, that makes squatter settlers open to political engagement and mobilization.

In this chapter, I illustrate how urban informality provided a fluid backdrop for the pro-Kurdish party to design and implement programs against the established (state) order. I show how the "organizing logic of urban informality" shaped the activities of the urban poor in both public and domestic spaces. I posit that the organizing logic of squatter settlements—socially and physically—allowed the pro-Kurdish municipality to fill in the missing aspects of everyday life for the residents and draw connections among urban institutions, society, and action.[6] In doing so, the municipality amalgamated the links between society and the party through local foundations and associations.

Filling the Gaps

From the early 2000s until 2015, the pro-Kurdish party found itself enacting state power against "the state" (the central government in Ankara) through the channel of municipalities.[7] In other words, holding municipal power enabled the party to "see like a movement and act like a state."[8] By "state," I mean the status of the pro-Kurdish party holding municipal power; and by "social movement," I mean another status of the pro-Kurdish party as a social movement actualized by establishing networks of activism against the government's order in the city. Early activist advocacy helped party members establish strong links with social groups on the ground to mobilize support for the pro-Kurdish movement. Party leaders and party elites usually had a strong activist background, such as serving in administrative capacities in human rights associations, unions, women's organizations, bar associations, and NGOs.[9] For instance, the then-chair of the BDP (Peace and Democracy Party) Selahattin Demirtaş partook in the administration of the Diyarbakır Human Rights Association prior to joining the party. Before being elected mayor of Sur, Abdullah Demirbaş was a member of the Turkish Union of Education (Eğitim-Sen). Osman Baydemir, the mayor of Diyarbakır from 2009 to 2014, was vice president of the Diyarbakır Human Rights Association before his tenure in office. Strong connections with NGOs and unions helped the pro-Kurdish party forge strong alliances with a wide-ranging organizational network at the local level.[10]

The BDP not only built on existing social, economic, and cultural networks but also actively and strategically created new networks via institutions and programs that served to articulate a Kurdish bloc in the city.[11] Various pro-Kurdish social institutions and programs, established and operated directly by the municipalities, span diverse areas such as vocational training, art education, income-generating activities, and civic-participating programs. These organizations and centers, directly founded and conducted by the party or the municipality, were not the only platforms the party would use to build coherent Kurdish blocs. The party presided over a network of interlocking support groups that directly advocated for Kurdish politics and were reciprocally sustained by the party.[12] By 2010, Diyarbakır had over nine hundred civil society organizations, both large and small, over six hundred of which actively supported the party. In Diyarbakır, it was not uncommon for an ordinary citizen to belong to five different associations. These civil society organizations held activities that specifically addressed Kurdish rights and social justice, and they constituted crucial nodes of Kurdish political society. Among the largest organizations in Diyarbakır were the Human Rights Association in Turkey (İHD), the Movement for Kurdish Education and Language (TZP Kurdi), the Immigrants' Association for Social Cooperation and Culture (Göç-Der), and the Association of Poverty Fighting and Sustainable Development (Sarmaşık Derneği).

From larger-scale civil and political associations to smaller-scale neighborhood associations, the party built a strong network of alliances through which many of these organizations supported one another. Through these links, different social groups were able to collectively move in the same direction. Representatives of the neighborhood associations were from the local community, knew Kurdish well, and could easily communicate with local residents. The associations and the political party maintained close ties, frequently collaborating and sharing resources in different areas, such as reporting violations of human rights, mobilizing protests, or organizing signature campaigns. Party leaders, members, and activists worked face to face, street by street, and district by district on a foundation of personal relations.[13] Activists were also matched to residents in their neighborhood according to gender, age, and kinship ties, benefiting from loyalties between friends and neighbors.

In the next section, in further analyzing the relationship between the pro-Kurdish party and the squatter settlers, I focus on the Sur district of Diyarbakır. My selection of Sur for this analysis is intentional. As I discuss in the previous chapter, Sur was the largest quarter of squatter settlements, as well as one of the main hubs of Kurdish mobilization and activism—and its neighborhoods were targets of the state's project of urban renewal and settler relocation. Therefore, analysis of the activities of the party, municipality, and local associations in Sur affords critical insights into the mechanisms of this relationship.

My fieldwork in Sur aimed to assess the commitments and undertakings of the political party, the local community, and various associations, especially those operated or supported by the municipality. I sought to examine the relationship between the municipality and local residents because the former was one of the most obvious ties between the party and society. A particularly important point of concentration was how residents become involved in politics through service delivery or support centers. As part of this research, I conducted both structured and free-floating interviews with focus groups, including mayors, party members, residents, participants in local associations, and ordinary residents, both men and women. I tracked specific informants as they moved around the neighborhood and took part in associations during their daily lives. I repeated my observations and traced specific informants over the span of ten years. These informants appear in other chapters; however, this chapter addresses a two-year portion of this ethnographic fieldwork.

The Party's Urban and Civil Network in Sur

For most Diyarbakırians, Diyarbakır means Sur. Sur is the heart and the beginning of the city. In the history of the city, anyone over forty, if not a recent migrant, has likely lived in Sur at some point. Since the mid-1980s, Sur has sheltered thousands of squatter settlements built on private land or on lots left empty by the displacement of local populations. In Sur, narrow, short, dead-end streets punctuated with doorsteps are informal extensions of houses, fostering spaces where women and children engage in conversations and socialize, thereby establishing an open public space for broader interaction. These informal spaces serve as grounds for forging strong connections and nurturing social cohesion (figure 8).

The vast majority of residents are rural migrants, most of whom were internally displaced, especially during the conflict between the Turkish military forces and the PKK.[14] The armed conflict, internal displacement, and the austerity politics of successive governments since the mid-1980s increased poverty rates in Kurdish cities, leading to income figures approximately 54 percent less than Turkey's average and 70 percent less than Istanbul's.[15] And in Sur and similar squatter settlements in the region, income levels are even lower. Most of Sur's residents have few or no skills for the urban job market. They live below the poverty line, working largely in informal sectors or as temporary workers—as street vendors, construction workers, and daily carriers.[16] Many women, in particular, are not literate and speak only Kurdish—especially the rural dialects of Kurmanji and Zazaki.

FIGURE 8. Typical street layout view in squatter settlements in Sur in 2009.
Source: Author, 2009.

Almost the entire population of Sur has been oppressed by state interventions, such as by losing their houses during forced migrations. It is also not uncommon for families to have had at least one of their family members fighting with the PKK "in the mountains." On an ordinary day, in the streets, one often encounters "illegal" graffiti promoting a free Kurdistan or praising the PKK, or a group of children chanting well-known Kurdish slogans, such as "Biji Apo" (Long live Apo)—meaning PKK founder Abdullah Öcalan (figure 9).[17] During my fieldwork, the residents of Sur were remarkable not only for their politicized arrangement but also for their daily engagement and continuous mobilization around political action.[18] In Sur, it was common to see public demonstrations side by side with a tourist group exploring the walls or shopping in the old market.

Despite its highly politicized population, Sur was not isolated from the rest of the city, nor did its settlers fit the category of "being under class or [of]

FIGURE 9. Graffiti in the Hasırlı neighborhood of Sur, Diyarbakır. On the left "APO" and "PKK" refer to Abdullah Öcalan and the Kurdistan Workers' Party. The middle reads, "Kurdistan is a rebellion" (Kürdistan İsyandır, in Turkish). On the right it reads "Happy Resurrection Day" in Kurdish, referring to the PKK's foundation day.
Source: Author, 2009.

advanced marginality."[19] In fact, Sur was one of the hubs for Kurdish mobilization and activism and was well connected to the rest of the city. Its residents were active participants in the city's politics and social life. They were neither spatially alienated nor stigmatized but rather at the center of everyday urban life, identified with a growing sense of a politicized Kurdish community in Diyarbakır.

For instance, between 2008 and 2016, thousands of Sur residents militantly refused to pay their electricity bills. "This is the state's [*devlet*] electricity," said a resident of Sur in the İskenderpaşa neighborhood. "Why am I going to pay for it? In reality, the state owes this to me. The state forced us to move here. We lost our village; we lost our place." In the residents' minds, there were two types of state authorities. Residents would often refer to the central government as the state (*devlet*). Even though the municipality is technically a state organization, in residents' mind the municipalities administrated by the pro-Kurdish party are not the "state."

Among informal settlers in the Middle East, refusal to pay the electric bill is a common practice. Indeed, such activities are usually driven by the force of necessity—"territorially based action by the poor" striving for a share of urban services.[20] Quite often, such responses could also be interpreted as what Asef Bayat calls "quiet encroachment"—that is, "open and fleeting struggles without clear leadership, ideology, or structured organization."[21] But in the context of the Kurdish movement, such actions are part of a conscious political act—with clear leadership, ideology, and structured organization that constantly mobilize residents against the "state." In Sur, refusal to pay the electricity bill was not an individual act or a "quiet encroachment" but an engaged, collective action by residents and the political party.[22] In Sur, this urban condition was produced by pairing a political party with local associations in the larger politics of populist mobilization and the local struggle for political power. The salient feature of urban informality in Sur was that informal practices not only engaged with the built environment but were also embedded in organized political affiliation with the BDP, in the reciprocal relations among squatter groups, the political party, and the municipality. The leadership of the BDP actually sustained the condition of urban informality, which allowed the political party to blur its lines between municipal institution and social movement.

In the summer of 2009 I continued my fieldwork in Sur. When I met with Mayor Abdullah Demirbaş, he was well equipped in his effort to keep the squatter settlers living in Sur. He was once again embroiled in several ongoing trials because of his pro-Kurdish projects for expansion of the Kurdish language—including printing a children's book and tourist brochures in Kurdish and allegedly giving a blessing in Kurdish while officiating at a wedding ceremony. "No matter if this is a crime, I will continue my struggle for our rights to speak in our mother tongue. Language is a basic right of every human being," Mayor Demirbaş said, leaning back into his chair and pushing away from his desk, which was piled with files and paperwork. He then leaned forward and grabbed a group of folders. Handing them to me, he said, "Look at these files. These are ongoing prosecutions against me for our multilingual municipality projects, which makes 486 years in total prison sentences." He added, "Perhaps this is why my son went to the mountains."[23] He indicated a silver-framed photograph on his desk, a picture of his sixteen-year-old son wearing a school uniform. "It has been fifteen days since he left, and his mother is so worried for him. Because my son, my own son, lost his faith in peace, all of our efforts here are to make my son and other sons to return home."

When Mayor Demirbaş showed the file of investigations to me, he probably did not imagine that he would be detained as soon as he was. A couple of months after our interview, in December 2009, Demirbaş and several other politicians, along with a large number of journalists and activists, were rounded up under a Turkish court order for alleged links with the KCK (Kurdistan Democratic Confederation, or Kurdistan Communities Union) as part of a widespread crackdown.[24]

Throughout the summer of 2009, I wanted to take a closer look at how Sur's formal and informal local associations were organized and at their interlocking relationship with one another and the party, society, and the municipality. Demirbaş had intimate knowledge of every single civil society organization and neighborhood association in Sur. During one of my interviews with him—when I asked about ties between the local associations and the party—he suggested that I visit the Free Compatriot Association (Özgür Yurttaş Derneği, or FCA) and immediately called one of his assistants, Melih, to take me to the Hasırlı neighborhood.

The FCA was a locally based association that had started in Diyarbakır in the early 2000s. The association, most of whose members were male, had branches primarily in the informal settlements. It was known for its efforts to mobilize support for the Kurdish movement and for organizing protests and demonstrations against the state.

It was early in the morning when Melih, wearing a green polo shirt untucked over his jeans, took me to the FCA in Hasırlı. As we made our way through the neighborhood, I got to know Melih. His parents were among the first large wave of migrants that arrived in Diyarbakır from Lice, in the 1950s. In the beginning, they were living in Sur, but later, by the mid-1990s, they moved to Kayapınar, outside of Sur. While walking through the narrow streets in Hasırlı, Melih remarked that Sur was not always as it is today. "It changed a lot after the migrations in the 1990s. Here it became deteriorated. Now, everywhere is full of *gecekondu*. People are vulnerable; they are poor here." Indeed, most Diyarbakırians used to describe Hasırlı as a neighborhood of extreme poverty. As discussed in chapter 2, it was one of the neighborhoods from which the governor of Diyarbakır wanted to relocate the residents. Among Diyarbakırians, Hasırlı was known in particular for its Kurdish mobilization and support groups for the PKK. Melih remarked, "But you know what? The state's police cannot enter here! This is our territory here. Even if they [police] arrive, they cannot arrest anyone. One could move from one roof to another or from the tunnels connecting these houses here."[25] When we arrived at the FCA's two-story building, the group's representative, Hasan, in his late thirties, was waiting for us outside. Like almost all the houses in the neighborhood, the association's building was not legal. But lacking the proper building title was perhaps the least of the staff members' concerns. From Hasan's greeting, I gathered that Melih had explained to him that I was interested in learning about the association. Making clear the group's links with the municipality and the party, Hasan emphasized that, under normal circumstances, they would probably not grant an interview, but I was a guest of the mayor. While passing through the short corridor leading to the meeting room, I noticed the daily shift list of the members hanging on the wall. It had only male names. After removing our shoes, we entered the small meeting room—simply furnished as a living room in a traditional Kurdish house, with carpets on the floor and *diwans* to the side. On the middle column, under the traditional Kurdish *heybe*, hung a poster of the International Declaration of Human Rights (figure 10). The small bookshelf held several banned books on the ideology and history of the PKK, as well as some writings by Abdullah Öcalan and a poster of Öcalan himself. On the opposite wall was a large poster of Cihan Deniz and Hüsnü Albay, two former PKK members who died in a car accident in 2008. The poster displayed them in civilian clothes without labeling their names. Below the image it read, in Kurdish, "Şehîdê Kurdistanê Namırın," meaning "The martyrs of Kurdistan are immortal."[26]

Along with Hasan, three other members joined us on the floor; Hasan, however, did most of the speaking. I asked about the association's activities and outreach and how they see the contemporary conditions of Kurdish politics. Though the group was open to talking about their association's ideology and goals, the members were prohibited from sharing their individual stories, such as how they were recruited into the association. During our conversations, sometimes Hasan would spontaneously speak, carefully choosing which questions to answer. He spoke very slowly, pausing and selecting his words. Each of his sentences, coming intermittently, seemed almost chosen from Öcalan's writings.[27] I was not allowed to record our meeting or take any pictures of the members, so I took notes instead. Before he poured tea for us, Hasan rinsed all the glasses with boiling

FIGURE 10. The meeting room of the Free Compatriot Association in Sur. *Source:* Author, 2009.

water. "This is how we pour tea," he said while taking a puff of his cigarette. Then he explained: "This is the project of the leadership [*önderlik*; the word meaning "leadership" is commonly used to refer to Abdullah Öcalan]. This is a project that belongs to the city, belongs to the people. We take our support from people, and we support people. This is our struggle from the bottom up. We will not surrender. We prove that there can be life without a state. We don't need any state."

The organization had about one hundred members in the Hasırlı neighborhood, I learned. Their web of influence, however, was larger than that. The main outreach activity was a weekly meeting organized in the association's building. In the small room where we sat they would organize book reading nights or hold their meetings, which they called "meetings of awareness." Hasan continued: "Every week, we organize meetings here to bring the awareness of free citizenship to people and disseminate the message of the leadership. We have a lot of attendees not only from Hasırlı but from whole Suriçi."

Like several other local associations in Diyarbakır, the group relied on personal relations to communicate and was not using phones or the internet. "To invite people to our rally or a meeting, we have street leaders. We begin from one corner of the neighborhood, and we continue from there. We individually knock the doors one by one and invite the households to the protests, rally, or a meeting here." Sur's informal residential layout allowed this invitation activity. This way, the association was able to limit state surveillance and assess who was committed—or not—to the movement.

"We are strong here [in Hasırlı]," Hasan continued. "We also give support to women's laundry houses." These were called White Butterflies Laundry Houses. In Diyarbakır, civil society centers, particularly those in the informal settlements, were often gender-segregated. In these centers, while women's organizations mainly emphasized daily support for women's chores, male-dominated organizations aimed to raise awareness of human rights and justice through seminars and meetings. But why and how would a male-dominated platform politically representing itself as an organization for the full awareness of society concerning "state-free citizenship" support the municipality's laundry houses for women?

Following my visit to the FCA, I visited the laundry house, located a few houses away in the same neighborhood. The laundry houses were first established by the municipality in 2003 and 2004 in the Hasırlı, Ben-u Sen, and Aziziye neighborhoods, and expanded to Yeniköy in 2010—all informal settlements whose residents struggled with poverty. Most of the residents of these neighborhoods did not have washing machines or the infrastructure to install them. Most of the women were housewives with multiple children. The Hasırlı laundry house was in a large single-story house with a sizable garden, where women frequently sat together to converse or chat while waiting for their laundry to finish. It included a lounge for the women with a small kitchenette and satellite TV.

While these laundry houses appeared to be a simple response by the municipality to accommodate the household needs of women, their organization frequently went beyond that.[28] During three visits on different days, I noticed that ROJ TV, a pro-Kurdish channel broadcasting from Denmark in Kurdish, was constantly on the television, even when the lounge was empty. Next to the lounge was a children's room, where women could leave their children in a place with toys and children's books in Kurdish. Social workers who were party members worked closely with the women. "Laundry houses," said the municipality officer, "while easing the burdens of everyday life, also strengthen women's knowledge of freedom, self-awareness, and women's rights."[29] In these houses, while women did their laundry, they were also expected to participate in seminars organized by the municipality. Seminars were in the form of conversations with social workers on topics varying from women's rights, to human rights, to hygiene and child care. Through these seminars and organizations, the party aimed to emancipate women from their traditional roles and foster self-awareness and a sense of freedom. In fact, in the everyday life of the city, laundry houses were a crucial platform for the municipality—and therefore for the party—in establishing connections with the women of the neighborhood, recruiting women members for the party, and disseminating party ideology.

Cultivating Politics in Homes and Expanding the Networks

In February 2011 I again visited Mayor Demirbaş. After five months of imprisonment he had been released in May 2010 because of health problems and since had returned to work. A large black cloth, displayed to protest his detention in December 2009 along with that of other pro-Kurdish politicians, mayors, and activists, was still hanging from the walls of the municipal building. Following Demirbaş's return, one could easily recognize the change in the municipality. From the visual symbols to the interactions among municipality staff, the sense of Kurdishness had become even bolder and more pronounced. Despite his detention, Demirbaş did not seem cowed.

Upon entering the municipality building, visitors were greeted by ribbon bands in the red, white, green, and yellow of the "Kurdistan" flag. Mayor Demirbaş had already put his project of a multilingual municipality into practice. The Turkish signs inside the building had been replaced by trilingual signs, in Kurdish, Turkish, and English. Even though the official language was still Turkish, several staff members consciously opted to use Kurdish in their interactions. Meeting with the mayor, I immediately noted that he had not lost an ounce of his activist energy and excitement. His son was still in the mountains. He was preoccupied with a queue of visitors outside his office. As soon as I sat down with him, he eagerly delved into discussions about his latest projects.

They were making efforts to hire new staff members who knew Kurdish, in order to provide better services to the local residents. "They are migrants with little or no school education," Demirbaş said. "The only language they speak is Kurdish.... We have to serve our [Sur] residents better." He was explicit about party politics and was aiming to take care of not only Kurds but all minorities. The party was very careful about presenting itself as being about democracy and justice for all, not just a Kurdish nationalist party. Demirbaş was eager to carry out his Street of Cultures project, which involved restoring a local mosque, a synagogue, and an Armenian church, and rejuvenating the multicultural atmosphere of Sur. "See," he said, "our movement is not only about Kurds. It is our aim to bring back the multicultural environment of Sur and restore its cultural rights." Yet the majority of the projects focused on generating a new Kurdish identity.

In the span of two years, party activism and the party's network had visibly expanded from local neighborhood associations to individual homes, further strengthening connections. Sur municipality's "Every Night One Story, Every House Is a School" project, organized as a house meeting, exemplified this networking. The project aimed to restore and strengthen traditional Kurdish culture. Neighbors would gather each night in one of their houses with a *mamoste* (teacher), *dengbej* (musical bard),[30] and *şesyda* (imam) to tell Kurdish folktales to the children of the neighborhood; 365 stories for children, in Kurdish and other minority languages, were planned for publication. Demirbaş invited me to one of those house meetings organized by the municipality in the İskenderpaşa neighborhood. The house occupied the second floor of one of the squatter settlements. The owner's strong ties with the party were recognizable from the way he and Demirbaş greeted each other. That night, the small living room, decorated simply with *sedirs* on the floor, was filled with about fifty people, with children in front, men to the side, and women at the entrance side of the living room. Mayor Demirbaş, Levon (a famous Turkish Armenian author and a former Armenian resident of Sur), Afran (a prominent local author and former consultant for the Diyarbakır mayor) were sitting together with the *mamoste*, the *şeyda*, and the *dengbej*. Those unable to find a spot in the living room floor moved to the hallway of the house. In the middle, on a large tray, traditional snacks—dried figs and dried mulberry pulp—were presented for the guests to taste.

It was an evening of acute nostalgia for everyday Kurdish culture. Mayor Demirbaş began in Kurdish, explaining the importance of the project to regenerating Kurdish culture, particularly among children. "In our culture," Demirbaş said, "there have been three important features: our mothers, our *dengbej*, and our *şeyda*. Thanks to them, our Kurdish culture is still alive today. Today, here in these houses, we bring these features together." The *mamoste* began, emphasizing the importance of the Kurdish language for the following generations. The *şeyda* followed, telling a short religious story about honesty. The *dengbej* continued by chanting a short *kilam* (recital). The participation of the *dengbej* was symbolic. Using a poetic style (without music), *dengbejs* have been crucial oral historians, passing down traditions and memories of the Kurds. Because written Kurdish could not be developed among Kurds, *dengbejs* told stories about agonies, love, aspirations, nationalism, wars, and clashes between families.[31] And yet, several times, *dengbejs* have been silenced and prohibited by Turkish officials under the ban against the Kurdish language.[32] After the mid-2000s, pro-Kurdish municipalities began to reactivate the *dengbej* tradition in the cities, organizing festivals or opening *dengbej* houses.

As each speaker took his turn, a hushed admiration filled the room. Sitting next to me on the floor, a young female journalist from a local newspaper diligently took notes and photographs during the event. Later, Levon began speaking. Under the multicultural municipality project of Sur, Mayor Demirbaş had recently named the street of the Armenian author's childhood home after him. Talking about vivid memories of his childhood, Levon expressed a yearning for Diyarbakır's past, with its "multicultural streets and traditions." Finally, Afran began, wistfully speaking about his youth and friends in Diyarbakır and completing his speech with a wish, in Kurdish, to "free Kurdistan." *Every Night One Story, Every House Is a School* was just one of the BDP's projects, with political and civil society interacting to develop and reinforce Kurdish identity among the local communities. It was regulated by highly organized actions of the party under an umbrella of "Kurdishness" that tied households to one another and to the party. Organizers were to ensure that each component of the project was implemented properly and that various other houses in Sur were already listed as venues for following events.

Municipality Facilitating the Informal Economy

In the spring of 2011 I saw the spectrum of local associations expand, not only in number but also in content. Domestic, commercial, and social and political relations were intertwined, each becoming a resource for the others.[33] Women's organizations had grown from daily support activities, like the laundry houses, to income-generating activities, coupled with political empowerment initiatives. These income-generating activities, organized by the municipality, were heavily embedded in multiple dimensions of everyday domestic life, such as women's abilities to cook and bake, and incorporated child and family care. For example, women would bake breads at *tandır* houses, next to the laundry houses, and sell them at local markets (figure 11). The municipal officers actively participated by designating the market and supporting the women in selling their home-produced goods.

Women's Support Houses (Kadın Destek Merkezi, or KADEM) were founded by the municipality initially to provide services in five different neighborhoods.

FIGURE 11. A view of women getting ready to distribute the *tandır* bread by a laundry house in Sur.
Source: Author, 2011.

They not only supported women in their daily activities but also promoted income-generating organizational centers that connected civil society to the party. I was introduced to KADEM by Saliha, the vice-mayor of Sur municipality, who was in her late twenties. Born in the Hasırlı district, Saliha held a bachelor of science degree in agricultural engineering. She had joined the municipality board after the 2009 local elections and was subsequently elected vice-mayor. In fact, Saliha filled the mayorship for a while when Sur's mayor was detained in 2009. She had a small office, and I rarely saw her there except when she had visitors. Wearing jeans with a khaki or a black blouse, and with her long brown hair in a ponytail, Saliha was usually in the field supervising micro-level women's projects and associations, especially KADEM.

KADEM offered informal types of home-based micro-projects that women could undertake as a form of poverty alleviation. Through KADEM, women took literacy courses as well as vocational courses in embroidery and other needlework, jewelry design, mushroom cultivation, and pickle production, typically producing these products at home and selling them in local markets or grocery stores with the help of the municipality. Women cultivated produce in their courtyards, gardens, sheds, and basements. Saliha, with her agricultural background, was leading these projects. In the afternoons she would often audit these women's support centers and follow up with advising ongoing projects. Notably, the pro-Kurdish party's approach to women was not unique to Sur municipality but was within the scope of their larger political agenda. Especially since 2002, the pro-Kurdish party's campaigns included "Women's Liberation" among the main party goals.[34] The DTP was the first party to introduce the cochair system (*eş başkanlık*) for joint leadership of a man and a woman at all levels of the party.[35]

In March 2011 I accompanied Saliha as she audited home-based projects. One afternoon we were checking mushroom cultivation in Sur. Residents of these houses would sell the mushrooms to the local market. Because of the natural humidity in the basements of squatter settlements, Saliha explained, "mushroom cultivation is one of the best ways to somewhat alleviate poverty in our community." When I asked how she had come up with the idea of growing mushrooms in the houses, she responded that it was actually a project of the "leadership" (*önderlik*). For a second I paused, since for the party *önderlik* meant Abdullah Öcalan; but how could a home-based project like mushroom cultivation in a squatter settlement be related to Abdullah Öcalan? I pressed for more information: What did she mean by a project of the *önderlik*? As we walked from one house to another, Saliha explained: "This is part of our ecological society project. He [Öcalan] wants every house to sustain its own economy. He sees this as a part of Kurdish identity and an important path to achieve freedom." The project of mushroom cultivation was initiated by the Democratic Society Congress (Demokratik Toplum Kongresi), under the commission of economy and employment, in collaboration with the Sur municipality. Mushroom cultivation, like several other locally based projects, was part of Abdullah Öcalan's wider project of "democratic confederalism" and "ecological society," inspired by the ideas of Murray Bookchin, a socialist political theorist whom Öcalan read and followed intensively beginning in the early 2000s while he was in prison, according to Janet Biehl.[36] Biehl, who collaborated closely with Bookchin especially in developing the concept of "social ecology," notes in her piece "Bookchin, Öcalan, and the Dialectics of Democracy" that:

> to create an ecological society, cities would have to be decentralized, so people could live at a smaller scale and govern themselves and grow food locally and use renewable energy. The new society would be guided, not by the dictates of the market, or by the imperatives of a state authority, but by people's decisions. . . . The confederation of citizens' assemblies would form a counterpower or a dual power against the nation state. He [Murray Bookchin] called this program libertarian municipalism. . . . Libertarian municipalism was a way to do that, to get a firm toehold against the nation-state.[37]

Drawing on these ideas, Öcalan developed his concept of "democratic governance and confederalism" whereby society governs itself, and supervision of societal work is conducted through clusters of local councils, commissions, and assemblies.[38] The "Democratic confederalism of Kurdistan," wrote Öcalan, "is not a state system, but a democratic system of the people without a state. With the women and youth at the forefront, it is a system in which all sectors of society will develop their own democratic organizations."[39] Within this idea of "democratic confederalism," Öcalan proposed "autonomous democratic self-government," which "builds on the self-government of local communities and is organized in the form of open councils, town councils, local parliaments and larger congresses."[40]

Inspired by Öcalan's democratic and self-governance model, these micro-level projects in the city aimed to have every household sustain itself in a cooperative neighborhood network.[41] As we walked in the streets of Sur, Saliha explained, "With a goal of expanding to over a hundred homes, the project began with fifteen women growing mushrooms in their homes to help with their home economy through self-employment, self-governance. We aim to help households through participation of Sur women in the local economy." In fact, following the thread of Öcalan's idea of self-governance, the creation of "independent communities" was language I heard repeatedly from party officials and activists. The social component of "democratic confederalism" sought to address the gaps created by economic exploitation, with cooperatives and institutions of communal saving practices helping to overcome regional and class inequalities.[42] In another interview with Mayor Demirbaş, when I inquired about the sustainability of these local projects, he said, "This is a response to the politics of impoverishment. Our goal is for our people never to depend on those who put us in this condition. The revenue gained from the sales is collected into a pool and redistributed equally to the participants so that we are developing a culture of communion."[43]

While alleviating poverty, these social networks, local projects, and NGO programs established strong ties between society and the Kurdish political party and made communities more accessible for urban mobilization and political engagement. Creating an informal urban regime, these initiatives bolstered household economies while strengthening not only the social networks among residents but also the political party's control over residents. For the party, however, being both in the position of municipality and the advocates of informal economy came at a cost in the city.

One incident exemplified this dilemma. One afternoon, I was at the municipality waiting for Saliha to complete the office work before she would head out to inspect the projects. Saliha's office was bustling with residents seeking aid for poverty relief, as well as activists bringing to her various problems from the neighborhoods. A man in his early forties insisted on speaking with Saliha. It seemed a bit out of the ordinary because, leading women's projects, Saliha usually had women visitors from the neighborhood. Curious, Saliha welcomed him into her office. After introducing himself, the man, an owner of a local bakery market in Sur, said, "Look, you have to listen to us [he meant the local registered bakeries]. Your women's *tandır* bread sales disrupts our business. Because you sell them so cheap to the markets, several [local markets] stop buying from us." Saliha was taken aback by the complaint. She paused. She was caught between her dual roles: an activist advocating for the local women's economy and a municipal officer obligated to regulate informal sales. Her immediate response reflected her activist side: "These families are hungry; we have to support them." The baker was not convinced and continued to talk about his family's and his friends' economic struggles because of the decrease in their bread sales. He concluded by vowing his loyalty to the Kurdish movement. "If they [women who sell bread] are supporters of the party, we are also members of this party. Think about us as well." There was a slight tone of threat in man's words, in terms of voting power.

It was striking to see how, even in this conversation about commerce, the subject would inevitably arrive at party politics. Saliha immediately sensed his subtext and countered from a municipality position. She responded in freighted language: "We may come and visit you for health inspection." Health inspection was a nightmare for local restaurants and bakers. Although she used one of the powerful tools of municipality, she did not want the encounter to escalate. Local elections were close, and the party did not want negative rumors to circulate. They had to talk further about this, Saliha concluded. "I have to leave now, but come next week."

After two weeks, I was again waiting at Saliha's office as she wrapped up her meeting with Ahsen, a representative of the Bağıvar neighborhood of Sur. The network between the local associations was even stronger when local association leaders reported back to the municipality on a regular basis. Ahsen was complaining about the low participation of the women in the Bağıvar KADEM because they had to take care of their children. Saliha and Ahsen went over names together, household by household. They were working on the idea of opening an additional child-care center that would teach Kurdish children so their mothers would have time to participate in classes. When I followed up with Saliha on the baker's situation, I learned that, after several days of negotiations with local bakers, the municipality had decided to organize *tandır* bread sales at selected grocery stores where local bakers would not sell. At the same time, they made local bakers in Sur lower their bread prices. By intervening in the bread market in this manner, the BDP swiftly shifted from a social movement to a municipal authority. Through grassroots initiatives, the municipality not only spearheaded local micro-scale home-based projects but took an active role in facilitating the "informal economy," notably by designating and restructuring the market rules.

From Embroidery Course to the Street

Several times during my fieldwork in 2011, I saw members of KADEM participate in activities concerning Kurdish rights and freedom (for example, protesting the imprisonment of Kurdish journalists, or discrimination against women). These commitments were also evident in the party's agenda. "We do not simply support women," Saliha said, "but we also encourage them to be active participants in politics." Although I hadn't initially inquired about the political participation of women, Saliha brought it up, and I was eager to understand how the party connected home-based poverty alleviation projects with political involvement. Therefore, I asked about how she encouraged women to be active participants in politics. Saliha responded, "It is all about being conscious." As women became "economically independent, the Kurdish consciousness grew in them." Whether it was poverty alleviation or cultural programs, the common theme was "Kurdishness" or "struggle against the state"; a vocational center or a laundry house would host a Kurdish language class, or "weekly group meetings" would be thematized around "state violence against Kurds."

The structure of pro-Kurdish politics emphasized the local, whereby politics were conducted as a well-organized and integrated triad of municipality, party, and local associations—directly working with both male and female activists and party members. Unlike other parties in Turkey, in the early 2000s the pro-Kurdish party could not rely on media or social media to get its message out.[44] The party had very limited influence within the national media. One of the reasons for avoiding social media was to prevent the organization's networking and protest activities from becoming known to governmental authorities. Each street had a community leader, who also served as a representative of the pro-Kurdish party, connecting neighborhood leaders with district and city-level leaders. The street leaders maintained regular communication with the political party. For rallies and protests, they were responsible for mobilizing the neighborhood, ensuring high attendance. Typically, on the evenings before a protest day, residents were called upon from their homes by individuals knocking on their doors, engaging in face-to-face conversations. On a protest day, each resident was taken to the protest area, with transportation provided by the municipalities. When the politicians and local leaders visited a neighborhood, they organized meetings with the help of these leaders. The leaders knew the residents' affiliations with the party and the PKK (for instance, whether they had family members fighting in the mountains with the PKK) and the activism level of individuals; they kept track of who attended the rallies and protests and who did not. These leadership and network organizations provided a durable link between the people and the BDP. In fact, this everyday politicization arrived with a growing sense of Kurdishness.[45] Kurdish citizens—both women and men—came to be politicized as conscious Kurdish activists in the cities.[46] The cultivation of Kurdishness allowed residents in each activity,[47] in Anderson's terms, "to think about themselves, and to relate themselves to others" whose "imagined world is visibly rooted in everyday life."[48]

One afternoon in late spring 2011, I was at the Bağıvar women's center watching a group of women who came for an embroidery course. Before the class began, Saliha arrived. She greeted all the women individually and then began her address. She explained the plan to participate in the rally "for the right to educate our children in our mother tongue." She continued: "We are Kurds, we live in Diyarbakır, and our language is Kurdish. Certainly, our children should learn Kurdish. Speaking in our own mother tongue is our right. Otherwise, this is an injustice! This is a tyranny! A tyranny which has lasted for hundreds of years. Tomorrow, we are all gathering here to rally to the city center, to stop this injustice!"

The next morning, when I arrived at the center at eight o'clock to follow up with the protest invitation, several women had already gathered, and many more were coming to the center. They dropped off their children who were not of school age, to be taken care of by volunteers at the center who were also party members. It was a typical protest day. After half an hour, Saliha arrived to lead the group. The women walked through the neighborhood to where buses had gathered. The municipality assigned the buses to take them to the Diyarbakır Municipality Guest House in Yenişehir—the designated location for joining up with other protesters from different parts of the city to begin marching. Participating in rallies was evidently common practice among these women, although it wasn't exclusive to women.

Beginning in the early 2000s, until 2016, urban informality allowed the pro-Kurdish party to perform like a movement and act like a state. Almost all programs and urban activism organized by the party in informal settlements were funded by the municipal budget. Particularly in Sur, civil society organizations, founded and operated by the municipality, served a bridging function by providing an organizational framework in which mobilization and political articulation could occur.

The Party's Link to Distinct Civil Society Groups

The party's link to Kurdish society was not limited to poverty alleviation projects and vocational courses. Condolence houses, *dengbej* houses, and Quran-reading courses were other venues that maintained links between the party and civil society. For example, the local municipalities in Diyarbakır officially opened condolence houses, particularly in poor informal neighborhoods. Condolence houses follow an important Kurdish-Islamic tradition. Following the death of a society member, neighborhood dwellers visit these houses to express condolences for three days. Over time, condolence houses evolved into gathering centers, offering space for various purposes, such as weddings, engagement ceremonies, temporary seminars, and neighborhood meetings. In these houses, genders were usually divided. Visitors predominantly engaged in political discussions; however, when a member of the PKK died, the conversation would shift to the topic of state violence.

Additionally, Quran courses, under municipalities' rule, were popular in the peripheral districts of Sur, in small villages and in religious neighborhoods; residents would send their children to these courses especially during summer holidays or on weekends. When party members visited these neighborhoods, pious-looking women with headscarves would accompany them. For example, Saliha would usually visit peripheral villages on weekends, and each time she would take Nur, a graduate of Imam-Hatip High School in her late forties, with her. I met with Nur in front of the Sur municipality building one Saturday morning when we arrived with Saliha from a breakfast meeting of KADEM. Nur was waiting for Saliha inside the car, in the back seat. While Saliha ran into her office to pick up some documents, I chatted with Nur. When I asked about her objectives for visiting villages, she explained, "We sometimes go to villages just to listen to women's problems. Women find it easy to confide in me. Sometimes I read Mawlit, I pray with them; if they have a problem, you know about their children or with their husbands, I lend an ear, guide them to the relevant organizations. But don't think I leave it there. Later I follow up with those families." Nur's compassionate duties demonstrate the pro-Kurdish party's strategic efforts to establish strong ties with pious segments of the society that have helped the party expand its base and increase the amount of support in Kurdish cities. Especially after the period following Öcalan's democratic confederalism, the pro-Kurdish party as well as the left wing of the movement began to develop a more inclusive approach to distinct segments of the society, which also included those with pious and conservative positions. Many aspects of the movement moved from an orthodox Marxist, secularist, absolute-independence-oriented position to a socially liberal, inclusive, and "democratic autonomy'" position.[49] The pro-Kurdish party's political competition with the AKP in the region also amplified the party's effort to establish strong links with the conservative, pious segments of civil society. In alignment with this political repositioning, the pro-Kurdish parties (first the BDP, and later the HDP) began to include in their ranks well-known religious and conservative figures like Altan Tan and Adem Geveri, and organized and supported conferences and commissions on Islamic matters such as the Commission of Peoples and Beliefs (Halklar ve İnançlar Komisyonu). In 2013 and 2014, following a call by Öcalan, the movement organized Democratic Islam Congresses in Diyarbakır and Hagen, Germany. In the meantime, the movement supported the foundation of Muslim civil society led by organizations like DİAY-DER (Religious Scholars Assistance Solidarity Foundation) or established alliances with religious organizations in the region like Mazlum-Der (Association for Human Rights and Solidarity for the Oppressed).[50] Founded in 1990, Mazlum-Der has its headquarters in Istanbul but also has branches in several other cities, including Ankara, Adıyaman, Konya, and Diyarbakır.

DİAY-DER was founded in Diyarbakır in 2007 and later expanded to other Kurdish cities and to Istanbul. Later in 2011, DİAY-DER worked with the party in conducting "Civil Friday Prayers," public demonstrations in the form of

Friday prayers defending the right to pray in their mother tongue, Kurdish.[51] Remarkably, the party's pro-Islamic endeavors were not merely an effort to support Islam or Islamists; their goal was to intertwine Islamist rights with Kurdish rights. They advocated for the right to speak and pray in Kurdish as an Islamic right and organized a commemoration ceremony for past Kurdish religious figures (for example, in 2011 the BDP organized a commemoration ceremony for Sheikh Said in Diyarbakır on the anniversary of his execution). The pro-Kurdish party's inclusive approach was not limited to conservative and pious groups but included a variety of minority groups, particularly those excluded by the AKP, such as environmentalists, LGBTQ rights activists, and secular Turks. It is noteworthy that the party's organization toward these groups was more active in western Turkish cities such as Istanbul and Izmir than in Kurdish-populated cities.[52]

Oscillating between Powers

Diyarbakır squatter settlements—both socially and physically—allowed the pro-Kurdish party to fill in the blanks between urban institutions, spaces, society, and action. Over the past few decades, a rich and diverse body of knowledge has developed to account for how nonstate actors can take up urban planning, particularly in the context of squatter settlements.[53] Scholars examining the multilayered forms of urban informality have looked "at the nature of exchanges and interactions between citizens and apparatuses, agencies, and agents of state power and control."[54] In this vein, scholars have aptly interrogated the innovative urban strategies of residents' resistance as well as nongovernmental organizations' actions against the state's policies toward informality.[55] While existing analyses often present NGOs and residents as against the state and the municipalities, the Sur case expands these arguments. It demonstrates how urban informality in Diyarbakır unfolds within intricate relationships between state, the municipality, and nongovernmental actors; but it does so by relying on the pro-Kurdish party's shape-shifting abilities, functioning as a political party, municipality, and social movement—all simultaneously.

While performing like a social movement, the party would often implement state power through the channels of municipality and act against the central government. Hence, in the Kurdish context the "organizing logic" of urban informality has operated not only through relations among residents, agencies, activists, and governmental organizations within binary exchanges, but also in multiple directions. The case of Sur demonstrates how the pro-Kurdish municipality creatively harnessed the "organizing logic" of informal settlements, allowing them to strategically blur the already absent boundary between social movement and political party, helping to politicize citizens. As I note in the case of bakers, urban informality led the party to quickly fluctuate between social movement and municipal power. But more than anything, these associations, and organizations such as laundry houses, helped the party to establish strong ties between party and resident, even recruit membership, and disseminate party discourse. Through municipal service, the pro-Kurdish parties managed to forge strong connections with local communities, activists, union organizations, and NGOs. This facilitated formidable networks among these diverse groups and bolstered the party's discourse. Additionally, the foundation of several women's, youth, and conservative organizations enabled pro-Kurdish parties to mobilize a wider section of society.

Collaboration between civil society organizations—from women's organizations to pious associations—ultimately strengthened the Kurdish bloc in the city. As mentioned in the previous chapter, the strength of political articulation in Sur also explains why the AKP's government zealously sought to demolish the squatter settlements and relocate settlers to the fringes of the city.[56]

The pro-Kurdish party had absolute control over members of society—from their public activism to activities in their domestic lives, from youth's after-school Kurdish education to women's micro-entrepreneurship. Party programs such as poverty alleviation associations and organizations provided "a collective public space for politicized debate,"[57] commemorating past violent events, animating antistate views, and promoting thinking collectively about concepts of justice and equality, frequently introduced through party activities. Waiting for their laundry or their bread at *tandır* houses, women formed a robust sense of collectivity. Men in local associations (like the FCA) and at condolence houses chatted constantly about politics, injustice, and inequality. These debates were oftentimes fueled by local urban rumors or news of violence used by the Turkish state. A statement from President Erdoğan, the detention of a neighborhood resident, or news of a neighbor's relative killed while fighting for the PKK in the mountains would bring new topics to the table, news to spread in the community, sites that correspond to Hannah Arendt's notion of the political, whereby people come together and cultivate their capacity for action.[58] These everyday encounters and debates—listening to others' comments on the incident, expressing thoughts about recent events, receiving verbal confirmation from others—provide power to the community "as it keeps [preserves] the public realm, the potential space of appearance between acting and speaking men, in existence," in Arendt's words.[59] At the same time, as for organized meetings, party leadership was recognizable in cultivating participants. Almost all meetings (including city council or neighborhood meetings) had a party representative or municipality representative who would advocate and shape the conversations, discussions, and activities of the participants.

In the early 2000s, the mobilization of Kurdish society extended beyond the urban poor and migrants to encompass various groups within the city, including the upper middle class and conservatives who merged in politicized Kurdish identity. The provision of social services to the poor was not the only channel to help the pro-Kurdish party leverage mass support and form a large Kurdish bloc in the city.[60] In articulating the Kurdish bloc, pro-Kurdish parties have employed unique urban politics, effectively utilizing urbanism to bring diverse classes of citizens together. As for the urban poor, this articulation was often influenced by the idea of "self-administration"—ranging from "nonstate" thought, as in the case of the Free Compatriot Association, to "ecological society" in the mushroom-cultivation projects of KADEM, to the BDP's rhetoric of struggle and rights, including the right to pray in Kurdish—and even, in some cases, fed off the rhetoric of "one Kurdish nation."[61] When it came to upper-middle-class Kurds, however, the party's rhetoric and urban strategies for articulating this bloc were different; therein lay the creativity of the party. While the municipality was battling to preserve the squatter settlements in Sur, it continued modernization efforts for the rest of the city at full speed. In the next chapter, I turn to the Kurdish political party's way of practicing "urban development" and its ties to the urban Kurdish middle and upper-middle classes.

4
BRANDING THE CITY
"Diyarbakır Is Our Capital"

While the municipalities undertook a formidable urban battle to sustain the squatter settlements in Diyarbakır, they were also actively seeking to "modernize" the rest of the city and thus cleanse it of visible poverty. In the course of the Sur negotiations with the central government, the pro-Kurdish municipalities doggedly worked building roads and highways, setting up recreational sites, revitalizing sidewalks, issuing new zoning permits for Diyarbakır, and expanding the city.

How was it possible that the municipalities were protecting squatter settlements downtown while carrying out large-scale modernization projects elsewhere? Outside the city center, urban development became the main concern, despite the anxieties of the local government to control and hold the residents in urban informality in Sur. A major arena of municipal entrepreneurialism and pro-business urban development was the redevelopment of residential urban areas and the proliferation of material culture in the city.

In this chapter, I discuss how the mobilization of Kurdish society and the rise of nationalism in Diyarbakır were entangled with commodification and neoliberal modes of urbanism.[1] I study the sites of everyday consumer culture and urban development to elucidate how they embraced the aspirations for the rise of an autonomous Kurdish nation. While the previous chapter focused on the urban poor and rural migrants, this chapter turns to the pro-Kurdish party's ties to the urban upper middle class and the rich. In this chapter, I demonstrate how neoliberal urban development served the imperative of nationalizing the city, proposing Diyarbakır as the Kurdish capital to be. City expansion, major urban construction projects, and even new sites of consumption intended to serve as tangible proof of the movement's inexorable journey toward Kurdish autonomy in Turkey.

Architectural historians have often studied modern architecture and planning as primary tools of nation-building processes.[2] I contend that nationalism is not necessarily, or solely, a modern project, but can equally be a neoliberal project, as it was for the modern era. As urban scholars Neil Brenner, Nik Theodore, and others have already demonstrated, neoliberalism comes in many guises. It is not a monolithic affair. As I demonstrate in this chapter, neoliberalism in fact shapes itself through multiple localities and historical trajectories.[3]

The first half of this chapter focuses on the intimate links among urban development, the construction industry, and nationalism. I examine the ways in which neoliberal urbanism can augment the reach of nationalism by constructing spaces that represent the prospect of development and progress. I show how urban development, from road construction to opening parks and public squares, was charged with allegories of progress and nationalization in the city. In the second section I study everyday sites where nationalism intertwined with ordinary objects and consumption.[4] I examine the ways in which neoliberal urbanism and everyday consumption propelled Kurdish nationalism in Diyarbakır.[5]

Speculative Practices: "Land Prices Went Insane in Diyarbakır"

In February 2011, the week I returned to Diyarbakır to explore the Arab Spring's influence on the Kurdish movement,[6] I registered a somewhat unusual setting when I attempted to meet with one of my local informants, Cemil, a former car rental owner at Ofis. In his midforties, Cemil has switched businesses multiple times in the course of our friendship. When I first met him in 2007, he was managing a gas station while he also worked in the cheese trade. For a period he was also interested in treasure hunting, but he dropped that pursuit quickly. Then he opened a car rental business and finally a real estate brokerage with two other partners. He had also become a council member for the Kayapınar municipality—at the time a relatively new municipality for the emerging well-off district of the city—to represent his uncle, a prominent tribal leader (*aşiret lideri*) in the city. Because of his family ties, Cemil never truly relied on money or took these professions seriously—except for the new real estate business. Cemil had never sounded this excited about a job.

In a brief conversation over the phone the day after I recontacted him, Cemil offered to show me his new real estate office in Kayapınar. They had just opened the office two weeks ago, renting a storefront and getting to business so quickly that they did not even have time to put up their business sign. On our way to his new office, he began to talk about the rising land sales in Diyarbakır. "This is crazy here! People lost their minds, forgot about their work [*insanlar kendilerini unuttu*]; they keep buying and selling land. Even the women, housewives, are selling their gold to buy land. Nowadays, people are buying the land even without seeing it. Everything happens in paper, and no one even sees the area. People do not even know where or what they are buying." Strikingly, as Cemil was depicting the insane new land speculation in Diyarbakır, he was also describing his part in this real estate frenzy. When we arrived at his office, it reminded me of scenes of traders on a busy stock market trading floor. Both the front and inside rooms were crowded with men pacing up and down talking hungrily on the phone about land sales.

A large cadastral map was pinned on the wall behind an expansive table, which was apparently Cemil's. When I asked if all the parcels they were selling had zoning permits, Cemil assuredly answered, "Some, yes, but some not for now—but if it goes like this, very likely they will have permits." Cemil sounded confident.

During our meeting in his office, Cemil even asked me if I would like to buy any land. He was, at the same time, conscious that this was speculation, a land bubble that could end very soon. As he made this proposition, he shared a bit of insider advice: "Sister, if you are planning to buy one, buy as soon as possible, otherwise this drift will end soon. Then you may end up with it blowing up in your face [*yoksa arsa elinde patlar*]." It was not only Cemil; everyone I spoke to in the city during those days was talking about the crazy land sales.

Events were developing rapidly. Around a week later, by the first week of March 2011, national newspapers captured this abrupt land speculation with sensationalist headlines such as "Land Prices Went Insane in Diyarbakır" (Diyarbakır'da arsa Fiyatları çıldırdı).[7] News articles highlighted that "land prices increased ten times in a year" and proclaimed that the madness was even "suspending everyday life in the city."[8]

Diyarbakır, the hub for the Kurdish movement and known for its antigovernment demonstrations and street clashes, was again in the news, but this time for a very different reason. Media interviews with leading businesspeople in the city sought to present a clearer picture of the reasons for the inexplicable hikes in land value. An interviewee in one national newspaper noted, "We call this business 'land exchange' among ourselves. Prices rising at terrible rates are the work of land speculators."[9] A news outlet reported that, because of the intensive land purchases and sales, the number of transactions in four separate land registry directorates in the city center had increased by 50 percent.

Complicating the picture, this unusual price hike was happening shortly before the national elections, which were to be held in three months, while demonstrations aligning with the Arab Spring were to begin in ten days.[10] Several Kurdish politicians and activists I interviewed in early March feared that this speculative market would bring the political activism and campaign of the pro-Kurdish party to a standstill, as citizens busied themselves with land transactions rather than supporting their party and campaigning for the elections.

The pro-Kurdish Party reacted to such speculation immediately. Diyarbakır mayor Osman Baydemir, in a joint statement with the city chambers of commerce, warned that the land prices were speculative. He made it very clear that agricultural land on the outskirts of the city would not be zoned for construction.[11] According to public perception, Baydemir's statements were determining the city's future zoning plans. And, indeed, over the following two months, land speculation dropped. Even Cemil, who was very enthusiastic about his new venture, transferred his shares to his partners in June and returned to his car rental business. Some popular newspapers described the radical shift as the bursting of the "land balloon" in Diyarbakır.[12] It is true that what Diyarbakır experienced in those four months of 2011 was real estate madness, a clear case of speculation. But it is not true that the hikes in land prices were entirely unprecedented or new to the city.[13] In Diyarbakır, urban speculation was merely a symptom of typical neoliberal urbanism seeping through the hands of both local governments and local elites (the latter oftentimes with tribal family backgrounds).[14]

In the first decade of the twenty-first century, the total number of registered construction firms almost tripled in Diyarbakır.[15] Beginning in 2004, under the pro-Kurdish party's administration, Diyarbakır had undergone massive change. Between 2004 and 2008, the city quadrupled in size. The zoned area of Diyarbakır, which had been twenty-six thousand hectares (one hundred square miles) until 2004, in a span of only four years reached 110 thousand hectares.[16] Likewise, Diyarbakır had 43 neighborhoods before 2004. This number increased to 126 in 2008.[17] In fact, the expansion of the city beginning in Osman Baydemir's term was remarkable. While 6,672 building permits were issued in Diyarbakır in the more than four decades between 1961 and 2004, in the four years between 2004 and 2008 the number of titles issued was 2,466.[18] Concurrently, land prices had multiplied almost sixty-fold between 2004 and 2018.[19] During this period, the lucrative contracts and alliances between the municipal administrations, local landowners, and emerging developers shaped the new urban landscape.[20] With ambitions to prove its ability for self-administration, the city oversaw hundreds of instances of agricultural land becoming urbanized, projects of land acquisition and urban development along with booming housing and shopping mall construction. But all of this work—as elsewhere in the world—began with highway construction and infrastructure.

The Politics of Infrastructure

In Turkey, since the republican period, the construction of dams, infrastructure, and roads has often been associated in popular culture with prosperity and development.[21] Nationalism has always had a territorial aspect according to which "urban design is used as a technique for turning cities into fields of social, cultural, and national identity production."[22] Diyarbakır was no exception to this pattern. It is this bond between city and nation that the pro-Kurdish municipalities sought to build in "modern Diyarbakır," where Diyarbakırians could imagine themselves as a booming independent and autonomous nation. Thus, new zoning plans and highway and construction projects were regarded as manifestations of autonomous governance—embodiments of the party's success.

Fashioning an autonomous governance also entailed controlling the physical landscape. The party's Kurdish politics obviously had to facilitate utilitarian transactions. The Turkish state had long overlooked Kurdish cities, failing to engage or invest in urban development—a disregard perceived as an affront by Kurdish society. Now it was time for the Kurds themselves to prioritize self-investment and development. Beginning in the early period when the pro-Kurdish party municipalities came to power, they placed special emphasis on highways, viaduct, and infrastructure construction. Particularly during Mayor Osman Baydemir's tenure, the municipality worked determinedly on infrastructure projects, constructed new roads, converted agricultural fields into residential or industrial land, and approved hundreds of building permits for new residential blocks and towers. In one of his routine highway construction audits in 2012, Baydemir highlighted the imminent rapid development. He told the local press, "See, we are building these roads ahead of the housing development."[23]

The outcomes of urban development were considered significant milestones for the Kurdish movement, carrying both tangible and symbolic weight. In the city, highway inaugurations were often scheduled to coincide with a commemorative event, highlighting that such ceremonies were part of the narrative of progress and prosperity. The new Diyarbakır had a pedagogical purpose for its citizens: the individual components of urban development and practice were signposts along a larger narrative of self-administration and advancement. At the same time, as one moved through the city, these projects were constant reminders of Kurdish historical narratives and nationhood. Similar to public parks and memorials, which I discuss in chapter 5, the structures and streets that composed this new landscape were named after Kurdish heroes, authors, or Kurdish territories that often transcended Turkey's borders.[24]

The case of Mahabad Boulevard—a seventy-five-meter-wide road, often referred to as *75' lik yol* by Diyarbakırians—illustrates this co-narrative of nationhood and development. The name of the boulevard commemorated Mahabad—a short-lived, unrecognized Kurdish state within the borders of present-day Iran from January to December 1946. At the time of its inauguration, Mahabad Boulevard represented a new benchmark of successful urban development and an extension line for the city. Even before the inauguration ceremony, information about the boulevard—its width, and narratives around its challenging construction—spread by word of mouth. In everyday encounters while grocery shopping, in cafés, and at social gatherings and house meetings, people exchanged stories that turned the boulevard into the stuff of legend. Esra's dialogue with her son exemplifies this tale. A housewife in her mid-forties, Esra lived in a high-rise residential block built in the late 1990s in Kayapınar, which at the time was a newly established middle-class district. After losing her husband, she was alone with her five children. They had an income source from their agricultural lands in Mardin, but one of her main concerns was securing jobs for her children. Esra would always complain about how one could find a job in the city only through acquaintances. One afternoon in July 2008, Esra and I were cooking dolmas together in the kitchen when her son Miran, a cab driver in his midtwenties, returned from his shift. As we stuffed dried eggplant, Miran sat down for a late lunch. He suddenly turned to us and said, "You see Osman Başkan did what he said. He really completed this seventy-five-meter-wide road [Mahabad Boulevard]." He looked at me and said, "You know, first he asked this road to be built from the general directorate of highways. The state should have built it. But they didn't. Then Osman Başkan said, even if you [state directorates] don't build it, I will build this road for this city. And he did. He kept his promise. The man is really developing our city."

Even in the way that Miran called Osman Baydemir "Osman Başkan" (Osman the mayor),[25] one could feel Miran's sympathy toward the BDP. Miran's brief, unsolicited celebratory praise of Osman Baydemir and the completion of the road reveals multiple meanings. For Miran, a resident of a middle-class apartment block, there was a great distinction between the state on one side and the Kurds and the Kurdish movement on the other. It was an attitude no different from that of the squatter settlers. What made Miran's case interesting to me was not so much his sympathy for Baydemir and his excitement about the road opening, but his family's political background. I had met Esra in 2008. Her husband had been a member of the AKP (Adalet ve Kalkınma Partisi, Justice and Development Party), and until this death Esra had been working for the women's branch of the party. Esra was pious; she would wear a long coat and a headscarf outside and pray five times a day. Miran was not as observant as his mother. But as former members of the AKP, both Esra and Miran provided me an interesting opportunity to better understand how the pro-Kurdish party was able to bring diverse constituents of society together. Through progress and development, the party was attracting pious middle-class citizens. In my contact with the family over the years, I observed how family members grew more and more sympathetic toward the pro-Kurdish party.

Quickly eating his lunch at the table, Miran said, "You will see, these neighborhoods will be highly valued. Mom, we should sell this house and get one in those new blocks close to Mahabad." Esra responded to Miran with affirmation: "Yes, indeed, they [the municipal officers] work.... Let's wait and see first. Kismet—we need you to find a proper job first." Almost ten years later, in 2019, Esra and her family moved into a luxurious new apartment block by the Mahabad. As I elaborate later in this chapter, their decision mirrored a primary objective shared among other middle-class residents of Diyarbakır—to move into the new prestigious neighborhoods of the city. Every day, ordinary conversations over the infrastructural achievements of the BDP or its members provided venues to facilitate a sense of "nationness."[26] Daily talk about the work of the party, of party members, or the mayor—particularly when the state in Ankara did not deliver services—forged assemblages of fellow citizens who came to proudly share the BDP's success in the city.[27]

Elaborate ceremonies inaugurated the modern infrastructure and road construction projects. While displaying the hard work of the party, these projects provided great venues for conducting opposition and conveying anxieties about state coercion. During the inauguration of Mahabad Boulevard in 2009, party officials took every opportunity to make clear what was at stake. The opening ceremony was as crowded as a political campaign event. In front of the gathered people stood Parliament members and several party members, along with Mayor Baydemir and Ahmet Türk, then-chairman of the Democratic Society Congress (DTP).

The inauguration ceremony testified to the party members' links to new infrastructure, progress, and national pride. One after another, party leaders delivered speeches addressing the political implications of Kurdish national progress and fashioning a narrative of a unified nation. (Indeed, these infrastructure and road construction projects frequently involved flashy public speeches and press releases targeting the central government.) Ahmet Türk began by critiquing the central government's lack of economic and infrastructure support for Kurdish cities. He denounced government discrimination in Kurdish cities using the case of Mahabad Boulevard:

> We know from the past that the share received from the budget of the Ministry of Transport in twenty-one provinces where Kurds live is not as much as in Bursa or Adana.... Police stations were built here, service was not provided. If roads to the mountains are built today, they are built for different purposes [implying militarization of the land]. Ports and subways are being built elsewhere. How will a government that hesitates or even refrains from construction of these roads, embrace these [Kurdish] people? ... If you cannot embrace the identity, diversity and freedom of these people, investing in this region becomes an unattainable endeavor. You cannot please the people of the region. We have a long road ahead, we will walk this road together, and we will cover this distance shoulder to shoulder. Our way is the way of freedom. Our way is the free future of our people. With your struggle, we will demolish all obstacles, we will realize the brotherhood and freedom of the people.[28]

During the inauguration speeches, two main themes emerged: freedom for Kurds and the national interest in peace. The speeches abounded in double meanings, like paving the road and paving the way for peace. The unveiling of Mahabad was no exception. Following Ahmet Türk, Osman Baydemir proclaimed, "Economic social development will hopefully lead us to freedom. It will lead to an honorable peace. Now we are together to pave our way for peace."[29]

Indirectly and directly, these road and infrastructure inaugural speeches hinted at a Kurdistan to come. The municipalities' urban actions were seen as a harbinger of future Kurdish city administrations. In a way, the ongoing self-administration of the Kurdish movement was being realized in the form of urban development and infrastructure—or as Ahmet Türk said, "If they [the state] don't deliver, we will build for ourselves."

These inauguration speeches often emphasized collective achievement despite the vulnerability of Kurdish people. They promoted experiences of belonging that transcended the borders of Diyarbakır, of citizens becoming aware that their concerns were shared by hundreds of thousands of anonymous others.[30] For example, during the official unveiling of Qamishli Boulevard in 2013, Mayor Baydemir's oration clearly traced an arc between Diyarbakır and other historically Kurdish territories. And Diyarbakır—the Kurdish capital to be—was placed at the center of this network. The roads served as a metaphor for the promise of uniting Diyarbakırians with Kurds from other territories. The name of the boulevard, Qamishli, was also that of the de facto capital of the canton of Rojava, a Kurdish autonomous region in the northeast of Syria.

These speeches deliberately made reference not only to historic Kurdish territories but to heroic experiences and traditional loyalties. In this spirit, Baydemir noted during the inauguration, "With the Mahabad Boulevard, Diyarbakır met with Mahabad. With the Qamishli Boulevard, Diyarbakır will once again meet with Qamishli, below the border. I believe that our friends, who will take over the flag from us, will add Hawler Boulevard [Hawler, or Erbil, is the capital and the most populous city in the Kurdistan region of Iraq] to these boulevards. In this way, borders will once again lose their meaning. With the permission of the people of Diyarbakır, I dedicate the Qamishli Boulevard and the Zoxê viaduct to the people of Rojava."[31]

As Baydemir illustrated, the Kurdish community was bound by the larger, contested territory divided among Turkey, Syria, Iraq, and Iran. Party officials carefully chose the names of these new roads to link Diyarbakır to a transborder Kurdish heritage. The narrative arising out of these acts of naming reframed an overarching Kurdish history in order to lend exclusive legitimacy to the party and its municipalities in Diyarbakır.

The same year that Mahabad Boulevard was introduced, the municipality opened Marwani Bridge as an alternative to the historic On Gözlü Bridge, passing over the Tigris River. The name of the bridge derives from the Marwanis, a Kurdish dynasty between 935 and 1085, centered in the city of Amid (Diyarbakır). With the symbolic meaning behind naming boulevards—Mahabad, Qamishli, and Hawler—Osman Baydemir was gesturing to the geographical distribution of Kurds in Iran, Syria, and Iraq to the south and the east of Diyarbakır. As demonstrated in several public speeches, he yearned for Diyarbakırians to imagine themselves as part of the larger Kurdish community. During the inauguration of Qamishli, by connecting Diyarbakır to Kurdish territories in three other countries, and even dedicating the boulevard to the Rojava, Baydemir sought to bring every inch of Diyarbakır into the collective imagination of a larger Kurdistan. Hence, beyond a statement designated to support the people of Rojava (at war while the inauguration was taking place), Baydemir's words should be interpreted within the idea of nationhood, invoking both a distinct populace and the territory they occupy.

The new urban development projects clearly served nationalistic and pedagogic functions by fostering confidence in self-administration and prosperity among Diyarbakırians, proving that they could own and administer their city. During one of the interviews I conducted with Baydemir in 2011, he told me, "Thanks to the municipality work, we have proved that we can govern both the city and ourselves." By "ourselves," he meant Kurdish society. The emphasis on self-governing without the central government's—the state's—budgetary support reflected the aim of an independent Kurdish territory. Along the highway, the city reaches its gated communities, shopping malls, and upscale cafés and restaurants, perceived as markers of the anticipated economic prosperity of the Kurdish nation-to-be.

The pro-Kurdish party treated urban development as a tool to assert and symbolize Diyarbakır's "modernity," first to the country and then to the world. All these infrastructure and urban development projects—built as symbols of pride for the Kurdish people, representing a modern Diyarbakır—also led Diyarbakırians to regard themselves as residents of the modern capital of the larger Kurdistan territory.

The urban development of Diyarbakır was advertised in municipal publications and billboards around the city. Some the most striking of these promotional efforts were a series of hard-copy, two-hundred-page activity reports. Published annually and quadrennially, these heavily illustrated reports documented the development and progress made under pro-Kurdish party administrations in a range of areas: infrastructure, social work, environment, media, public relations, culture, budget, and finance. While displaying the fruits of their labor, the pro-Kurdish party also used these reports to condemn and "reveal" what the documents explicitly label as "the systemized impoverishment policies of the state" (*devletin yoksullaştırma politikaları*) deployed against Kurds.[32]

Rather than city residents, the intended audience of these reports seemed to be other politicians, other municipality members in Kurdish cities in the region, and visitors to municipal offices. Each time I conducted an interview in any municipality in Diyarbakır, at the end of the interview the mayor would proudly present one of these reports to me, which over the years amounted to a hefty collection. Not surprisingly, the reports highlight urban planning, zoning, infrastructure, and road construction projects. The activity report for the period from 2004 to 2008 published by the Diyarbakır Municipality was titled *We Made It Together. This Pride Belongs to Diyarbakır*. The report begins with images of Osman Baydemir's engagement with civil society and facsimiles of press releases. The presence of the municipality's work in the international and national press was a source of pride for the municipality. In the very first pages, the report presents newspaper clippings, foreign and domestic, discussing the municipality's work with the following words: "The local administration model created by our Metropolitan Municipality has found wide coverage in the local and national press. Diyarbakır, which claims to be a world city with its city diplomacy studies, was also discussed in the international press."[33] The first 120 pages of this 250-page document are devoted to infrastructure and zoning developments and are heavily illustrated with images of newly built and paved roads. The rest of the report covers environmental work, health inspection, social work, culture, and tourism, and includes a section called "city diplomacy," with informational copy catering to foreign and international visitors to the municipality.

Attesting to the activity reports, construction never stopped in the city. Each time I revisited, a new development would be underway in Diyarbakır. Right after landing, on my way to the city center I would take a longer route from the airport toward these recently opened boulevards to see, one block after another, what was new. Sometimes several blocks would rise over a period of six months, and at other times change would occur in shorter periods. The cityscape would be different and yet typical: along the newly asphalted roads, new multistory residential blocks would arise; right next to them were prairies of recently dug brown earth and construction machines preparing for another project (figure 12).

Interestingly, except for a few voices from the Diyarbakır Chamber of Architects and within the party ranks, the party did not seem much concerned with these mushrooming concrete blocks. Amid the peace process and the ongoing conflict with the governor in the city, these gated communities were obviously not at the top of the party's agenda. Further, in the eyes of many Diyarbakırians, rather than "ugly concrete blocks,"[34] the characteristic structures of this new neoliberal city were associated with urban development and progress. Whereas Sur represented the city's past, these new development areas—especially Kayapınar—spelled the future of the city, almost as a brand for the new Diyarbakır.

FIGURE 12. A typical view from Kayapınar, showing rows of new-looking high-rise apartments behind a billboard advertising a new gated community.
Source: Author, 2016.

New Construction Paradise: Kayapınar

One can leave Sur behind—either through Ofis and Yenişehir, passing by the governmental sites, or through Ben-u Sen out to Bağlar—and reach Kayapınar, observing the rapid change in the built environment: asphalt roads, an increasing number of neighborhood parks, wider sidewalks, and greater distances between residential blocks. Driving farther, one finds more luxurious artificial enclaves for the upper class surrounded by shopping malls and private schools. But even at such distance from Sur—the hub for mobilization in Diyarbakır—one cannot escape the feeling of Kurdishness suffusing the city.

By 2008, Kayapınar was a predominantly residential district boasting the city's most expensive real estate and gated communities (*siteler*). In fact, during the late 1990s, what is now known as Kayapınar had been constituted from small villages. The urban Diyarbakır would end around the Diyarbakır–Urfa road. The peasant villages of Kayapınar produced dairy and wheat for the city.[35] Newroz Park to the south and the industrial zone in the north delimited the city. By 2017, the Diyarbakır–Urfa road seemed like one more main thoroughfare in the middle of the city. Kayapınar stretched through a triangular area, flanked on the northern side by Üçkuyular ve Huzurevleri and in the south by Çölgüzeli; all three were largely TOKİ housing projects. Wedged between militarized and state-owned land, Diyarbakır had no choice but to expand westward (see figure 2 in the introduction for the urban development map).

As the city expanded, new residential units were built by converting former farmlands.[36] First, in 1991, Peyas, one of the villages of Kayapınar, was declared a subdistrict (*belde*) municipality under the jurisdiction of the Diyarbakır municipality. Next, Kayapınar's status was upgraded to first-tier municipality in 2004 and to district municipality in 2008.[37] The city's 2006 master plan envisioned Kayapınar as the city's primary residential zone.[38] Thus, of the total 4,880 hectares of planned land in Kayapınar, around 2,700 hectares were devoted to residential areas and 824 hectares to green areas.[39] While the overall population of the city center almost doubled in only fifteen years, between 1990 and 2015 the urban population of Kayapınar grew more than thirty-fold, increasing from almost ten thousand to more than three hundred thousand by 2020.[40]

The rapid urbanization and the burgeoning service sector—spanning construction, private health, education, and tourism—have expanded the Kurdish middle class.[41] This newly emerging class found its home in Kayapınar, transforming the district into a popular destination for the working middle class and upper middle class alongside high-ranking HDP officials and their families. With newly asphalted roads, high-rise concrete housing blocks, new road-lighting systems, and striking aluminum façades, interspersed with gated communities and private schools, Kayapınar became the new face of Diyarbakır. Kayapınar houses the largest shopping malls of the city (Forum Diyarbakır, Ceylan Karavil Park, Ninova Park) as well as lavishly decorated chain restaurants. The architecture of the malls and the restaurant interior designs compete with high-end equivalents in Istanbul or Ankara. This new profile, the new imagery of the city, is no different from that of any other major city in Turkey.[42]

Gated Communities of Diyarbakır: "Our Mayor Also Lives Here"

In tandem with the infrastructure projects, by the early 2000s the number of construction companies and new development projects had almost tripled in Diyarbakır. Most of these new developments were concentrated in the former outskirts, now part of the city. Plot by plot, acres of agricultural lands were zoned for residential construction, giving way for rows of hundreds of ten-to-seventeen-story apartment blocks. Between them mushroomed private hospitals, shopping malls, and private schools, projections of the future modern capital.

Typically, these apartment blocks consist of gated complexes—called *site*, a common form of gated community in Turkey. Depending on the size of the plot, a typical *site* can be constituted from three to six apartment blocks. For the ones facing main streets, the first two floors are allocated for luxury home decor stores. Often surrounded by some form of fence or wall, *sites* usually have gated entrances, with barriers and twenty-four-hour security guards checking individuals upon entry. Most gated communities have children's parks and walking tracks. The more luxurious ones include basketball courts, swimming pools, saunas, barbecue grills, and cafés. The swimming pools are often gendered, open for males or females in different time slots.

Most of the time the new complexes cater to working middle- and upper-middle-class families who prefer to live in a secured environment with parks and other facilities. Compared to their equivalents in Istanbul, these residences have much larger living room and kitchen areas, as they address the needs of larger families. The majority of the residents send their children to private schools and private swimming and music lessons. They shop at shopping malls and dine in Kayapınar restaurants.

Gated communities have frequently been studied as a form of "urban pathology"—another detrimental social impact on cities, typically related to issues of urban segregation and social exclusion.[43] Moving beyond conventional scholarship on gated communities, in this chapter I offer a nuanced perspective on the ways these new developments became an inseparable part of everyday life.

In fact, the residents of these gated apartment blocks provided me one of the most illuminating insights into how the party brings diverse constituents of society together under one Kurdish political identity. Sustained support for the party by the upper and middle classes did not mean there was no resentment against the Kurdish middle class among the urban poor, however. Even in the party and among some civic organizations, from time to time the lifestyle of the Kurdish upper middle class was a subject of criticism.[44] However, the essence of Kurdish identity persisted within these developments, albeit expressed in different forms. The rising trend of "being Kurdish" in the city could also be traced amid upper-class housing—expressed by its own material culture, its façades featuring the colors of the Kurdistan flag, or in names associated with Kurdish culture and its past. (Following the military intervention in 2015, almost all the Kurdish flags were removed and replaced with Erdoğan's posters across the city.)[45] Strikingly, the only HDP flags I was able to see in the city during my visit in 2016 were at a few of the gated communities. Despite the income difference between the residents of Kayapınar and the rest of the city, the inhabitants of these upscale apartment blocks—educated migrants, businessmen, merchants, landowners—would primarily define themselves through their Kurdish identity, much like the residents of Sur. As in the case of Miran, I frequently encountered supporters of the AKP (which received 20 percent of votes) and popular sympathy toward the HDP, particularly Osman Baydemir. Further, and strikingly, during the local elections, the pro-Kurdish party would receive an almost equal percentage of votes from the middle-class communities of Diyarbakır as it did from Sur (table 1).

TABLE 1. Chart showing the percentages of pro-Kurdish party support between 1999 and 2019 in major districts of Diyarbakır. In parentheses are the names of political parties at the time of the election.

YEAR	SUR %	KAYAPINAR %	BAĞLAR %	YENİŞEHİR %
1999 (HADEP)	69.4	—	67.3	56.2
2004 (SHP)	56.6	58.6	61.9	53.7
2009 (DTP)	65.4	63.10	68	59
2014 (BDP)	54.4	54.6	58.5	53.7
2019 (HDP)	60.76	66.35	70.34	62.32

Source: Compiled by the author using election results provided by the Supreme Election Council of Turkey.

The account of Selin and Arda, a couple living in one of the gated communities in Kayapınar, exemplified this trend of HDP support. I got to know Selin and Arda through Oya, one of the planning officers at the municipality. Both Selin and Arda graduated from Dicle University, Selin as a gynecologist and Arda as a surgeon. They worked at one of the private hospitals in Kayapınar. They had two children, both with Kurdish names (and attending a private school near their house). Selin was from Kulp, and Arda was from Silvan, two peripheral villages of Diyarbakır. Though proficient in Kurdish, they mostly spoke in Turkish to each other. They had a babysitter who would arrive in the afternoon, cook for the family, and meet the children when they arrived home from school. On the weekends, the couple would take the children to music and art classes or organize cultural tours in nearby cities.

One day, Selin invited me for dinner at their house. After work, they picked me up with their brand-new Volkswagen Passat, which had an Izmir registration plate number (35). In Diyarbakır, among the middle class particularly, it has become common to have plate numbers registered outside of Diyarbakır, as a tactic to avoid being pulled over by police. Along the way, Selin made a quick call to the babysitter to check if the dinner was ready and that everything was all right with the kids—if they had had their snacks and done their homework.

As we were driving on Şanlıurfa Boulevard toward their home on Mesopotamia Boulevard—a new boulevard designed to alleviate traffic from the city—Arda complained about the rising congestion. "Here it is very developed, but it is still getting very crowded." As we arrived at their site, Arda hailed the security guards with his hand. Without exchanging a word, the guards recognized him and lifted the barriers. One of the early wealthy gated communities in Kayapınar, their site had playgrounds, basketball courts, and walking pathways. Arda parked in a designated spot in front of their apartment block. We were moving upstairs to their floor when Selin excitedly asked, "Do you know, our mayor [*başkanımız*—she meant Osman Baydemir] also lives here?" For Selin, the fact that they lived in the same site as Osman Baydemir was cause for pride and excitement. In fact, it was not the first time I heard residents proudly describe their gated communities as homes of prominent party members. These *sites* would become more popular and yet more expensive if a prominent party member resided there. Selin was not an active party member, but she was a strong supporter. During dinner, when I asked about her stance with the party, she explained her support:

> Maybe I can't join the demonstrations every day—I need to work, I have children to run after. . . . I can't take the day off from the hospital to participate in a protest. But I would never give up supporting our party.

If we are not going to support HDP, who else are we going to support in this city? Look [indicating the new pedestrian project outside her window], they are doing what the state didn't do for us. They showed us how we can be proud of our Kurdishness. We [Diyarbakırians] have been despised for years. I see this every day in the hospital. Some of my women patients don't even know Turkish; they need a doctor who can speak Kurdish. But where is that doctor? The state has banned Kurdish for years.... So now you tell me, whom should I vote for?

Selin began expressing her support by highlighting her absence from the demonstrations while stressing her willingness to participate in them. For a typical middle-class working family that had never been active in party politics, the ability to feel "Kurdish" was an important reason for supporting the HDP. But what does being Kurdish mean for someone like Selin? When I confronted her with this question, she replied, "When we go to the West [meaning a western Turkish city like Istanbul or Izmir] for vacations or something, from our accent people immediately tag us as easterners [doğulu].[46] I feel their treatment changes. This is wrong! We don't deserve this. They don't treat us like humans. We are Kurds, and Kurdish is our roots."

For Selin, a distinct contrast remained between Diyarbakır and the West, an enduring polarity in the minds of residents since the foundation of the republic. Rather than mentioning the specific cities she visited, she would broadly label them as "the West." Not only for Selin but also for several of my interviewees—Havin, Miran, Esra—"being Kurdish" was almost sacred. Selin's words reminded me of a statement from Havin, whom I met back in 2007: "When I grew up, I didn't know that I was Kurdish. As I lived here, I learned that I was Kurdish."[47]

While we were chatting about the idea of being Kurdish, Arda participated in our conversation. Expressing his frustration with the perception of Kurds in society, he explained: "Look, why do you think we [the residents of Diyarbakır] cannot, we don't get 21 plate numbers. Because we are tired of being [seen] as terrorists. Our party [the HDP] is now altering that perception." Here it is important to note that the peace process between the PKK and the state—along with the party's liberal policies in the city and the pro-Kurdish municipalities' urban development projects—helped the pro-Kurdish party garner support from the middle and upper-middle classes.[48] For Arda and others, especially within the middle class, the HDP's capacity to "defend Kurdish rights peacefully" stood out as a significant reason to back the party. At the same time, Arda acknowledged the party's success in earning the confidence and trust of residents from entirely diverse backgrounds in the city. He continued: "My mother raised us by herself.

Poor woman, she didn't even know Turkish. She struggled as she was forced to speak in Turkish. We suffered a lot from this state. But now everything is changing. We are showing them we can also live and administer ourselves. Thanks to this party [the HDP] we don't fear to say we are Kurds. We [Kurds] deserve to live better. We deserve to live."

People from various backgrounds—intellectuals, the pious, merchants, businessmen with tribal backgrounds—choose to live in these gated communities. Another example of pro-Kurdish party support came from Mehmet, a well-known intellectual among Kurdish circles, who was also living in one of the latest and most upscale gated communities. A university professor in his early forties, Mehmet was known for his publications on the Kurdish issue and his newspaper columns. Because of his pious and intellectual background, even though he was a supporter of the Kurdish movement he was respected among the AKP as well. I have known him since 2008 and frequently interviewed him about his work and on the right to speak Kurdish. He was one of the founders of a major local NGO focused on human rights and lifting the ban on Kurdish-language use. Mehmet's wife, Elif, was an attorney and also a human rights activist like Mehmet, working for a well-known NGO in the city.

In the summer of 2018, during one of the interviews at his office, I accidently found out that Mehmet was living in Med City Mahabad. I would always pass by Med City Mahabad but never imagined Mehmet and his family would live there. Med City Mahabad was one of the well-appointed gated communities, sitting at the corner of the famous Mahabad Boulevard. While a three-bedroom flat in the city in Yenişehir would cost around 120,000 to 200,000 TL at the time, in Kayapınar a gated community flat would be around 500,000 TL. In upscale sites like Med City Mahabad, the price would climb to around 800,000–900,000 TL. Med City Mahabad was constructed by An-Yapı, a developer renowned for the Sümer Park Cultural Center project as well as for hospital construction in the city.[49] I asked Mehmet about his choice of housing, to which he responded, "For us [his family] Med-Mahabad was a rational choice. It is close to our kids' school, their afterschool, and courses. You know, robbery became so common in Diyarbakır. We feel safe here, and there are many facilities and playgrounds that our kids can enjoy after school."

Indeed, for many residents, security was the top reason to live in gated communities.[50] Med City Mahabad consists of twelve-story apartment blocks, seven in total. Most apartments are single-level, with four bedrooms, a spacious living room, and a balcony. Med City provides 24/7 security and private parking. It offers walking and biking trails, a basketball court, a playground, a swimming pool, and indoor and outdoor cafeterias.

The name Med City Mahabad also carries symbolic meaning. In the last ten years, it has been common to encounter the name "Med" in Diyarbakır.[51] The Medes, an ancient Iranian people, lived in the same territory where Kurds now live (the south of Turkey and in northern Iran). Kurds believe the Medes were their forefathers, a claim supported by some Kurdish intellectuals. "Ey Reqib" (Oh, enemy), a famous poem written by Dildar in 1938, contains the lines "We are the sons of the Medes. . . . Our god is Kurdistan." "Ey Reqib" became the official anthem of the autonomous Kurdistan Region of Iraq and is widely listened to and sung by the PKK and its supporters.[52] The name "Med" connotes the territory of the Medes and therefore the territory of the Kurds. The term appears frequently in Diyarbakır—Med-Land amusement park, Medya Park, and Med City Mahabad. Using the English word "city" is common for gated communities across the country and implies a certain status in the popular imagination. Emphasis on Kurdish identity also appears in the buildings' ornamentation. The white façade of the apartment blocks is explicitly decorated with the colors of the Kurdistan flag—red, white, yellow, and green in descending order. Further, at the top of the café and at the entrance gate, "Med City Mahabad" appears in a similar color scheme (figure 13).

FIGURE 13. The gate of Med City Mahabad in Kayapınar. The lettering over the gate is in red and green on a yellow background. The twelve-story apartment blocks display red, green, and yellow stripes on a white façade.
Source: Author, 2018.

As I noted, Med City Mahabad is not the only gated community imparting Kurdish symbolism. The names of these communities frequently draw upon figurative representations of Kurdish history. Zana Marina Sitesi, Sur Amed, Bahoz sitesi, Azel sitesi, Welat, and Med Park are but a few of those gated complexes bearing Kurdish names. Bahoz sitesi is another gated community with green, red, and yellow cladding on its apartment blocks. The Arçel blocks, located on Mesopotamia Street, represent a similar trend, featuring connections to Kurdish history on their façade. The blocks depict a double-headed eagle (Çift Başlı Kartal), a well-known Mesopotamian figure, which carries an apotropaic significance (the ability to ward off evil). This iconic eagle functions as a powerful symbol in the city, adorning the historical city walls and serving as the emblem of the Diyarbakır municipality.[53]

The symbolic expression of Kurdishness was not limited to residential blocks. It appeared in diverse venues of consumer culture, such as restaurants and shopping malls, blending with everyday life and signifying the rise of diverse forms of Kurdish nationalism in the city. The "new Diyarbakır"—as one the main housing contractors I interviewed in 2011 claimed—"could be only completed with large shopping malls located at the newly opened roads." In the eyes of many upper- and middle-class Kurdish residents, the shopping malls, elegant restaurants, cafés, and residential complexes were putting Diyarbakır in competition with Istanbul and Ankara. Constructed by two prominent families of Diyarbakır in 2014, the Ceylan Karavil Park Mall was launched as "the largest shopping center of the East and Southeast," marking a significant milestone in the region's commercial landscape. Three years earlier, the Ninova Mall had been launched as the largest shopping center in the southeast. Ninova—Nineveh in English—was a famous ancient Assyrian city and trade center and is recognized as one of the most important Kurdish cities (where now Mosul is located in Iraq).[54] These complexes not only showcase the city's urban achievements but also demonstrate how the local economy intermingles with an urban image defined through Kurdish economic success, Kurdish freedom, and Kurdish development.

Mainly through business-friendly projects, the pro-Kurdish municipality successfully established and tapped into networks of economic and political interdependence by promoting an emergent Kurdish capitalist class in the city. Between 2000 and 2015, the urban development ambitions of the municipalities matched the interests of the Kurdish business circles. Key construction firms in Diyarbakır—An Yapı, Baran İnşaat, Çeysa Yapı, Azel Holding, and Bir Tane İnşaat, among others—several of which were established in the early 2000s, actively contributed to the city's expansion toward the northwest. These firms built large apartment complexes alongside shopping malls. Diyarbakır's new urban landscape took shape amid large housing and shopping-mall colonies, private clinics, and smaller-scale business centers, connected by wide roads. As the municipality invested in critical infrastructure (roads, schools, improvement of the sewage system), Diyarbakır experienced a transformation into a burgeoning business hub. This growth coincided with increased trade opportunities, also fostering connections with Iran and Iraq. The city's hospitality sector flourished, witnessing a significant rise in luxury hotels from a mere two to dozens, catering to both tourism and business. Additionally, Diyarbakır hosted its most expansive business expos during this period.

To understand speculative urbanism in Diyarbakır, we cannot simply apply Hernando De Soto's well-known formula: converting "dead capital" into "liquid capital."[55] Neoliberal speculation in Diyarbakır was not undertaken directly by local governmental bodies, which would, for example, allow (or create the opportunity for) the transformation of old city markets into central business districts. On the contrary, the pro-Kurdish municipalities often opted to retain rural migrants within squatter settlements and informal jobs as peddlers, vendors, and temporary workers, aiming to leverage their participation in political life. This approach did not prevent the already existing landlords and upper-class residents from capitalizing on the urban modernization of Diyarbakır. During this time, while landlords prospered (as did contractors), most rural migrants remained in the poor districts of Diyarbakır. In the city, the developers' political view has usually aligned with that of the party: the republic's long-lasting policies had exploited and impoverished the Kurdish cities. It was now the municipalities' and the business leaders' role to "lift Diyarbakır where it deserves to be," or turn it into "a prosperous and wealthy city, as the capital of the Kurds deserves to be"—two phrases I would hear frequently from businesspeople in almost the exact same wording.[56]

For business leaders especially, lifting Diyarbakır to its just position was associated with urban development, usually enacted in the form of building. Ahmet's account exemplifies the ways in which businessmen personally pledged to develop Diyarbakır through a blend of nationalism and profitable construction projects. In his mid-forties, Ahmet was one son of a very large tribal (aşiret) family in Diyarbakır. After his father died, he and his three brothers managed a construction firm and car dealerships in Diyarbakır. I met him at his car dealership at Şanlıurfa Road in 2009. In 2010, the brothers began focusing on housing construction, but they had also built a marble factory in the region. While showing me their ongoing projects, Ahmet compared Diyarbakır to Istanbul: "What are we missing from Istanbul? Nothing. This state left us behind. This city has always been associated with terror. It is wrong. We are now lifting Diyarbakır to where it deserves to be. Of course, we should have a share in our city's development." Indeed, the contribution was taking place through construction, through the rise of housing blocks built of concrete. In Ahmet's and other developers' view, construction projects were shaping Diyarbakır's new image as the Kurdish capital city to be. The marriage of capitalism and nationalism also led to the establishment of several business associations in the city. In 2014, for example, a group of businessmen founded the Kurdistan Industrialists' and Businessmen Association (KÜRDSİAD), and Ahmet was one of its members.[57]

In the early 2000s, Kurdishness rapidly entered into the marketplace and popular consumer culture in its various forms. Rogers Brubaker remarks that nationness is embodied not only in political claims and nationalist rhetoric but also in everyday encounters, practical categories, commonsense knowledge, cultural idioms, cognitive schemas, mental maps, interactional cues, and discursive frames, as well as in social networks.[58] Likewise, what suffused this sense of Kurdishness was not only the party's urban political strategies in the city; it was also the material consumer culture, constantly reproduced by residents. The party managed to forge social cohesion around the imaginaries of Kurdish nationhood. This sense of nationhood was not only reproduced in terms of territorial investment (as I discussed in the context of urban development projects); Kurdish nationhood was also strongly enmeshed with popular and material culture, constantly shaping a shared consciousness about the city.[59] During this period, being Kurdish in Diyarbakır was popular. Orchestrated by the party, this popularity was a form of everyday life determining how Diyarbakırians "practice[d] their nationness" through the political positions the party designed.[60] Kurdish identity was not something to be hidden; it was something to be proud of. In 2015, at the height of everyday Kurdish nationhood, one would experience the rising sense of Kurdish nationalism just by walking in the streets of Diyarbakır. The food, the colors, the signs, the informal conversations, and the music played in the streets all offered explicit experiences of "national belonging."[61] This experience permeated the city through Kurdish material culture.

Everyday Kurdishness

The following vignette describes a typical weekday afternoon in Diyarbakır as citizens from distinct backgrounds—from pious to leftist—convene in one of the popular cafés to practice Kurdishness in their own ways. In July 2015, after completing my appointments at the Sur municipality, I met with Havin.[62] It was a typical hot, dry day in Diyarbakır. The streets, emptied by the noon heat, began to crowd again around four o'clock. Havin and I frequently met at Sur in the afternoons; he would drive there from his job at Dicle University. Together, we walked through Gazi Street. We checked out the stores. We looked for shady spots to hide from the sun. It was good to walk through the passages and narrow backstreets. We entered the *Bedesten* (a traditional covered market where fabric, jewelry, and similar valuable items are sold) and went through the back gate; we could hear Kurdish pop music from the open doors of the shops. We also heard Kurdish pop music through the cracked windows of the cars passing by. After we passed the coppersmiths, we arrived at Sülüklü Khan,[63] originally built in 1683. The khan had been restored in 2010 and since then run by a collective as a café; Sülüklü Khan quickly became one of the favorite spots in the city. Upon entering through a brief, narrow passage, we were welcomed by a vast courtyard space. The khan had a typical basalt stone courtyard plan with a surrounding arcade. A large sycamore tree stood right in the middle, and small palm trees grew in a few flowerpots to the side. As in a traditional Diyarbakır house in hot summers, the stone floor was dampened, aiding in humidifying the courtyard air during the day. Above, mist floated down from time to time from a mist system installed over the courtyard. But the air was so hot the mist evaporated before it fell on us. Occasionally, sunlight streaming through branches, mingling with the water droplets, would create tiny rainbows in the air. That day, Sülüklü Khan was crowded. The dark wooden tables in the courtyard were almost full. We found a table beside the entrance near the arcade.

At the end of the corridor, to my right, a photo of Charlie Chaplin was hanging on the stone wall. In the other corner, the poems of the famous Kurdish poet Ahmet Arif covered the entire wall: three short poems appeared on a white panel; below was a head silhouette in red, beneath which his name was transcribed with big, bold red letters. The young customers, some conservative and pious, some liberal, sat side by side. Next to our table, behind Havin, was a group of men and women who appeared to be in their late twenties, engaged in an animated conversation. They drank a local Syriac wine. Two more young men joined the group. After greeting one another in Kurdish, they continued their conversation in Turkish. Among Kurdish youth, greeting in Kurdish was a sign of their advocacy and support of the Kurdish movement.

Next to them was a group of six: two children and their parents, accompanied by another couple probably in their thirties. They had combined two tables. The family, perhaps tourists in the city, were taking selfies and photographs of the khan, and later asked the waiter to take a group photo with the other couple. Behind them, at a separate table, were two women wearing headscarves and loose clothes, with their little daughters. One of the women was swaying her head to a Kurdish song playing at the back, while the other woman tried to make her baby fall asleep. The little girl was playing with sugar cubes inside the sugar bowl on the table.

Across the courtyard, on the other side of the sycamore, two young women smoked cigarettes and drank tea. Closer to the kitchen, in a silent corner by himself, was a young man probably in his late twenties. He was reading a book and drinking tea. He seemed to know the waitstaff; he would have long chats with them in Kurdish when they approached him to refill his tea. Two men who looked older greeted him in Kurdish and spoke with him for five minutes or so and then moved to another table to talk with two other men. They dove into deep conversation in Kurdish.

There was no official menu. The front side of a red-paper flyer on the table was bordered with white lines. Under the image of a black cat, it read in Kurdish, "Xana Zêlûyan in Comben, 1683" (Sülüklü Khan Collective, 1683). Centered on the paper was a poignant excerpt from Kurdish poet Cemal Süreyya. At the bottom was a piano and a silhouette of the courtyard tree to the left. The drinks menu was presented in Kurdish, with Turkish translations in the margin. Beverages ranged from teas and local Kurdish fruit sherbets to local Syriac wine. Our waiter greeted us in Kurdish and took our order: two cold sweet basil sherbets, a local drink. After a while, as the sun was setting, the khan became even more crowded. More families with children replaced the young couples, and more young groups arrived from after work. Some drank wine, and some drank tea. Havin saw one of his colleagues from the university arrive with his family. They greeted each other from a distance.

From the music that was playing, to the array of beverages served, to the diversity of the visitors, the Sülüklü Khan epitomized many of the shifting features of everyday culture—and the pervasiveness of Kurdishness in Diyarbakır. While popularly known for its support of the Kurdish movement, Sülüklü Khan was also one of the first cafés in Diyarbakır to serve wine. Evidently, the café's political position and offerings did not prevent its patrons, coming from different educational and class and religious backgrounds, to convene. To the Sülüklü Khan came the pious and the secular, leftists and university students, housewives, tourists, businessmen, university professors, and merchants, together and all at once, to practice "Kurdishness" in their own ways.

Michael Billig argues how various daily practices constitute "banal nationalism," creating intense nationalist experiences.[64] With this concept in mind, he considers food one of the crucial cultural objects fostering strong aspects of national belonging, particularly at times when "nations declare some aspects of their cuisine unique."[65] Testifying to Billig's point, between 2010 and 2015, cafés and restaurants boasting Kurdish cuisine flourished in Diyarbakır. Traditional courtyard houses in Sur quickly converted into cafés; restaurants flooded onto the pavement in Ofis; and luxurious chain restaurants appeared in Kayapınar. It was Kurdish cuisine's declaration of independence. Likewise, typical confectioneries in the streets of Sur advertised "Kurdish coffee" with signs. Some even rebranded Turkish coffee brands by literally placing "Kurdish coffee" stickers over their logos (figure 14).

In many herb and nut stores, Turkish delight signs were replaced with "Kurdish delight." Here, rebranding Turkish coffee as Kurdish coffee and

FIGURE 14. Turkish coffee bags rebranded as Kurdish coffee displayed at a sidewalk stand. The paper sign reads, "Diyarbakır stone-ground Kurdish coffee 5 TL."
Source: Author, 2015.

Turkish delight as Kurdish delight allowed both vendors and buyers to express Kurdish identity in relation to mainstream Turkish society. Banal consumer products were transformed in the context of everyday Kurdishness, emerging as heavily coded objects.[66] Such everyday cultural materials simultaneously produced an exclusionary group identity premised on opposing Turkish identity. In parallel, Kurdish culinary books became common in bookstores. In 2015, the Diyarbakır municipality published a thick book titled *Meyir*, dedicated to Kurdish culinary culture and brimming with an assortment of traditional Kurdish recipes.

The reinvention of Kurdish culinary culture in Diyarbakır penetrated a collectively shared practice of Kurdishness that could be observed in distinct spaces the city.[67] Each time I visited the city I checked out the souvenir shops at Hasan Paşa Khan, a sixteenth-century khan in Sur. Following its latest restoration in 2008, the khan became famous for its souvenir shops and breakfast cafés on the second floor. The shop I regularly visited was on the ground floor, right across from the entrance gate. It sold a variety of objects, from silver jewelry and rosaries to decorative lamps, clay bowls, handmade cloth purses, and traditional shawls and *shalwars*. But the most compelling part of this store was the decorative tapestries hung outside. These eleven-by-seventeen-inch black-and-white tapestries depicted well-known figures. Organized side by side, they included Musa Anter, known as "Apê Musa," a Kurdish author and intellectual who was assassinated in September 1992; Seyid Rıza, a prominent religious figure and leader of the Dersim uprising in Turkey in 1937–1938; Molla Mustafa Barzani, Mesut Barzani, and Che Guevara; and, right next to the Latin American revolutionary, Sheikh Said, the leader of the Naqshbandi order and the principal organizer of the Sheikh Said Rebellion, who was hanged in 1925.[68] In other visits to the city, I spotted silhouettes of political activists like Deniz Gezmiş, Kurdish film director Yılmaz Güney, and Kurdish singers Ahmet Kaya and Şivan Perwer on tapestries outside the shop.

Checking these decorative objects helped me measure the political spirit of the city. From time to time I could even see Atatürk's image among them, close to the religious figures. From 2011 to 2014, the store increasingly featured more leftist Kurdish figures, more than Kurdish sheikhs. During that time, Atatürk's image disappeared. In 2015, I saw—for the first time—an image of the pro-Kurdish party leader Selahattin Demirtaş. He appeared among tapestries with Mesut Barzani, Ahmet Kaya, Che Guevara, and Deniz Gezmiş; 2015 was the peak of the Kurdish movement and of the popularity of Selahattin Demirtaş in the movement (figure 15).

Simultaneously, more and more bookstores began to proudly display pro-Kurdish history books on their shelves. Kurdish dictionaries appeared in

FIGURE 15. Souvenir shop in Hasan Paşa Khan displaying decorative tapestries: *Left, top to bottom*, Molla Mustafa Barzani, Ahmet Kaya, Abdullah Demirtaş, Yılmaz Güney, and Che Guevara; *at back*, Deniz Gezmiş; *right, from top to bottom*, Ali, Said-i Nursi, Ehmedê Xanî, Seyid Rıza.
Source: Author, 2015.

bookstore windows. Clothing stores displayed traditional women's dresses, shawls, and Kurdish *puşi* (a Kurdish scarf, keffiyeh, with yellow, red, and green colors). Multiple versions of fake Adidas "Kurdistan" soccer jerseys appeared beside the Amed Spor (Diyarbakır's official soccer team) jerseys (figure 16).

The rise of nationalist consumer culture in Diyarbakır did not necessarily cater to tourists; it was part of an everyday exchange among Diyarbakırians. Indeed, this growing sense of Kurdish consumer culture made the citizens believe in Kurdish autonomy within the illusion of a little Kurdistan in the city. The market and everyday consumption amplified the reach of nationalism.[69] Quotidian objects that "effectively circulate and spread through simple market transactions and consumer preferences" represented a distinct Kurdish identity.[70] They also helped generate a strong sense of Kurdish belonging among the residents.

Branding the Nation

The scholarship of nationalism has long portrayed neoliberal frameworks and nationalism as incompatible. This view deems globalization and neoliberal practices as a challenge or a weakening force to nationalism.[71] However, in

FIGURE 16. Street shop in Sur displaying jerseys and scarves for the Diyarbakır soccer team, Amed Spor.
Source: Author, 2015.

the past few years, scholars have interrogated this view, and it is now widely accepted that certain nationalist policies and neoliberal practices can actually be harmonious and even mutually reinforcing.[72] Extending these debates, the case of Diyarbakır allows us to understand how neoliberal urbanism might resonate with nationalism even in the absence of state power. Conceptualizing the relation between neoliberal urbanization and nationalism as an antagonism eventually resolved through a process of absorption leaves little room for discussing the symbiosis between the two.[73] Diyarbakır shows instead how neoliberal urbanism and identity politics can engage in a relation of reciprocal reinforcement, which may open up space for political struggles and contestations.[74] Of course, suturing together the two rationalities is tenuous and far from complete.[75] But one can study the reconfiguration of neoliberal urbanism and nationalism by looking at urban development projects and everyday life practices.

Nationalist politics and neoliberal urbanism can be dependent on each other while conjointly evolving. Similar dependency can be traced in the AKP's emphasis on economic nationalism, especially after 2013, in the way AKP officials re-created state institutions in the form of corporations and channeled financial flows, and in the sectors of energy and construction implicated within the concept of "authentic and national" (*yerli ve milli*).[76] Turkey's recent urban transformations under the AKP, as I discuss in chapter 2, took shape around such neoliberal populism—what scholars have called "economic nationalism."[77]

The relationship between neoliberalism and nationalism I explore in this chapter is slightly different from this corporate nationalism. Here, rather than examining the reorganization of the state in the form of a corporation, I look at the city under neoliberalism as it weaves together a sense of progress, national identity, and power for its residents.

The Kurdish movement has been, on the one hand, strongly oppositional to neoliberal discourse, as shown in the movement's approach to the urban poor and its poverty alleviation projects discussed in chapter 2. But, on the other hand, under Turkey's presiding market logic, which has vigorously pushed for capitalist accumulation, urban mega-projects, gentrification, and the formation of class-exclusive neighborhoods, neoliberal urbanism was not something that the pro-Kurdish municipalities could easily avoid. Hence, to gain legitimacy and power in the eyes of Kurds, the party needed to compete with the AKP's pervasive neoliberal governance. At the same time, the HDP's leaders saw public infrastructure projects as a great venue for demonstrating power while promoting sentiments of national belonging and justifying autonomy. As Ernest Gellner comments, "Nationalism is not the awakening of an old, latent, dormant force, though that is how it does indeed present itself."[78] The movement's pursuit of national identity needed careful recasting to serve political ends in how it wanted to present itself as progressive and sovereign in contemporary Turkey. As amply evidenced in the inauguration speeches of party leaders, public infrastructure projects served as concrete proof that Kurds could administer themselves despite state coercion. According to Benedict Anderson, the essence of the nation rests in its capacity to foster a sense of national identity while collectively imagining a range of things—past and future.[79] The performative strategies the party officials devised[80]—ranging from commemorative ceremonies of other Kurdish regions to inauguration speeches—were designed to convey the founding myths of a Kurdish past and progressive future for an imagined national geography. The newly asphalted roads, new road-lighting systems, aluminum-clad façades, high-rise luxury apartment blocks, shopping malls, as well as the objects of everyday life, were all part of the new national identity and Diyarbakır's ability to equal Istanbul or Ankara on its own terms. Indeed, these new construction projects played a significant role in forming an everyday experience of nationhood, somewhat similar to nation-building projects and early republican attempts to create the unified, homogeneous territory that Zeynep Kezer calls "Nationalizing Space."[81] In the case of Diyarbakır, nationalizing space happened by branding the city, representing progress and creating spaces of "Kurdish consumption" with the help of markets and business circles. Consumer culture repeatedly reproduced the sense of national belonging at the very sites of neoliberalism in Diyarbakır. During this process, networks of pro-Kurdish financiers invested billions of dollars across urban projects.[82] By doing so, they have had a noticeable influence on propagating the imaginaries of Kurdish nationhood in the city and retooled local urban governments to present Diyarbakır as a world-class city, the capital of a nascent Kurdistan. Such neoliberal urban practice, in the form of both urban infrastructure and everyday culture, allowed the pro-Kurdish party to perform sovereignty. The municipality's interest in pursuing (neoliberal) architecture and planning was also tied to issues of economic independence, which the party sought. The co-articulation of neoliberalism and nationalism has had visible consequences in the reframing of urban governance in the post-2004 context in Diyarbakır. In fact, the pro-Kurdish party's blend of nationalism and neoliberalism proved to be a very timely political project, as the party secured repetitive victories in local elections, in 1999, 2004, 2009, 2014, and 2019. The success of the party did not only stem from the mobilization of the urban poor. As this chapter shows, it also resided within its urban strategies directed to, and by, the local elites and the city's Kurdish business classes. The everyday culture led by the party helped to integrate diverse identities into a Kurdish bloc,[83] as seen in the example of Sülüklü Khan. As such, Kurdishness in Diyarbakır was created not only during speeches by HDP party members or in municipality events or political campaigns. Kurdishness sprang up in everyday material culture: through ordinary consumer objects, in the names of gated communities and symbols decorating their façades, in books being sold, in Kurdish jokes—full of confidence—that people told each other, on restaurant menus, in pop music blasting from cars, and in the colors of dresses sold in stores. The parallel emergence of a dynamic culture made citizens believe in the manifest future of Kurdistan and an experience of nationness. Thus, Diyarbakır became a brand associated with Kurdish national identity.

This everyday nationalism was very much entangled with the memorial landscape created by the party, feeding the nationalist sentiments of the city. In fact, making Diyarbakır a capital required building a landscape that would capture and sustain Kurdish culture and keep Kurdish memories alive. The following chapter studies the memorial landscape of Diyarbakır, examining the ways in which pro-Kurdish municipal officials appropriated public space: from the construction of public parks and memorials expressing state violence to the diverse forms of mass demonstrations associated with these spaces.

5
SCULPTING VIOLENCE, ACTIVATING THE STREET
"Freedom or Freedom"

On the night of November 6, 2013, two trucks pulled up in front of a twenty-meter-long sign spanning a wide avenue in downtown Diyarbakır. As the trucks blocked the roadway, several men dismounted from them and began to dismantle the towering structure, all amid applause and cheering from citizens surrounding the trucks. As this gateway-like sign was coming down, the crowd increased, and cars honked to celebrate the event. While some local TV stations aired a live broadcast of the removal, citizens on the street recorded this moment with their phones.

The gateway sign was one of the few remaining self-assertions of the Turkish state in the city. Featuring Mustafa Kemal Atatürk's famous adage, "Ne mutlu Türküm diyene" (How happy is the one who can say he is a Turk) in red and white—the colors of the republic—across its center, the sign bore Turkish flags on each side. On top at its center was a large reproduction of a watermelon, Diyarbakır's renowned fruit, sitting atop a model of the city's famous wall and bastions. Installed by state officials following the 1980 military coup d'état, the gateway sign commanded attention on a heavily trafficked road in the city center. Further, it was situated directly between the governor's office and Anıt Park, the city's only remaining memorial park attributed to Atatürk, built by the republicans. The sign was not an adornment of the space. Rather, it stated the very subject of that space: a formidable assertion of the Turkish state's presence in the city (figure 17).

It came as no surprise that, following its installation, this mammoth state sign was received with hostility in the city, and the Kurdish movement repeatedly

FIGURE 17. Trees growing in the median strip veil the middle of a sign stretching over a wide, empty roadway. Turkish flags are at either end of the span, and an oversize replica of a watermelon, partly obscured, nests atop a castle-like model in the center.
Source: Author, 2009.

demanded it be removed. Thus, its dismantling was the culmination of a years-long heated debate that had exacerbated already acute tensions between the Kurdish political community and state officials in Diyarbakır. The removal of this sign—with the permission of the governor—was actually a rare event in Diyarbakır. Perhaps for the first time, a nationalist symbol was removed by the governor's decision. Notably, the timing of the sign's removal in November 2013 was not accidental but rather a symbolic gesture, coming amid the peace talks between the PKK and the Turkish state.[1]

Of the sign, what was perceived as most offensive was its emphasis on "Turkishness." Prior to its removal, the Greater Diyarbakır Municipality had placed fully grown ornamental pine trees to purposefully veil the word "Türk."

In 2011, during an interview I conducted, the mayor of Diyarbakır, Osman Baydemir, stressed his frustration with the sign: "It is offensive! It is insulting! Imagine our Kurdish people passing under this fascist nationalist arc every single day. Since we couldn't remove it, we veiled it. But it is not only about the word "Turk"—insulting. What's with that watermelon? For years, they [state officials] have been trying to associate our city with watermelons, but they cannot. We will not let this happen. Diyarbakır is a Kurdish city. And they cannot identify our city with a fruit, a watermelon."[2] Indeed, in almost every publication produced by the offices of the governor or the central state—from the public festivals they organize to the posters they design—a watermelon was used to symbolize Diyarbakır. For me, this representation was a way to quickly determine whether a publication or a poster I came across in the city belonged to or was funded by the governorship. Nevertheless, the polemic of the watermelon—whether it represents the city—has long been on the table. The debate over the symbolic representation of the city exceeded this discourse, however.

Beginning in the late 1930s and into the early 1940s, monuments, busts, and equestrian statues of Kemal Atatürk, along with plates inscribed with his sayings, appeared widely in the cities of Turkey, especially after his death in 1938. As I discuss in the first chapter, in addition to the new monuments, it became common in this nationalist climate to rename streets and boulevards "Atatürk," "Gazi" (veteran), or "Cumhuriyet" (republic).[3] These urban practices, whose effects linger today, extended to Diyarbakır. However, unlike in other cities in Turkey, especially beginning from the early 2000s, statues of Atatürk in Diyarbakır were no longer common; nor were his slogans endorsing Turkish nationalism. The night of the gateway sign's destruction was not the first time Diyarbakırians had convened to witness the remaking of the memorial landscape. During the time it stayed in power, the pro-Kurdish party purposefully and continuously utilized urban space to re-create the city's memorial landscape. While gradually erasing Turkish nationalist symbolism from urban space,[4] pro-Kurdish mayors installed dozens of monuments and memorials, opened hundreds of public parks and tens of museums, conducted archaeological excavations, and led restoration and cultural heritage projects with an aim to cultivate collective Kurdish identity in the city.

This chapter examines how pro-Kurdish municipal officials appropriated public space—from the construction of public parks and memorials expressing state violence, to the diverse forms of mass demonstrations linked to these sites. It demonstrates how these appropriations of public space mobilized Kurdish society, established the collective experience of Kurdish citizenship, and provided an extra-parliamentary channel for disseminating political messages to the rest of the country. What does it mean to present a national identity, in the absence of a nation-state, through memorial landscape? What is it like to construct a narrative of a nation under the yoke of another state? These conditions required urban creativity. The pro-Kurdish party deployed alternative methods for creating a memorial landscape that belongs to the city. This chapter delves into the intricacies of these alternative and often nuanced approaches in shaping the city's memorial landscape.

The Memorial Landscape of Diyarbakır

The memorials of Diyarbakır were not gathered in one site to which people could come and engage in the "rituals of citizenship."[5] They were dispersed across the city, located in places where Kurdish citizens lived their everyday lives. Especially until the armed conflict in 2015, the memorial landscape of Diyarbakır—with over fifty sites in public parks and memorials—registered state oppression and violence. The party effectively linked these sites to particular uses in terms of street actions, such as funerals, commemorations of Kurdish rebellions and activists, and public sermons and festivals. Together, these sites conjured a collective memory that animated residents' sense of Kurdish identity as they walked past them, protested in front of them, or even spread stories about their own narratives.

The city has no single, collective martyrs' memorial. Instead, Diyarbakır offered representations of the ongoing struggle for an autonomous Kurdistan across a dispersed constellation of sites. Diyarbakır's memorial landscape did not merely attempt to tell the history of Kurdish culture—it also drew from current events and state violence. As individual memorials sprang up throughout the city, they became entwined with the complex realities of political conflict.

Rogers Brubaker, in "Rethinking on Nationalism and Nationhood," defines "nationness" as a contingent event that crystallizes and spreads through everyday practices and takes shape as "collective or individual action" that manifests a sense of community.[6] In this spirit, Kurdishness was not made merely via the tangibility of the memorial landscape but emerged from the narratives—what I call memorial activism—embedded within them. Crucially, the emotional experiences of memorial activism, as this chapter will explain, are not limited to these projects but rather merge with the everyday practices of the urban space, where citizens discuss, interrogate, protest, and encounter them.

In this chapter, I reconsider the cultural and political meaning of memory making. I examine the relationships between collective memory and public space, between the representation of violence and the formation of political identity. For the most part, scholarship on collective memory examines how memory assists individuals in forming membership groups and creating a sense of their past, present, and future.[7] These studies contend that group identity takes form by claiming and remembering sameness over time and space.[8] Scholars of public memory thus explain why nation-states spend so much effort on institutions of memory—museums, monuments, memorials—to create a sense of imagined community for the nation.

Similarly, historians have long studied how postcolonial states or newly forming nation-states have used memorial architecture and urban design to legitimize political power and promote a new national identity.⁹ The literature pays particular attention to the capital cities of nation-states, cities upon which this new memorial landscape frequently draws for a common heroic past and a promising future in service of establishing a new identity.¹⁰ More recently, however, distinct minorities and previously marginalized groups across the world "build their collective identities on a shared past of victimization."¹¹ Only a few scholars have analyzed how nonstate powers institutionalize memory, particularly at a time when that memory is alive and actively evolving.¹² Thus, this chapter is concerned not only with how the memorial landscape of Diyarbakır helped to create a sense of national community but also with how and why specific memories in the city are spatialized and institutionalized in such forms and yet still play a part in political campaigns.

Étienne Balibar, in pondering the question of what makes a nation a community, notes that "every social community reproduced by the functioning of institutions is imaginary, that is to say, it is based on the projection of individual existence into the weft of a collective narrative. . . . The fundamental problem is therefore to produce the people. More exactly, it is to make the people itself continually as national community."¹³ Thus, it is not necessarily the memorials or places themselves but the constant strategic lived events they support or elicit—protests, press conferences, everyday interactions, and rumors—that render meaningful the commemorative structures in the city.¹⁴ During my fieldwork, I often had to change my daily schedule in the interest of observing such public meetings, which would occur rapidly, sometimes organized in a matter of hours by party and municipality members at a selected memorial. Taking into account these practices, I not only analyze memorial sites in formal terms but also consider them as "spaces of engagement" and look at how individuals and the party in the city engage with this memorial landscape.¹⁵ By looking at diverse cases of memorial landscapes, memorials, parks, and museums in the city, I elucidate how these spaces of engagement established the collective experience of Kurdishness.

Right to Life

For someone moving across the city, it is almost impossible not to come across Koşuyolu Park, the former racetrack.¹⁶ Completed in 1999, Koşuyolu Park is one of Diyarbakır's largest urban parks. It is located between Ofis and Bağlar, where most of the city's lower-class migrants reside. Koşuyolu Park has been the epicenter of hunger strikes, proclamations, antigovernment marches, and funeral demonstrations.¹⁷ On my several visits, I witnessed more than a dozen protests at the park. Typically organized by party officials and civil-society organizations, the protests generally began with a crowd gathering in front of the party building, then continued through the streets of Ofis, where Diyarbakır's prison is located, and ended at the gate of Koşuyolu Park. Such events were usually accompanied by a press release from party officials that emphasized a discourse of state violence, Kurdish rights, social justice and freedom, or the diversity of Kurdish culture and nation.

Koşuyolu Park was also distinctive because it memorialized state oppression and violence through monuments that recalled an array of historical events. The first of these pieces was erected in 2002, when the pro-Kurdish municipality installed a Human Rights Monument. In an act that sought to strengthen the discourse of Kurdish rights, the monument presented the articles of the "Declaration of Human Rights" on an ornamented tablet. In 2008, the *Right to Life* (*Yaşam Hakkı* in Turkish) memorial was installed. Located at the west entrance to the park, the gray aluminum piece was elevated atop a concrete base clad with dark gray tiles (figure 18) and was accompanied by two wall panels facing each other (figures 19 and 20) Together, the three pieces, designed by local artists, commemorated seven children (out of ten) killed when a bomb exploded along the wall of Koşuyolu Park on September 12, 2006—an event for which no side claimed responsibility.

FIGURE 18. The *Right to Life* memorial.
Source: Author, 2009.

FIGURE 19. The wall panel depicting victims of the bomb blast.
Source: Author, 2009.

FIGURE 20. The wall panel depicting Kurdish society engaged in the *halay*, symbolizing solidarity.
Source: Author, 2009.

While state officials contended that PKK militants, targeting security forces, executed this bomb attack, pro-Kurdish party members and some civil-society organizations claimed it to be an act of state-orchestrated violence, without citing the perpetrator. During my interviews in the field, I heard competing narratives from state officials and pro-Kurdish party members.

Immediately after the blast, the memorial was commissioned and named by Osman Baydemir, the mayor of the Diyarbakır Metropolitan Municipality at the time. In April 2011, I tracked down Eylo, a local sculptor in his early thirties and the artist behind *Right to Life*. I met him for an interview in his workshop, located fifteen minutes from the park. Eylo was working as an art teacher in a small elementary school in the city, and on the weekends he worked in his own atelier, a twenty-five-square-meter space on the ground floor of an apartment. When I arrived at his studio, he welcomed me from atop scaffolding. He was working on a statue of Aram Tigran, a famous Armenian singer who sang primarily in Kurdish. There was almost no space to move; all his easels were filled with paintings of Kurdish symbols and models of various figures. He later showed me his models for a forty-meter-high Kawa,[18] the Kurdish blacksmith who led the rebellion against King Dehak, an episode that has long been accepted as the founding myth of Kurdish history. The Kawa project was commissioned by the municipality to be installed at the Newroz Park, a large park in the city designated for annual Newroz celebrations.[19] After we sat down on low stools to drink tea, I asked Eylo about the design of *Right to Life*. His source of inspiration for the memorial was quite striking: he drew from his own experience of the blast. "When the bomb exploded," he began, "I was in my apartment right across the park. Hearing the blast, I ran to the street to see if I could help. But it was too late." He continued, "I couldn't stop myself from designing the first draft of this memorial when I saw a mother, by the bus station right in front of the gate of the park, her legs maimed by the blast, creeping on the ground and looking for her children. . . . I tried to depict those moments: the dead body of a mother in pain trying to reach eternity and free her children from torture." He added, "This memorial is the abstraction of frozen moments of violence." *Right to Life*, Eylo said, "is actually the desperate plea of a mother, like we [Kurds] feel for our freedom." In representing the traumatic violence of the bombing, Eylo associated the mother's plea with the Kurdish nation's, its struggle for autonomy. From Eylo, I learned that another artist, Feras, a sculptor in his late thirties, created the accompanying wall panels.

When I later met Feras, he was working as an art and ceramics instructor in the municipality's Sümer Park cultural center. In terms of form and symbolism, the wall panels were relatively more explicit than Eylo's sculpture in narrating the violence. During our interview, Feras also showed me his other work, displayed in Sümer Park, on "the state violence over the Kurdish villages," which he represented with red military tanks to explicitly symbolize violence. The Koşuyolu Park panel featured in relief the wounded heads of people killed by the blast. Feras even used red paint to depict the blood coming from their wounds. Scattered over the surface of the panel, the heads frame an open book with the handwritten names of the children who perished (figure 19). Thus, visitors can recognize collective and individual loss. When I asked about the significance of the book, Feras said, "It represents our search for justice for those children who died. But at the same time we are also very hopeful for the peace; this is why I added the two pigeons."

Feras explained that in the second wall panel (figure 20), "the eye cries for the Kurdish society, carved over united Kurds engaged in the *halay* [a traditional folk dance]." He continued, "This panel does not simply narrate the bomb blast. It represents the united Kurdish nation. The upper portion of the panel features a sun, representing hope and peace for the future." During our interview, Feras stated that he did not want his piece to be pessimistic. He noted, "I added the figure of the sun because I didn't want to end this memorial solely with the representation of pain. The sun is also an important symbol for Kurdish culture." Both Eylo and Feras witnessed the tragedy of that day and were supporters of the party. They designed memorials freighted with meaning that went beyond the traumatic event to encompass Kurdish society's "struggle for freedom and . . . search for peace and justice."[20]

The memorials were installed at the very place where the bomb exploded, presenting an explicit narrative of death and a powerful acknowledgment of ongoing oppression and violence against Kurds. On September 12, 2008, two years after the bomb blast, the memorials were revealed in a large commemorative event with the participation of mayors of Diyarbakır, prominent party members, activists, hundreds of citizens, and the relatives of those who died from the blast. The opening speeches confirmed the artists' acute awareness of the significance for these sculptures to Kurdish society. Expectedly, the inauguration was not merely about the bomb blast but was more widely addressing state violence against Kurds. In his speech, Osman Baydemir invoked other violent incidents, recounting the names, in plural form, of children killed in such violence:

> Here are Mizgins, Evins, Uğurs, Şilans, Ferhats. One was a baby, a pacifier that fell out of his mouth, a breast; one was twelve years old when he received thirteen bullets. Enes, who was shot in front of me, was only nine years old. The loss was a life, a future, our future. . . . We have lost mothers, children, and young people dreaming of peace in this war. We

have been living this pain for thirty years. Despite all this, we repeat our call for peace at every opportunity. We know, the pin pulled, the trigger dropped hits both those in front of the barrel and the ones behind it. We made our calls for peace, democracy, and freedom. We built this monument to share our call with our city, where we were born, grew up, lived, and buried our children in its bosom.[21]

Baydemir's speech was not only about the pain of the victims of the blast; his words, by memorializing children who died in similar incidents, expanded the memory to encompass the city of Diyarbakır and even the Kurdish nation. As Baydemir reemphasized the call for peace, democracy, and freedom, he was territorializing, embedding the pain, the hope, and the future of the Kurdish nation in the city. Thus, the *Right to Life* exceeded its role as an artifact of national solidarities or a common past.[22] While building a discourse of Kurdish identity among citizens of Diyarbakır through an imagined future of hope and peace, the sculptures also embodied a critical memory and sense of a collective traumatic history. With the display of wounded heads, the memorial enforced a strong relationship with the visitor, condensing the ongoing atrocity and the suffering of the Kurds. *Right to Life* exposed Diyarbakırians and other visitors to the emotional experience of the past, fostering a new collective memory—a poignant lesson accessible even to those who hadn't witnessed the bomb blast.

The Act of Civil Disobedience

The memorial landscape of Diyarbakır was not constituted only by symbolic, fixed representations of Kurdish identity and culture; most of the time that landscape was a source of urban activism, cultivating specific histories and politics. Over the years, Koşuyolu Park became an epicenter for thousands of protests and demonstrations. On March 15, 2011, Diyarbakır's residents awoke to discover that a large tent had been erected in Koşuyolu Park. The result of a collaboration between the Peace and Democracy Party (BDP) and the Peace Mothers Initiative, a grassroots pro-Kurdish organization, the tent was inspired by the occupation of Tahrir Square in Cairo, as part of the movement now known as the Arab Spring.

Dubbed the "Democratic Solution Tent" by the BDP, the massive tent was also conceived as part of a larger project of civil disobedience. Erected three months prior to the Turkish national election of June 2011, the tent highlighted both the ongoing grievances by Kurds against the Turkish government and specific election laws that prevented Kurdish parties from gaining seats in Parliament through national elections. Its installation followed a joint press conference with the Democratic Society Congress (DTK), at which the BDP called on Turkey's Kurds to stage acts of civil disobedience to draw attention to four demands: the right to Kurdish-language education, the immediate release of jailed Kurdish politicians, an end to Turkey's military operations against the PKK, and the abolition of Turkey's 10 percent threshold for parliamentary representation.

The first tent—among several in other Kurdish cities—was erected in Diyarbakır two months after the fall of the Tunisian government, a month after the overthrow of the Mubarak regime in Egypt, and on the very day the Syrian uprising began. There was no doubt that its appearance owed much to the stirring images of Tahrir Square, occupied by tens of thousands of people in tents, which had inspired diverse movements in the region and across the globe. Immediately, the events in Diyarbakır appeared in headlines across Turkey. Political commentators dubbed it the "Kurdish Spring" (or, by then, a Kurdish Summer).[23]

Unlike the popular uprisings tied to the Arab Spring that were experienced in most of the countries in the Middle East, the Kurdish Spring was neither "uncoordinated" nor "leaderless."[24] Instead, it was a well-organized and coordinated project directed by pro-Kurdish party officials. From the choice of location for the installation of the Democratic Solution Tents, to the orchestration of various types of activities, the party's project of civil disobedience was deliberately aimed at engaging spectators in highly symbolic forms of political activity. For example, attendance at the tents was coordinated twenty-four hours a day, with each municipality arranging nightlong shifts to staff them and pro-Kurdish groups providing meals for visitors during the day. Unlike in Tahrir Square, there were no street clinics; nor was there a permanent kindergarten. There was neither a baby born nor a wedding celebrated in the squares of the Kurdish movement.[25] And unlike the popular unfolding of the Arab Spring or the Occupy movement elsewhere, the initial networking of participants was not primarily sustained by social media. Throughout March and April social media expanded the movement, and indeed social media helped the movement bring large numbers of people into the streets; but in the city the BDP very much capitalized on its own in-person networks, as neighborhood representatives simply knocked on doors to organize volunteers to support the effort.

The very first morning of its installation, I went to see the tent in Koşuyolu Park. With the capacity to shelter almost one hundred people, the Democratic Solution Tent was strategically placed at the center of Diyarbakır's memorial landscape. This large new structure was yellow—one of the main colors of the BDP and of the proposed red, green, and yellow Kurdistan flag. Outside its entrance hung the four demands of the civil disobedience campaign, clearly printed as large posters in both Kurdish and Turkish. Moreover, since the Kurdish text was written in red and the Turkish in green, all the colors of the Kurdistan flag were displayed as part of the installation. At the time, it was unlawful (and it still is) to fly the Kurdistan flag in public in Turkey. Bringing these colors together in indirect ways, such as in one's clothing, has been a frequent form of protest at pro-Kurdish demonstrations. Deliberately, the day the tent was raised coincided with the local commemoration of the poison-gas attack against Kurdish civilians on March 16, 1988, in Halabja, Iraq. And following an early morning gathering in front of the city's Municipal Guest House, a crowd of citizens—activists, party members, municipal officials, and mayors—marched with banners in hand to the Democratic Solution Tent. The journalists and plainclothes police recording the events accompanied the demonstrators to the park. When the crowd arrived, a short press conference was organized commemorating the Halabja massacre and emphasizing demands for Kurdish rights.

After the press conference, I stayed with the crowd at the park to observe what was happening. Within a couple of hours, the Democratic Solution Tent became the political and social hub of the city. The images and messages it conveyed were disseminated via traditional and social media; students, activists, politicians, and neighbors all took turns visiting. Some came just out of curiosity, while others came to show their support. Inside the tent, elderly Kurdish women and men passed a microphone among themselves, singing traditional songs and sharing stories about the Kurdish struggle. Eventually, the tent, the center of attention, attracted other activities in the park. Street vendors selling tea, water, and *simit* set up around the tent, and groups of youth began holding picnics and other gatherings on the grass in front of it. Ultimately, the pervasive character of this orchestrated demonstration united a variety of political groups, NGOs, and individuals of diverse ages and backgrounds—businessmen, housewives, activists, students, and youth—in the public space.[26] In the span of one week, as organized protests continued at the Democratic Solution Tents in Diyarbakır and elsewhere, other acts of civil disobedience were staged in cities with large Kurdish populations across Turkey's southeast, including Batman, Van, Hakkari, Şırnak, Bingol, Siirt, Adıyaman, Gaziantep, and Tunceli. In parallel with its program of Democratic Solution Tents, the BDP organized several other demonstrations as part of its larger campaign of civil disobedience. In Diyarbakır, one of the most notable of these was a campaign of Civil Friday Prayer—initiated to protest the state requirement that a designated script (written by the Directorate of Religious Affairs) be used in Friday sermons. During one of my visits to the tent, I learned about the Civil Friday Prayers while chatting with Sami, the director of cultural affairs for the Diyarbakır Metropolitan Municipality. The Civil Friday Prayer campaign was initially inspired by the massive

Friday prayers conducted in Tahrir Square during the Egyptian uprisings. "It is important for them [the public and the state] to see us in a mass, how high our numbers are," Sami explained; that was one of the motives for organizing the prayers in a public space. The Civil Friday Prayers, like the Democratic Solution Tents, were initiated concurrently in several cities, including Diyarbakır, Batman, Hakkari, and Istanbul, with an invitation to all Kurdish citizens to participate. One of the earliest significant instances of protest prayers occurred on April 8, 2011, in Diyarbakır, when around three thousand Kurdish Muslims attended Friday prayer in Dağkapı Square, the main square of the city, instead of going to mosques.[27] I observed the gathering. It was one of those warm, sunny spring days in Diyarbakır. When I arrived, prior to the prayer, Dağkapı Square was surrounded by police. Worshippers were gathering, and some straw mats were already on the ground, but many men brought newspapers or cardboard or simply put their jackets on the ground to pray on. Journalists, plainclothes policemen, and other individuals were recording the prayer. The *mele* (Kurdish imam) at the podium had already begun the civic version of the Friday sermon in Kurdish. In Turkey, imams are appointed by the state, and the state strictly controls the content of the Friday sermons (*hutbe*) by distributing weekly texts prewritten by the Directorate of Religious Affairs. In this case, however, the imam was selected by the BDP to conduct a sermon using a text entirely different from the one prepared by the government. In his *hutbe*, the imam explicitly defended the right within Islam to conduct prayer in one's mother tongue and to live one's religion in one's own culture.

The selection of Dağkapı Square for the Civil Friday Prayer was noteworthy. Centrally located at the entrance to the city's historical quarters and market, the square had been remade in 1931 after the foundation of the Turkish Republic. Subsequently, like many other public spaces in Turkey, Dağkapı Square came to be adorned with a clock tower and a statue of Atatürk. Installed on the western side of square, the statue depicts Atatürk holding children under his arms. It has long attracted attention and criticism from Kurdish residents of the city. The statue is not the only prominent representation of Atatürk on display in the square. At one end of the public space, a massive mural on the side of an eleven-story military building (demolished later in 2015) showed Atatürk in military apparel. An inscription below read: "Those from Diyarbakır, Van, Erzurum, Istanbul, Thrace, and Macedonia are the children of the same race, the veins of the same one"—quoting Atatürk's address to the citizens when he visited the city. Across from the mural, another portrait of Atatürk surveyed the square from the top of the citadel, with a Turkish flag to its side. All three of these monumental works stood as powerful reminders of a Turkish nation-state imbued with Kemalist doctrine. The transformation of Dağkapı

Square into an outdoor prayer hall not only provided a religious challenge to the Kemalist secular nation-state, but also served as an act of eradicating state power (figure 21).

Shortly after a sit-in in front of the Atatürk statue, the Civil Friday Prayer began, under tight police surveillance. As the crowd of men expanded for the prayer, I moved to the section of the square with the non-praying attendees. In Turkey, it is usually the men who practice the Friday prayer. And it is not usual (for instance inside a mosque) to have separate sections for praying and nonpraying attendees. Here it was different. As the men were forming their lines to pray, at the western side of the square a large group of nonpraying attendees was arriving to show their support. They gathered in front of the street by a small park facing the square watching the Friday prayer. That the prayer was held in an outdoor public space allowed it to also enact a public protest. Among the nonpraying attendees was a group of veiled women. They were sitting on paving stones or on the little plastic foldable benches they brought. Some were silently chatting in small groups, while others were raising their hands to follow the prayers of the *mele*. Next to the women were municipality officers, party members, and activists, both male and female—many of the women not covered.

As the prayer continued, some of the nonparticipants were standing and sipping tea from a buffet behind the gathering, while others were squatting and chatting. I recognized several members of community organization groups,

FIGURE 21. Civil Friday Prayer in Dağkapı Meydanı.
Source: Author, 2011.

human rights activists, and members of leftist pro-Kurdish organizations I knew from prior demonstrations. Among them were Saliha (from Sur municipality) and Hasan (from FCA, the Free Compatriot Association, in the Hasırlı neighborhood), engaged in a lively conversation with another woman, Meryem, from the Sur office of the party.[28] Behind them were Ahsen (from Kadem) with Onur and Murat (from the FCA), and in front of them was a group of three middle-aged men, squatting as they conversed. Saliha and I briefly talked. As I continued standing with the group and watching the prayer, Sami approached me. Looking at the men praying, Sami said, "We have plans for this square. We are planning to install the sculpture of Sheikh Said right in the middle of this square. And there is another project for Salahaddin Ayyubi, pride of our [Kurdish] nation."[29] This would be one of the first few urban projects in which the pro-Kurdish municipality afforded significant space for prominent Kurdish Muslim figures. Though I said nothing, Sami saw my surprised expression and continued: "We are planning on installing forty-seven gallows representing their execution by the state"—he was referring to the hanging of Sheikh Said and forty-six of his friends in 1925 in the square—"so the people can remember and think about this violence. We also want to change the name of this square into Sheikh Said Square." The party was seeking to represent the direct violence of the state at the very site of the trauma, as well as to engage with important Kurdish religious figures in a publicly visible way.

When the prayer ended, many of the participants—pious, secular, leftist—marched back to the Democratic Solution Tent while chanting antigovernment slogans under close police surveillance. Following each instance of Civil Friday Prayer, major news organs reported on the event in print and online, under such headlines as "The Friday Prayer with the Apo Poster," "Alternative Friday," and "Civil Disobedient Prayer."[30] These reports featured excerpts from the speeches of party officials, mentioned the slogans used by demonstrators, and described clashes between the police and participants. The civil disobedience created a space of engagement for the Kurdish residents to feel solidarity. From the tent gatherings to "Civil Friday Prayers," these events facilitated interactions among different segments of society, bringing pious, religious, and traditional groups into the movement's fold.

The power of the party-organized spectacle of civil disobedience did not reside only in its symbolism, popularity, and public visibility; it also stemmed from the reorganization of the urban space during the events. For almost three months following the initiation of the campaign, the everyday life of Diyarbakır was scheduled around it. During weekly Civil Friday Prayers, shops were frequently closed at midday as thousands participated and then marched to the Democratic Solution Tent. Koşuyolu Park, too, became a meeting point for all sorts of civic groups that organized their own small art festivals or workshops. Most of the hotels in the city were fully booked with journalists, authors, and Kurdish visitors from elsewhere who either wanted to participate or document the events. Merchants sold out of BDP flags and other items representing the movement, and the municipality and related bureaucracies slowed down their work, as most of their employees and officers were participating in the demonstrations.

In May 2011, the movement of Democratic Solution Tents was shut down by a government court order. Hannah Arendt wrote that "the space of appearance comes into being wherever men are together in the manner of speech and actions and disappears not only with the dispersal of men . . . but with the disappearance or arrest of the activities themselves."[31] The performance of civil disobedience may thus not only target a government and its police power but also aim to engage a public audience, whether committed to the act of defiance or not. It is further through media representations of scenes of protest, including political speeches and clashes between protesters and the police, that those involved in such actions may seek "anticipated communication with others" by means of a dialogical attempt to invoke judgments of support and sympathy.[32] The rapid dissemination of images of these events through new and traditional media encouraged distant observers to become participants. Commentators from major newspapers were likewise moved to discuss Turkey's restrictions on political and cultural expression, the denial of citizenship rights to Kurds, and punishments for the expressions of Kurdish identity in public. Beyond this, commentators questioned whether these events might have revolutionary effects similar to those in Egypt and Tunisia. Television stations interviewed residents of Diyarbakır who were staying in the tent, organized political debates, and invited politicians and well-known commentators to discuss the demands of the BDP. Such a public "space of appearance" could be re-created whenever individuals gathered politically—that is, "wherever people gather in the manner of speech and action."[33] Even though the government eventually removed the Democratic Solution Tents from public space, the pro-Kurdish party was able to sustain intermittently the Civil Friday Prayers for close to thirty-one months.

Representing Violence in the City

The memorial landscape of Diyarbakır not only marked traumatic incidents within the city but also reflected a broader history of violence beyond its borders. One example is the Uğur Kaymaz memorial, designed by Eylo. Uğur Kaymaz was a twelve-year-old Kurdish boy who was shot repeatedly by policemen in November 2004 in Mardin, a city one and a half hours away from Diyarbakır. Within a year of the incident, the memorial was installed in a small park in front of Sur municipality. In the memorial, Uğur Kaymaz's abstracted body shows thirteen small, identical round holes carved into the stone, for the thirteen bullets that took his life. Bordered by an iron fence, the sculpture of the pierced body stood on a concrete base, with the United Nations' Rights of the Child engraved on glass in Turkish (figure 22). In 2005, immediately after the installation of the monument, a court investigation was opened to look into the sculpture and also at Sur mayor Abdullah Demirbaş, who had allegedly "spent the municipality's budget unlawfully."[34] The monument was vandalized and reinstalled several times; in 2016 it was removed by state officials.

Narratives of children and mothers are central to the Kurdish movement's representations of state violence and oppression. Ceylan Önkol Park, named after a Kurdish girl killed in October 2009 by a mortar shell while she was grazing sheep

FIGURE 22. The Uğur Kaymaz memorial stands across the street from the Sur municipality building.
Source: Author, 2009.

in the town of Lice, in Diyarbakır Province, is another example. Önkol's death drew considerable attention from the municipality, local media, and human rights organizations.[35] With the organized collaboration of the BDP and human rights organizations, thousands in Diyarbakır participated in marches protesting state military practices in southeastern Turkey. The campaign, which began in October 2009, emphasized the state's violation of the right to live and culminated in the opening of the park in June 2010 to honor Önkol.

With an urgency of expression and a need to transmit and preserve the memory of citizens exposed to violence, the municipalities acted quickly to install these memorials across the city. One could see a similar rationale at the Roboski memorial, marking the Roboski incident of December 28, 2011. Near the Turkish-Iraqi border, Turkish jets fired at a group of villagers and smugglers; the military asserted that PKK militants were crossing the border. When I returned to the city in 2015, Havin told me, "They just installed a new memorial about Roboski. It is a little vulgar, but you should see it." I visited the memorial. Just two years after the incident, the Kayapınar municipality had installed a memorial at a newly named Roboski Park. Representing the attack, eight rocket-like steel tubes—each ten inches in diameter and ten feet tall, with fins—surrounded a motherly figure mourning for the victims. The mother, depicted in bronze and wearing traditional Kurdish dress and a hijab, kneels with her hands raised to the sky. With a grief-stricken face, she wails and prays to God. The structure sat on a roughly circular granite base with the names of thirty-four victims engraved in stone (figure 23).

At the time the sculptor installed the work, many in the city found the Roboski memorial ugly. But perhaps that "ugliness" also made residents discuss the piece and stirred enough curiosity to draw others to visit it.

In 2015, I reached out to Aras, the sculptor of the Roboski memorial. We met in May at the Hasan Paşa Khan in Sur. When I arrived at the café, Aras had already ordered tea, and he greeted me with a smile. In his mid-thirties, Aras was a graduate of Dicle University and an art educator in Diyarbakır. After we finished our breakfast, I asked about the criticism that the memorial was ugly. Aras responded with the following words:

> I know some people see my sculpture as ugly. But isn't this atrocity ugly itself? Isn't the massacre of forty people ugly? I wanted to express this pain and the massacre bluntly. This is why I wanted to represent the bombardment, the missiles, with cold steel and the mother wailing in the center. She symbolizes the anguish shared by all mothers who mourn for our children daily.... Some of those murdered there were children, and they didn't have any weapons or anything. Then, in the sculpture, purposefully,

FIGURE 23. The Roboski memorial.
Source: Author, 2015.

> I exaggerated the brutality of the event. I used raw, unadorned materials to underscore the power imbalance. That way, visitors of the park can imagine the magnitude of the violence that transpired there.

Previous examples have shown that sculpting violence into the human body was central in making the memorial landscape of Diyarbakır. The Roboski memorial's use of a motherly figure was not accidental. The mother's body recurs regularly in Kurdish memorials, either mourning for, or dying with, her children. Recording violence, the mother figure symbolizes community pain and evokes attachments to the imagined nation.[36] But the symbol of the mother is not limited to visual representations of suffering. The party has a strong activist history embodied by women, such as the Peace Mothers Initiative or the Saturday Mother's Initiative. Women participate in many party initiatives, from organizing protests, marches, or hunger strikes in the city to protesting state violence toward the Kurdish people.

The Edi Bese memorial in Sur also records violence through the female figure. "Edi Bese," meaning "enough is enough" in Kurdish, represents "the women's revolt against the man-dominated system," said Mayor Demirbaş in a 2010 interview. The memorial is composed of three tall female figures on an elevated platform. While two of the women look down, the third looks up to symbolize rebellion. On March 8, 2010, on International Women's Day, the monument was unveiled with a public ceremony that included the participation of activists, women's organizations, and mayors. The Diyarbakır municipality organized free tours to women visiting the monument.

Memorial Landscape as a Form of Protest

In creating a landscape symbolizing national collectivity, Medya Park exemplified the politically contentious subject of Kurdishness. Constructed by the Kayapınar municipality, the park provoked immediate conflict between the municipality and the state-appointed governorship because of the shape of its ornamental pool, which was designed to resemble an imagined map of Kurdistan. During its construction, the governor of Diyarbakır forbade the park from being inaugurated and filed a suit against the Kayapınar municipality for "promoting separatist ideals." After settling several lawsuits and distorting the shape of the pool, the municipality finally opened the park on June 5, 2007. Many pro-Kurdish members of Parliament, party officials, and representatives of civil society organizations attended the event. Once again, the opening speeches were heavily publicized and built on ideas of Kurdish identity and freedom. Although the shape of the pool had been altered, residents of Diyarbakır still referred to it as a map of Kurdistan. Their insistence indicated its continued symbolism. What has made Medya Park most distinctive is not only the shape of its pool but also its name, derived from the root "Meds," the ancestors of present-day Kurds.[37] In this context, for some, "Media" (Medya in Turkish) also connotes the land of the Medes. Medland, an amusement park, and the Med City Mahabat housing project in Kayapınar, which I discussed in the previous chapter, are other examples of the frequent use of the root "Med-" in the city.[38]

Giving parks Kurdish names, or names that commemorate particular events in Kurdish history, was another practice the pro-Kurdish party commonly used to express resistance to the state. In 2008, the Yenişehir, Bağlar, and Kayapınar municipalities attempted to give Kurdish names to several parks within their jurisdictions, including Beybun, Şilan, Berfin, Rojda, and Roşna Parks. But since the use of the Kurdish language was banned in public, the names were rejected by the governorship (another instance illustrating the urban contestation between governors and mayors, as emphasized in chapter 2). In response, the municipalities developed a strategy of "unnamed parks," installing blank nameplates or nameplates with ellipses (. . .) at the entrance of each park, with notes explaining the obstacles imposed on the use of Kurdish iconography. With a sophisticated rhetorical strategy, the blank nameplates included—and typographically emphasized—the Kurdish names in the explanatory texts (figure 24).

During an opening ceremony in December 2008, the former mayor of the Kayapınar municipality, Zülküf Karatekin, highlighted the conflict and contradictions between different government authorities regarding permitting or rejecting the use of the Kurdish language and Kurdish names. He exclaimed, "While one [government authority] broadcasts a Kurdish channel on one of the state's television channels, another bans the use of Kurdish in public space. How democratic is that?"[39] Karatekin was charged and imprisoned in 2009. One of the charges was for fomenting unnamed parks. The rejected names for the parks were not all in Kurdish, however; for instance, the name "33 Bullets," in Turkish, was rejected allegedly because the "state was presented as an object of accusation and antagonism."

FIGURE 24. An "unnamed" park. The sign reads "The Municipality of Kayapınar . . . . Park." The park was named "Roşna" by the decision (no. 160) of the Kayapınar Municipality Council on November 7, 2008; however, the name was rejected by the decision (no. 212) of the Kayapınar District Governorship on November 19, 2008.
Source: Author, 2009.

In addition to establishing representations of past traumatic events, municipalities employed urban space to invoke Kurdish nationhood, culture, and history. From placing historic figures at the entrance gates of administrative buildings to naming streets, municipalities utilized every suitable corner in the city. In this process of Kurdification, the Kurdish movement broke ties with both Ottoman and republican pasts, instead establishing connections with pre-Islamic history. One notable example is the extensive use of the Lamassu figure, an ancient Assyrian and Mesopotamian protective deity, depicted as a winged bull with a bearded human head, believed to guard palaces and cities. The party incorporated Lamassu reliefs and statues into various public spaces, including municipality gates.[40]

Among public spaces, parks and squares occupied a special place, providing a venue for a broad range of discursive constructions and interactions among Kurdish citizens. Between 1999 and 2015, pro-Kurdish municipalities built more than two hundred urban parks in Diyarbakır, ranging in size from tiny pocket parks to six hectares (about fifteen acres).

Ayşe Şan Park exemplified how urban space could represent Kurdish contemporary culture. The park covered seventy-five hundred square meters (just under two acres) and included a free-speech square and a café, along with walking paths, children's play areas, ornamental pools, waterfalls, and a maze of plants. The park's primary symbolic importance lay in its recognition of the Kurdish language via the commemoration of the Kurdish singer Ayşe Şan, who died on December 18, 1996. Events organized within the park also aimed to honor *dengbej* culture via Ayşe Şan.[41] As memorialized in the park, Ayşe Şan was represented not just as a Kurdish singer but as a symbol of Kurdish activism and resistance, challenging the oppression of Kurdish identity. With a black-and-white portrait of Ayşe Şan installed on the roof of its café, the park identified itself with the common culture of activism. The park opened on December 18, 2008, the twelfth anniversary of the singer's death. Hundreds of people attended, including local mayors, Kurdish activists, and representatives of civil society organizations. The event was thus typical of the strategy according to which the pro-Kurdish party brings members of NGOs and civil-society organizations together in different contexts to forge a sense of popular grievance.[42] The opening of the park was also publicized months in advance, allowing merchants, coffeehouse workers, and people in the streets to talk over the summer about the songs and life of Ayşe Şan.

Before the opening ceremony, an introductory meeting for the commemoration of Ayşe Şan was staged by a joint organization of the Diyarbakır Metropolitan Municipality and the Mesopotamian Cultural Center (Mezopotamya Kültür Merkezi). A group of Kurdish women activists and artists spoke about Ayşe Şan's

Kurdish identity, her exile, and her symbolic role in the Kurdish movement. In one speech, the Kurdish artist Şilan Dora described Ayşe Şan as a "revolutionary." Dora added, "She is the voice and the heart of the people whose language is banned." Mayor Baydemir followed suit, stressing Şan's unmet wish to be buried in Diyarbakır: "Ayşe Şan, with her identity as a woman, represents the resistance to exist. She suffered greatly. In her residences in Istanbul, Germany, Baghdad, Hawler [Erbil], and Izmir, she amassed her agony. There was no doubt that one day that exile would come to an end. Today is that day."[43] Throughout the speeches, Ayşe Şan was once again embedded in a discourse of oppression, a symbol of Kurdish suffering.

Notably, Ayşe Şan Park, like many other parks in Diyarbakır, was visited not only by the Kurdish party supporters but also by Kurds not affiliated with the party. Indeed, the park embraced all visitors with its Kurdish environment, which is how I met Salih there. Salih identified himself as an "apolitical, pious Kurdish person," unaffiliated with the party. He described his interaction with urban Kurdish identity at the park: "I come to Ayşe Şan on a regular basis, almost every night. Sometimes we come here with my sisters-in-law and brothers. We love it here because we listen to Kurdish music, we picnic, and sit in a traditional way on divans. Ayşe Şan is ours! I like it here because this place reminds me of my roots. I don't support the party, but I understand them."

Ayşe Şan Park created a space of engagement that allowed people across the political spectrum to convene and listen to music together. Through such urban practices, the articulating logic of the pro-Kurdish party succeeded in bringing society together in public spaces. In fact, the Kurdish culture injected into the park by the pro-Kurdish party could be seen as one of the factors bringing a pious person and a leftist activist together, as I discussed earlier in this chapter.

Festivals: Performing the Nation

The organization of festivals and cultural events constituted a key part of making the Kurdish memorial landscape. These events allowed the party to perform like a nation-state. Further, the festivals and diverse cultural organizations demonstrated a level of public opposition to the state (the government in Ankara) that could not be realized through other forms of political action. Particularly, the annual Newroz celebration created new opportunities for popular mobilization and Kurdish activism in the city. Newroz, also known as Persian New Year, celebrates the arrival of spring (the vernal equinox). It is celebrated annually on March 21 by a number of populations in Central Asia and the Middle East.[44] For the Kurdish movement in Turkey, Newroz, with its narrative of resistance and resurrection, garnered new meaning, symbolizing the struggle of a nation seeking its freedom.

Before the 1980s, Newroz was mostly celebrated in rural areas. People lit bonfires, jumped over the fire, and sang songs around it. By the late 1980s and 1990s in Turkey, with the emergence of pro-Kurdish political parties and following the widespread displacement of rural Kurds to urban areas, the celebrations began to assume a more popular quality in Turkish cities with large Kurdish populations, sometimes becoming the scene of mass demonstrations against the state. These gatherings also saw clashes between Kurdish youth and the police.[45] In addition to street resistance, Newroz demonstrations in the 1990s included the self-immolation of several Kurdish activists.[46] But not until the early 2000s did Newroz festivals turn into high-profile spectacles, as pro-Kurdish mayors, municipalities, and party officials began organizing enormous events that attracted hundreds of thousands of participants. By the early 2000s, Diyarbakır had become home to Turkey's largest Newroz festival, with hundreds of thousands in attendance, drawing participants from nearby rural areas and neighboring cities.

To accommodate such a huge annual event, in 2005 the Diyarbakır municipality opened a large new Newroz Park, located in Bağlar. At the time, the site was on the outskirts of the city, a setting initially chosen by the governor to isolate the celebration. However, as the city rapidly expanded, by 2008 the Newroz site was in the middle of the city. Equivalent to the size of two soccer stadiums, the site included a main stage for political leaders and viewing podiums for journalists and foreign guests. Painted in the colors of the Kurdistan flag, the stage also displayed the images of popular martyrs on columns to either side of the rostrum. Reflecting timely events and current discourse, the images changed annually, chosen by the party and pro-Kurdish groups to represent ordinary citizens or activists who had either sacrificed themselves or been killed as a result of state violence. Above the stage, a large image of Kawa, the blacksmith of the Kurdish founding myth, appeared on a canvas banner, holding the Kurdish sun.

Newroz has been particularly important as a way to activate popular support for the Kurdish movement and to consolidate the pro-Kurdish party's power among an external audience. As Sami told me during an interview, "Newroz shows everyone in this country the unanimity of the Kurdish people and their support for our movement." At the Newroz festival, the images of martyrs beside the stage commemorated individual heroic sacrifice. Cultivating the symbolism of a heroic past, this artistic gesture sought to create national heroes out of ordinary citizens, thereby encouraging all spectators to struggle for the Kurdish nation. For example, in 2010, the festival presented the image of Ceylan Önkol (see the previous section on the park devoted to her). She appeared there alongside better-known cultural figures, such as the Kurdish Armenian singer Aram

Tigran and the pro-Kurdish militants Cihan Deniz and Hüsnü Albay. Two slogans accompanied these images: "Either a Democratic Solution or a Grand Resistance," and "We Say Enough to Cultural, Social, and Political Genocide." The following year, 2011, festival organizers chose to portray two PJAK militants in Iran,[47] Şirin Elem Hulu and Huşen Xizri, who had been executed by the Tehran government, along with Zekiye Alkan and Rahşan Demirel, members of the PKK who had immolated themselves on Newroz day. The Newroz slogans that accompanied them read, "Freedom or Freedom for a Dignified Life," and "National Democratic Solidarity for Freedom."

In addition to representations of individual martyrs, the image of Abdullah Öcalan was ever-present during almost all Newroz celebrations in the early 2010s. Although he had been serving a life sentence since 1999, Öcalan was typically shown in his guerrilla attire as a leader of the movement. Initially, Turkish law banned displaying posters of Öcalan or the PKK flag. Demonstrators holding these symbols were typically forced to hide their faces, clash with the police, or face arrest during these events. Nevertheless, Öcalan's image appeared alongside the stage—projected, to bypass the ban.

To increase the number of participants from peripheral towns, in 2011 the official celebration of Newroz in Diyarbakır was organized for Sunday, March 20. But the entire festival began days before. Almost a month earlier, the municipality had posted notice of the event on billboards including the Newroz slogan "An Azadi an Azadi" (Liberty or liberty). Pamphlets distributed by the municipality also read, in Kurdish, "Newroz, for 3,000 years, has been the key for freedom and victory. Winning the fight for freedom, come and participate in the Newroz of independence." Prior to the celebrations, city officials inspected the Newroz site with the press to encourage reports on the preparations in the larger media.

During the 2011 festival, celebrations were not limited to the Newroz Park but spread across the city. Thus, in the week leading up to Newroz day, political and youth groups organized smaller events in public squares, at the festival space of the Dicle University campus, and at conference venues. Local stores and BDP campaign buses blasted the popular song "Newroz Pîroz be" (Happy Newroz), inviting citizens across the city to participate in Newroz.

On the actual day of Newroz, thousands of participants arrived at Newroz Park. Some came on buses provided by the municipality. As the crowd grew, party leaders lit an enormous bonfire that was visible from miles away. Defying the government ban, the site was surrounded by PKK flags and posters of Abdullah Öcalan. The celebration included mini-concerts by pro-Kurdish singers, party officials' speeches, and the chanting of antistate slogans. There were also commemorations of Kurdish rebels, as demonstrators waved PKK banners and pictures of Abdullah Öcalan. After the political speeches, a crowd of citizens, with mayors and political party leaders at the front, marched to the city center to block the main roads and further broadcast their claims (figure 25).

At the festival, several participants wore traditional Kurdish attire. Men wore blue and khaki. Women dressed in the red, white, green, and yellow of the banned Kurdistan flag. Dressing thus on Newroz day did more than flaunt Kurdish culture. For some members of the pro-Kurdish political party who marched arm in arm in front of the crowd, this clothing expressed their resistance to state edicts designed to prohibit expressions of Kurdish identity.

Every year, the statements of Kurdish political leaders on Newroz day were awaited by the press and then debated for days.[48] Newroz celebrations produced an alternative version of national belonging that allowed spectators to recognize themselves as fellow citizens. From the music to the political messages and images, the spectacle of Newroz cultivated a dual, somewhat contradictory, sense of citizenship and resistance. Newroz dramatized aspirations for an independent Kurdish nation, as officials rehearsed the idea of an autonomous Kurdish regime in a way that conveyed ideas of freedom and Kurdish citizenship—as if Newroz were already the Independence Day celebration of an autonomous Kurdish state. Further, it promoted reciprocity: it encouraged citizens from different backgrounds to empathize with one another and engage in political action, anonymously linking them as citizens of a state yet to be realized.

FIGURE 25. Kurdish politicians lead crowds in a march from the Newroz site to the city center. At the left a flag carries the image of Abdullah Öcalan.
Source: Author, 2011.

Museum Politics

In the early 2000s, Diyarbakır was a vibrant stage unfolding the story of rising Kurdish nationhood. Festivals, streets, and parks with specific names, *dengbej* houses, tens of memorials. Practically every city corner signaled either state violence against Kurdish people or served as distinct Kurdish cultural markers suggesting liberation and freedom. Museums were an important piece of this memorial landscape in certifying the party to perform a broader nation-state narrative.

Constructing museums has long been a common practice to represent official ideologies. Especially since the nineteenth century, national museums have played an important role in inventing national histories, identities, and traditions, crafting nationalist imaginaries, and institutionalizing nationalist discourses.[49] The exhibitions—including art, history, military affairs, costume, language, or science—have typically been considered spaces for the reproduction of national history in terms of the didactic messages that objects on display communicate to visitors. In inventing a national history, whether artistic or heroic, national museums often construct a teleological narrative; their goal is to produce and reproduce collectivity among visitors.[50] These museum narratives are typically curated toward an idealized conclusion of national development.[51] Museums thus are spaces of historiography in which discourse makers can tell the same story in multiple and persuasive ways. From the interior design to the materials used on the façade, the entire museum prompts visitors to learn, experience, and reflect upon trauma or a past historical event. With their remarkable architecture, such museums also stand as memorials.

By the second half of the twentieth century, another genre of museum emerged, namely, the experiential or memorial museum, often designed to narrate the story of past violence, suffering, and brutality. Instead of representing the glories of the nineteenth-century nation-state, these new forms of memorial landscape seek to teach the lessons of past conflicts and violence in order to prevent future violence and to emphasize an understanding that respects diversity and human rights.[52] Examples include Holocaust, African American, and apartheid museums, which actively focus on visitors' emotional experiences by providing various modes of exposure to a specific traumatic history. Generally, such museums are either located at the actual physical sites of collective violence (prison museums are a common example) or re-create the experience through extensive, well-designed, and curated architectures. On site or re-created, these museums usually present a story of oppression "from above."[53] They cautiously take visitors from one room to another—one event to another. If they do not follow a linear construction of historical time, they present a well-curated, event-based or theme-based logic for visitors to follow.

Whether experiential or not, museums constitute significant educational institutions that shape public discourse. The pro-Kurdish party, in its efforts to build a narrative of a distinct Kurdish nation and collectivity, also employed museums. However, Kurdish municipalities did not establish a "national" museum one could go to and visit. Under the Turkish state's rule, it would be impossible to call a museum a "Kurdish museum."

Instead, abandoned houses in Sur were transformed into museums for diverse features of Kurdish culture (the Esma Ocak House, the Dengbej House), as were coffeehouses, especially ones belonging to prominent Kurdish authors or families. Layering museums over historic houses served two main purposes. First, they provided exhibition space for the municipality; and second—and more important—they helped keep citizens' memory of state oppression alive. It was not only the artifacts exhibited in these museums but also the architecture of the historic houses and the tragic stories of former owners that made their narration more influential and effective. In this regard, the Diyarbakır City Museum (DCM) presents a significant example of the party's museumification effort in displaying a distinct Kurdish past in the city.

The Tangibility of Everyday Culture and Memory

In Sur, the DCM is housed in the historic Cemil Paşa Mansion on the inner streets of the Ali Paşa neighborhood, surrounded by squatter settlements. The mansion, originally built in the nineteenth century, opened as a museum in 2014 after three years of restoration. Built on two thousand square meters and representative of the traditional residential architecture of Diyarbakır, the mansion is arranged around a large courtyard, comprising the *haremlik* (designated for women) and *selamlık* (designated for men) sections. Also characteristic of Diyarbakır houses, cut basalt stone and limestone lend the mansion a visual dynamism (figure 26).

The narrative of the museum overlaps with the history of the mansion. The mansion belonged to the Cemil Paşa family, one of the city's most prominent families, which played a critical role in shaping the Kurdish nationalist movement during late Ottoman and early republican periods.[54] Cemil Paşa and his family lived in the mansion until 1927. After the Sheikh Said Rebellion was suppressed, the whole family was sent into exile by the Turkish state in 1936.[55] Later, the mansion was transformed into a primary school, and still later into a site for sericulture and weaving.[56] The mansion was abandoned by the 1970s. At the request of the Cemil Paşa family, the restoration process was initiated in 1998 by the Çekül Foundation, but it could not be finalized. I first saw the mansion in July 2007, the very first day I arrived in Diyarbakır. Havin and I were wandering around the narrow streets of Sur when we came upon the house, which

FIGURE 26. Cemil Paşa Museum.
Source: Author, 2018

was derelict and stood out from its surroundings by its architecture and its size. Despite the many years and neglect, the house had maintained its main structure. At the time, a poor migrant family was informally living inside. In 2011, the municipality completed restoration with the family's permission. When I met with Sami in 2012, he was excited about work on the City Museum project:

> We see this museum as the memory of the city. They have tried to erase it since the beginning of the republic. In a way, this museum is our response to those who try to make us forget our past. This is why we will gather all the dynamics of this city in this museum. This museum will stand out as Diyarbakır's cultural and social memory. We envision a place where Diyarbakırians can renew their memory, learn about their past. Also, the visitors of our city can learn about the multiculturally rich history of our city.

Sami's words summarized the instructive qualities of the museum. In fact, DCM is not an ordinary history museum in which one finds the past; it is a living museum that constantly communicates the tangibility of everyday Kurdish culture. The DCM powerfully narrates the Kurdishness of the city—from the past until today—by depicting remarkable segments of Kurdish culture and daily life in the city. During my interview with Sami, as he explained the DCM to me, he mentioned future museum projects in the city, including a Kurdish Gastronomy Museum, where visitors could take part in a tasting experience, and the museum of Mehmet Uzun, a prominent Kurdish author known for reviving Kurdish traditional storytelling and who lived in exile in Sweden from 1977 to 2005 as a political refugee.[57]

The DCM gives the pro-Kurdish party a place to reproduce a Kurdish national history free from the strictures of the history imposed by the republican state. As I discussed in the first chapter, the republican version of this history has no distinct ethnicity: there are only Turks in Turkish territory, and Diyarbakır is a Turkish city. Yet the Diyarbakır City Museum not only embodies the city's culture but also asserts Diyarbakır as the yet-to-be capital of Turkey's Kurdistan. At the opening ceremony for the museum in 2014, Gültan Kışanak, co-mayor of the Diyarbakır Metropolitan Municipality at the time (imprisoned since 2016),[58] confirmed the museum's function as a response to republican discourses. The meaning she invested in the museum transcended a simple city museum or a response to state coercion. For Kışanak, the DCM signified the roots of Kurdish culture in Diyarbakır:

> We are holding an opening where the fate imposed on the Kurds is renewed and updated today. We have revealed this beautiful work that carries our history to the present. The herb grows on the root. Being rootless is the worst and most difficult situation in the world.... Thank God, the Kurdish people, Kurdistan is not without roots. It is our duty to find this past with its documents, to reveal it, to repair it, and to enable the new generations to meet this past. Our endeavor [protecting and keeping the Kurdish culture alive] will continue.[59]

Kışanak's words lucidly tied Kurds to the city as she described the Kurds as an organic nation, rooted in Diyarbakır. For Kışanak, the DCM served as the prototype for a national museum. She hinted at the effort to continue opening similar museums in the city, as well as in other cities.

The DCM portrays Kurdishness as distinctive and in so doing distinguishes Diyarbakır from the rest of the country, legitimizing the city as the capital of Kurdish culture. The museum itself signifies the discursive construction of the motherland; it tells the story of the city and simultaneously narrates Kurdish culture's territorialization in the city. The DCM neither displays heroic achievements carried out in the name of a nation-state nor imposes a set chronology on visitors. Instead, it presents a thematic expedition throughout the city's history, distinguishing Diyarbakır and its people from the rest of the country.

The museum's experience does not begin and end in the mansion's galleries. Because the museum is not accessible via car, its experience begins with a walk amid the squatter settlements of Sur. From the neighborhood walk to the galleries, to the courtyard, the DCM provides—as Sami described it—a "realistic" experience of everyday Diyarbakır that reinforces a sense of belonging, both inside and outside.

After visitors tour the exhibition galleries, the experience continues in the courtyard of this big mansion, where tea or cold beverages are served during summer. In the courtyard—the place in a house where Diyarbakırian life traditionally was sustained—visitors are invited to connect their own identities to the museum. The DCM does not isolate visitors from the outside world, as is typical of museums.[60] On the contrary, it exposes them to local everyday life. Several exhibition rooms are not dark; they receive sunlight directly from open windows, making the neighborhood immediately visible.

Because the rooms of the two-story mansion serve as exhibition galleries surrounding the courtyard, the transition from one theme to another is not smooth, as it might be in a traditional museum. The rooms are not necessarily connected to each other, so the visitor is invited—but does not need—to follow the signs and arrows from one room to another, or to climb the stairs. Each room reproduces Kurdish national history through a distinct theme. By displaying diverse segments of Diyarbakırians' lives, the rooms present a continuous development of the city with its people.

On the ground floor, after the entrance, one can find the "memory center," an archive for researchers. After that, the exhibition themes are lined up, side by side, in separate rooms: Language and Written Culture, Oral Culture, Music and Folkloric Dances, Education in Diyarbakır, Food and Culinary Culture, Water and Life, Religious Belief, Folklife and Cultures of Diyarbakır. Across from the cafeteria and the fountain, on the other side of the courtyard, is a room devoted to the Cemil Paşa family, with a family tree describing their history and displays of family photos and belongings.

The second floor is mostly devoted to everyday life in the city. The galleries of City Life and Housing connect to Production and Commerce. Animal Husbandry links to Agriculture. After this section, on the other side, Development of the City has exhibits on events and people of the city and a historical panorama of the city. The basement features multifunctional spaces for educational workshops. The objects in the museum are both multiple and discrete, with their importance for Kurdish culture narrated in both Turkish and Kurdish—but they all communicate an experience of Kurdishness.

When I visited the museum for two weekends in May 2015, I conducted informal interviews with museumgoers. "Our origins, this museum, is the testimony of our Kurdish identity and our Kurdish city," said Elvan, a retired bank clerk. For some of the visitors, the galleries were just glanced at in passing. "There is nothing inside that I don't know," said Erhan, an elementary school teacher in his late forties. "But," he added, "it is important to have such a museum." Rather than looking at the exhibits in the galleries, some of the visitors were more interested in just being inside the large Diyarbakırian mansion—observing the courtyard from the second-floor balcony, taking photographs of the house. Many took selfies or posed in front of the pool in the courtyard, or stopped for tea and a rest in the café, enjoying a moment of territorial kinship. During my interviews, most of the visitors shared their own or their relatives' stories associated with one or more of the themes of the museum. These stories usually included validation of Diyarbakır's, and thus the Kurdish people's, cultural wealth—a heritage that was forced to sink into oblivion—and the pride they feel about their own living memory. The visiting experience of Serdar, a chemist in his early thirties, exemplifies this point. Born and raised in Diyarbakır, he was living hours away in the city of Malatya, working in a lab in a private hospital there, and was in Diyarbakır for the weekend for a funeral. Serdar's words embodied how visitors internalized the concept of being Diyarbakırian, which was strongly evinced through the exhibitions:

> When I arrived to this museum, I felt so proud with our city and with this museum. This museum is a proof of our identity. Our food, our culture, our music is here—this is something that I can proudly show to my children. Diyarbakır has always deserved better, you know? My mom had a beautiful voice, but I remember how my dad would get so anxious if my mom would sing in the courtyard, if a soldier would hear her singing or speaking in Kurdish. We have gone through very difficult times. Now, it is as if this museum reminds us of those [difficult times] but at the same time makes you forget.

Serdar identified the museum as a center that tells the "reality" of Kurdish culture. It can even show and teach children what makes Kurdishness. In Serdar's and most visitors' minds, even though the museum does not explicitly display traumatic events, it establishes an intimate link between memories and the future by displaying the life of fellow Kurdish citizens. Thus, the exhibition evokes a troubled past but also encourages looking to the future.

The visitors I spoke with, when defining their identity, cited either their childhood or a relative's memory about experiencing Kurdish culture in the city. I met Yasemin, a woman in her early thirties, as I was walking around the exhibition. She asked me to take her and her daughter's photo in front of the coppersmith display. After I took their picture, she spontaneously began to speak about her memories with her grandfather. "My grandfather was a coppersmith here in Sur. More than being a coppersmith, he was an artist. They were all artists. We lost him years ago. But I wish I could have brought my grandmother here. They left Diyarbakır years ago, when it began to get messy here." Yasemin was referring to the rising conflict between the PKK and Turkish military forces. "But she is very old; she lives in Mersin. So I will take this photo to her instead." Yasemin was reestablishing her connection with Diyarbakır by reproducing the memory of her grandparents, who were forced to leave the city in the early 1990s.

The messages that the museum seeks to impart to its visitors are clear: Diyarbakır is a home for Kurdish people. Also, Kurdish culture—with its language, rituals, arts and crafts, traditions, music, and cuisine—is distinct from Turkish culture. "Kurds are not Turks," the museum conveys. In fact, the museum wants visitors to see that, "unlike the Turkish state, the Kurds never wanted to erase other cultures. Instead, they embrace diverse religions and cultures in the city"—as Sami once mentioned in an interview. This is also why, for example, the museum delineates Diyarbakır as a city loyal to multiple cultures, faiths, and identities—a place where visitors can read the historic Quran and an Armenian Bible in the gallery of Religions and Beliefs. Visitors associate the experience of Kurdishness presented at the museum with their own past or their relatives' pasts rooted in the territory of Diyarbakır. Both the DCM's collection and the building itself works to engage visitors in official and unofficial narratives.

Making of a Collective Memory

The experience of Diyarbakır's memorial landscape communicates that there is no one path to forming political consciousness. In the Kurdish case, what actually institutionalized memory in the city was not only the physical presence of these memorials or museums or commemorative objects themselves but the way these sites were utilized in the symbolic world—through what Achille Mbembe calls the "signification of events."[61] These events include opening ceremonies for these projects that commemorated the traumatic past, debates they stirred in the city, polemics and conflict they generated between the municipality and the governor's office, protests that began and ended at the site, press releases regarding court cases opened against these structures—what I have called "memorial activism." The power of the pro-Kurdish party's urban politics stemmed not only from its ability to embody the physical representations of state violence, but also from its capacity to create sites of engagement and to orchestrate memorial activism. These efforts help the party reproduce these past events in everyday life and prevent the diminishment of memories of violence, creating a forum of national membership in the city. Rather than an ethnicity constructed through blood ties or printed discourse, the spatial culture of the city—Diyarbakır—built territorial kinship for the citizens.

Here, Kurdish nationhood is not shaped by pre-given collectivities or facts. Rather, it is induced by the political dynamics of the pro-Kurdish party. In parks, tents, protests, prayers, hunger strikes, marches, funeral gatherings, house meetings, and so on, the pro-Kurdish political party created active spaces of engagement and articulated different groups of Kurdish society through an integrated claim of Kurdish nationhood. The "violations of human rights" by the state and the ban on the use of the Kurdish language, like so many other events, were all reported in local newspapers, featured on posters, and—more important—carried from one person to the next, in parks while drinking tea, or while waiting in line, sitting in coffeehouses, or during street conversations. Each narrative, each memory of violence, circulated through the everyday practices of individuals, setting the claims of Kurdish nationhood and producing a collectivity in which citizens—friends and strangers alike—imagine themselves belonging to the same Kurdish nation.[62]

And yet, the memorial landscape of Diyarbakır has been a site of contestation. In almost every installation of a new memorial or opening of a new park with a Kurdish name, the pro-Kurdish party and local mayors were subjected to juridical and bureaucratic pressure. Frequently, administrators from the pro-Kurdish parties, as well as artists connected with various memorials, were taken to court, fined, and even jailed. A case of vandalism on a memorial or a court case would be the perfect reason to organize a press release or a demonstration. All such incidents and events would generate gossip and rumors in the city, expanding in circles and thus keeping the collective and contemporary memory alive.

The lives and tragic deaths of ordinary citizens, like Uğur Kaymaz or Ceylan Önkol, resonated throughout the city in the form of hearsay, posters, and eventually a memorial that refused to obscure the pain and thus fostered citizen association with otherwise anonymous Kurds. In connecting violence and oppression of the past to the present, memorials aimed to harness the citizens together. The mother at the Roboski memorial could be the mother of any citizen; Uğur Kaymaz could be the son of any Kurd. Memorials and the practices around them brought the whole society together, from the pious to the atheist, from rich to poor. Nationalism operates here, in Anderson's terms, in the citizen's consciousness, with an individual's concern and bitterness "replicated simultaneously by thousands (or millions) of others of whose existence he is confident, yet of whose identity he has not the slightest notion."[63] The Kurdish case in Diyarbakır shows how instead of heroic or large-scale popular narratives, the stories of ordinary citizens may constitute and feed nationalism.

Indeed, the memorial landscape of the city—comprising the distinct scales of sculptures, memorials, and museums—fostered a collective Kurdish identity based on a shared past of atrocity. Such a memorial landscape is not necessarily akin to what many memorial museums offer, where visitors usually go through a fixed route and scenery of designed experiences—sections of photographs, artifacts, sounds, or catastrophic dark spaces where visitors vicariously experience trauma, in order to identify with the victims. Instead, the memorial landscape of Diyarbakır offered omnipresent reminders of state brutality. Each new incident of violence or recent tragic event would be commemorated and condemned by a memorial—whether or not that memorial was related to that specific event. In this way the monument's original meaning would be renewed each time another atrocity occurred, opening up a new horizon for collective memory. For example, the pro-Kurdish party and activist organizations not only commemorated the 2006 bomb blast with the *Right to Life* monument, but also had numerous press releases, commemorations, and sit-ins in front of other monuments, multiplying the recognition of the victimization of Kurds.

Following the armed conflict of 2015, the Kurdish memorial landscape was one of the first areas exposed to heavy vandalism and demolition. The trucks that dismantled Turkish symbolism in the city just a couple of years before subsequently dismantled the Kurdish signs and memorials in the city. Most of the memorials and sites I discussed in this chapter were demolished and vandalized following the events of 2015. In the next chapter, I discuss the destruction of the Kurdish memorial landscape and the correlative efforts to dismantle Kurdish mobilization in the city.

6

DISMANTLING THE KURDISH LANDSCAPE

"Hey, You People—Dreams Canceled"

What does the destruction of a twenty-year-long political articulation in two years look like? In this chapter, I examine how Turkish state officials deployed a pedagogy of urban development and municipal service premised on the idea of Islamic progress to disarticulate the Kurdish bloc in Diyarbakır, post-2015. Previous chapters demonstrate how urban planning may enhance political articulation for social change. This chapter discusses why—and under what conditions—urban planning may fail to produce the intended social change.

In 2013, the Justice and Development Party (AKP) government initiated a peace process to end the conflict with the PKK. In June 2015, the pro-Kurdish party benefited partially from the temporary détente and scored a historic victory when it secured 13 percent of the votes in the national election—for the first time exceeding the 10 percent threshold. Yet the peace process was short-lived and ended soon after the election. In July 2015, the two-and-a-half-year cease-fire broke down, and violence recommenced in the southeast. From November 2015 almost until March 2016, the armed conflict—"trench incidents" was how people described it—between the Kurdish militants and the Turkish army caused massive destruction to cities in the southeast of Turkey, including Diyarbakır, Cizre, Şırnak, Silopi, Yüksekova, and Nusaybin. The aftermath of the conflict was more devastating for predominately Kurdish cities, however. Following the brutal combat, even more destruction took place in reconstruction processes the Turkish government conducted. Scholars have argued how reconstruction, especially in postwar conditions, can be an act of "destruction."[1] This chapter demonstrates this complex relationship between the destruction and reconstruction by analyzing the Turkish state's unprecedented militarized urban intervention in the wake of the 2015 armed conflict between the Turkish military and the PKK in Diyarbakır.[2] It examines how the erasure of political articulation is targeted not only via destruction of the built environment but also via reconstruction.

Further, this chapter discusses how postwar reconstruction is not necessarily about recovery or repair of the city; in the eyes of the state, it might be more about the opportunity to instill new forms of urban regime and citizenship. Comparing destroyed sites and spaces to their previous condition, I study the extent of state action to outlaw public expression of Kurdish identity and to disassemble the former condition of urban mobilization. I look at subsequent state-sponsored projects (housing, museums, cultural centers, and mosques) to show how reconstruction itself can be a form of violence—particularly when such reconstruction displaces local residents and intends to ensure the erasure of public memory and cultural heritage.[3] In this context, the large infrastructure and city-beautification projects I examine reveal an authoritarian apparatus that has sought to subjugate Kurdish citizens to state power through new imaginaries of Islam, progress, municipal service, and consumption.

Destruction: Dismantling the Kurdish Landscape

When I left Diyarbakır in May 2015, I had never seen the city so confident of its Kurdish identity. From mayors, activists, and businesspeople to ordinary Diyarbakırians, people were confident and enthusiastic about the future of the capital of Turkey's Kurdistan. The sense of Kurdish nationalism was maximized in almost every aspect of everyday urban life—in public demonstrations, ordinary encounters, cultural idioms, and social gatherings. At the time, I saw a city in which a sense of Kurdish expression and nationness flourished, as if an autonomous Kurdistan had already arrived. The airport and the bus terminal were crowded and hotels fully booked with tourists and businesspeople, particularly from Iraq and Iran. Presenting the city as "a new opening gate to the Middle East," Diyarbakır was at the forefront of national media.[4] But in 2015, the events and the atmosphere of the city changed drastically. In August 2015, with the announcement by the KCK (Kurdistan Democratic Communities Union) of democratic autonomy and self-administration, a wave of public declarations emerged from grassroots groups and associations in the Kurdish cities of Turkey. Simultaneously, the YDG-H (Patriotic Revolutionary Youth Movement), known as the urban militant wing of the PKK, occupied at least a dozen Kurdish cities and declared them liberated. After the end of a cease-fire and two years of relative peace, the southeast region saw escalating violence, with the PKK and state forces engaging in armed clashes. Diyarbakır became the conflict's epicenter. In November 2015, Kurdish groups led by the YDG-H barricaded Sur and undertook a movement they labeled "self-defense." The armed group declared the neighborhoods autonomous and dug trenches to prevent Turkish police and military forces from entering. Later, the armed conflict escalated. Turkish military forces began heavy bombardments. Between November 2015 and March 2016, violent clashes destroyed hundreds of buildings, leveled tens of neighborhoods in Sur, and resulted in human casualties whose numbers are still disputed. Tens of thousands of residents were displaced. Months-long curfews imposed by the state prevented Sur residents from returning to their homes and merchants from opening their stores (figure 27).

In the summer of 2016 I returned to Diyarbakır to observe the post-conflict conditions in the city. Several small neighborhood parks had been turned into bases for special forces. T-walls (concrete barriers used in conflict zones) and armored security towers draped with large Turkish flags had sprouted across the city. Hundreds of new street surveillance cameras, secured with barbed wire, kept watch.

Diyarbakır and its people had changed drastically in one year. The city was uneasy. I had difficulty getting residents to consent to doing interviews with me. If they agreed, our conversations did not last longer than fifteen minutes or half an hour. People speculated about the factors leading to the fighting.

FIGURE 27. Aerial view of Sur in 2018. The photo, taken from a commercial flight, shows the demolished neighborhoods of Fatih Paşa and Hasırlı in the upper right corner.
Source: Author, 2018.

They had different theories about why it happened, why the PKK had dug war trenches, or what would happen next. But the streets showed no trace of HDP or Kurdish activism. The flags, posters, banners, colors—any symbols of the Kurdish movement I had seen over the years in streets, in parks, and on walls of the city—had all but disappeared. Miles of roadsides exclusively featured Turkish flags or President Erdoğan's posters. I saw banners of Islamist groups hanging in the streets. In the many years I had visited the city, I had never seen these kinds of displays or encountered such groups. At several popular spots in the city, the abbreviation of the Republic of Turkey, "TC," as well as the crescent and the star—the emblems of the Turkish flag—were sprayed on walls and on electric poles.

That same summer of 2016, I attended the pro-Kurdish municipality workshops and panels on how to restore the city from its post-conflict condition, with the participation of mayors, urban planners, academics, and lawyers. Even then, no one would have imagined that the city would see even more destruction in the coming months. Yet in the fall of 2016, the government directed a major crackdown on the HDP.[5] Government officials arrested several top Kurdish politicians and mayors in the region (including HDP cochairs Selahattin Demirtaş and Figen Yüksekdağ). Hundreds more activists, party members, and party officials were detained.

After the dismissal of the elected mayors of the HDP, the AKP's government appointed state officials (*kayyım*) as the mayors in Diyarbakır and in several Kurdish cities in the southeast of Turkey. As soon as the *kayyım* arrived at their offices, they dismissed hundreds of staff members by emergency decree (Kanun Hükmünde Kararname, KHK).

The new administrators set out to erase all evidence of Kurdish identity from the cities. On the first day of their arrival, state officials hung large Turkish flags on the façades of municipality halls—as if conquering a castle. Then they began to remove any signage and symbolism associated with Kurdish language and culture. As the following pages demonstrate, the post-conflict reconstruction of Diyarbakır was, in fact, an "act of destruction."[6] To further illustrate the government's attempts to dismantle the Kurdish movement and to erase Kurdish identity from the city, I now turn to the AKP mayors' urban actions against Diyarbakır's memorial landscape.

Paint It Black

In the fall of 2016, soon after seizing the elected mayors Gültan Kışanak and Fırat Anlı, the Turkish government appointed the *kayyım* Cumali Atilla as the new mayor of the Diyarbakır Metropolitan Municipality. The new mayor's first week in office was a busy one. He signed more than a dozen executive orders. He first reappointed staff members to unrelated positions until the emergency decree went into practice—for example, designating the municipality's chair of city planning, who is an architect, as a fireman. Atilla then fired several more municipality officers, including the municipality theater artists, abolished the municipality theater, and ordered major memorials to be removed from the city. He immediately ordered the dismantling of the Lamassu reliefs in front of the municipality, replaced the "Amed" signage with a Turkish flag, and had the Roboski memorial—which was erected to commemorate the killing of thirty-four Kurds—demolished (see chapter 5).

With a population of almost two million, Diyarbakır is one of the largest cities of Turkey. Given all the urban problems a city of this scale has, why did a mayor in his first few weeks of administration make it his primary business to dismantle the city's cultural and urban institutions? Andy Merrifield's approach to the relationship between urban and political space explains the situation. For Merrifield, "political space is nothing other than the urban itself, the real and normative battleground in which a new urban question continues to impose itself in evermore rapacious guises and disguises."[7] These rapacious guises and disguises—occupied by territorial battles, subversions, appropriations, possessions, and exclusions—constitute political space. As this chapter demonstrates, Diyarbakır has long housed all these urban conditions concurrently. After the fighting, in just a matter of months, most of the city's major parks, cultural centers, and sports complexes had been shut down. Public memorials and monuments had been destroyed. And several Kurdish names in public sites had been changed to Turkish or imbued with an unmistakable state military symbolism.

In June 2018, I sought to uncover the fate of the monuments and memorials I had documented in earlier phases of my fieldwork. Many of the smaller-scale reliefs and memorials like the Uğur Kaymaz and Roboski memorials had been completely destroyed or removed; the space they had occupied was already landscaped with ornamental flowers so that any sign of the monuments had vanished. Larger memorials, perhaps more costly to dismantle, were often vandalized. The practice amounted to a systematic campaign. Perhaps the most significant example of this sabotage was inflicted on the *Right to Life* statue and accompanying panels. As I discussed in chapter 5, the *Right to Life* memorial denouncing state violence was among the largest memorials in the city. When I returned to the site, I found that *Right to Life* had been heavily damaged, with the two flanking wall panels partially wrecked. One of the panels, which used to depict the Kurds dancing in solidarity, had been veiled with beige plaster. On the other panel, the reliefs of injured heads had been removed, the remaining traces veiled with plaster and painted black—amounting to a form of monument censorship. The most striking vandalism befell the central sculpture, *Right to Life*. The back side of the pedestal was covered in black graffiti: "Ulan insanlar—Hayaller iptal" (Hey, you people—Dreams canceled) (see figures 28, 29 and 30, and figures 18, 19, and 20 in chapter 5 for comparison purposes).[8]

Destroying the memorial landscape not only represented the state's views on Kurdish culture and past but also aimed to convey messages to Kurdish society. In the eyes of the state, indeed, the autonomy of Kurds was a dream. Now, at the end of the conflict, that dream was canceled. Even after the fighting, military symbolism literalized the seizure of public space and the attempt to establish state order—destroying monuments, memorials, and Kurdish symbols and replacing them with expressions enforcing state authority over Kurdish public space. While documenting the destroyed memorials and cultural sites in the city, I could not imagine what more destruction was to come. The urban intervention aimed at the erasure of Kurdish memory was not limited to the destruction of public memorials. The AKP also appropriated existing structures, refurbishing them to serve its ideology.

FIGURE 28. Censored art in Koşuyolu Park. The bottom half of the original piece is veiled with plaster.
Source: Author, 2018.

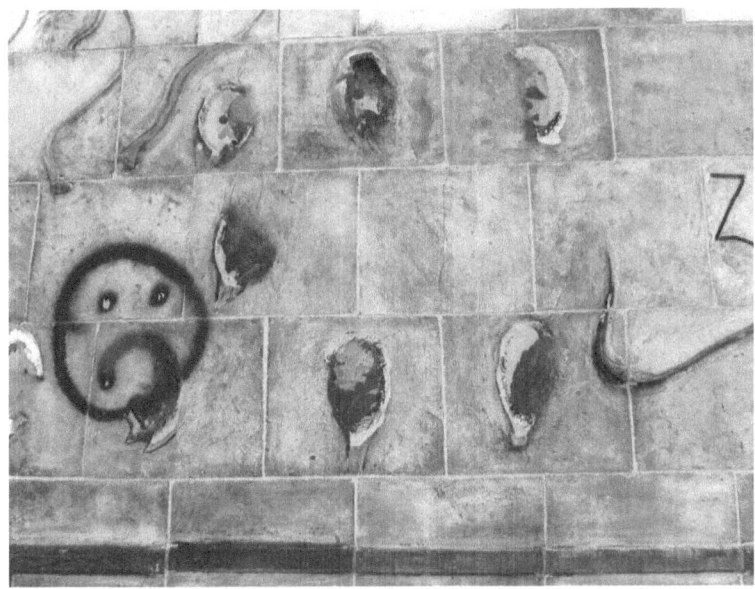

FIGURE 29. Censored detail of the wall panel. The sculptures representing wounded heads were removed, their traces covered with plaster or painted black. To the left appears a sad-face graffiti.
Source: Author, 2018.

FIGURE 30. The vandalized *Right to Life* memorial. Black graffiti at the tiled base reads *"Hayaller iptal—Ulan insanlar"* (Hey, you people—Dreams canceled).
Source: Author, 2018.

Islamification of Public Space

The AKP's post-conflict recipe did not simply constitute a process of destruction followed by new construction. Between these steps, party officials selectively appropriated major public spaces, parks, and cultural centers designed by the HDP municipality and refashioned them to suit their own "Islamist" identity. The AKP regarded these appropriations and urban interventions as an opportunity to manipulate society through targeted forms of citizenship. Such appropriation of public space was the initial step in the AKP's de-Kurdification and Islamification of public space.

The AKP was already experienced in the Islamification of public space. Since it came to power in 2002 in Turkey, the party has employed public space and infrastructure to signal the imposition of its style of political order in several cities, especially where it held mayoral power. As Bülent Batuman argues, this spatial expression of public order has been redefined under the AKP's definition of "nation" (*millet*), in which "Turkishness and Islam" present qualities of the same entity.[9] The AKP's quest for architectural representation of *millet*—incorporating nationalism and Islam—can be traced in Diyarbakır's public space. Such a form of representation serves to illustrate President Erdoğan's new political discourse for the country: "One nation, one flag, one state, one homeland" (*Tek millet, tek bayrak, tek devlet, tek vatan*), which intensified particularly after the coup d'état attempt in 2016. This four-faceted discourse rested on an essential understanding of Turkish nationalism blended with Islam, what Jenny White once called "Muslim nationalism."[10] In fact, "One nation, one flag, one state, one homeland" was a direct message to Kurds, responding to their desire to be autonomous.

For the most part, the AKP targeted the HDP's cultural centers—symbolically and structurally—for Islamo-nationalistic restoration. As I discuss in chapter 3, youth, women, and cultural centers were crucial hubs for Kurdish mobilization in the city. Echoing their treatment of public parks, the AKP's appointed mayors shut down several youth centers, schools, and sport complexes and renamed the remaining centers—in Turkish, and often with the names of Turkish "martyrs" who died during the failed coup d'état.[11]

Such was the case with the Cegerxwîn Youth, Culture, and Art Center (Cegerxwîn Gençlik Kültür ve Sanat Merkezi). Built by the HDP municipality and named after a prominent Kurdish rebel and poet, Cegerxwîn was among the most popular and largest cultural centers in the city. Hundreds of young people had taken art classes, Kurdish music and language courses, Kurdish folklore, and filmmaking classes there. In July 2017, the new administration moved to remove the name Cegerxwîn and rename the center "July 15 Millet Cultural Center," in reference to the coup d'état attempt that took place on that date in 2016. When the AKP mayors attempted to replace the name on the façade, it provoked a heated reaction from the citizenry. In response, the new administration kept the original name but added to the façade a large, shiny plaque with the Arabic letter و (*wāw*) next to Cegerxwîn's signage. Symbolically, in Islamic mysticism, the letter *wāw* is believed to represent obedience to Allah (God) and the universe. However, beyond its meaning, in the last ten years the *wāw* symbol has been a popular sign among AKP followers in the country as an affirmation of the AKP's authority and reign. Harnessing the center to Islam was not limited to a gesture on the façade; it also included radically altering the curriculum of the center. In de-Kurdifying the center, AKP officials canceled Kurdish classes and Kurdish cultural art courses and replaced them with Arabic courses. The state's disciplinary practices, its demolition of Kurdish memorials, changing of street names, revision of the curriculum at the cultural center, and so forth—all of this recalled a colonial form of city planning. Achille Mbembe's proposition on the post-colony, that "to exercise authority is, above all, to tire the bodies under it, to disempower them not so much to increase their productivity as to ensure the maximum docility,"[12] explains how AKP officials attempted to keep Diyarbakırians in check.

If Islamification was the formula for de-Kurdification, it is no surprise that the AKP administration promoted the construction of mosques and other initiatives associated with Islam. These new projects echoed the early phases of the AKP's Islamification efforts in Istanbul when the party first came to power. In erasing Kurdish identity from the city, the construction of new mosques in Diyarbakır was both symbolically and politically significant for the AKP. The party intended to utilize mosques as a spatial and symbolic means of dismantling the Kurdish bloc and bringing Kurds under the wings of the nation.

Diyarbakır Central Mosque: "A Little Mesopotamia, a Little Seljuk, a Little Ottoman"

Particularly after the armed conflict, constructing mosques was the one of the AKP's principal ways of symbolizing its reign and power, of leaving its own indelible mark on the city. In Turkey, once a mosque is built, demolishing it is almost impossible. The AKP needed a large, expansive representation of the party in the middle of the Diyarbakır, and thus the solution was to build a "Diyarbakır Central Mosque." AKP officials named it as such on the grounds that Diyarbakır did not have a "central" mosque; traditionally, almost every city in Anatolia has its own central mosque. But for Diyarbakır, this AKP construction signaled an attempt to create a new city center. The city already had the historic great mosque of Diyarbakır (Diyarbakır Ulu Camii) in Sur. By opening a new, larger central mosque, the AKP vied to decentralize the meaning of Sur for Diyarbakırians.

In fact, the AKP's intention in building a central mosque for Diyarbakır was not new. First, through several land law amendments and, later, land transfers, the government procured one of the most prominent sites for a mosque to be built. The 28,500-square-meter green site belonged to the General Directorate of Highways. The government first transferred the site to the Directorate of Religious Affairs, then converted it into a "Religious Facility Area" with the new plan amendment made by the Ministry of Environment and Urbanization officially approved in 2013. However, the AKP was able to begin construction only after it seized power in the city from the HDP. The choice of the plot for the new large mosque was significant both physically and ideologically: it was a central location whose visual and geographic presence asserted itself to every Diyarbakırian. The land sat right in the middle of two important sites: the governor's office and the memorial park associated with the republican period on one side, and the Diyarbakır Metropolitan Municipality building tied to the HDP's governance on the other side. With this mosque, the AKP was able to mark its own era and its own supremacy, clearly distinguishing itself from both the republican era and the HDP's rule in the city.

President Erdoğan himself oversaw both the mosque's groundbreaking and its inauguration ceremonies, accompanied by ministers and former and current Parliament members of Diyarbakır. In his speech at the groundbreaking, Erdoğan emphasized how the mosque would be used not only for prayer but also for social activities.[13] And, indeed, the complex was designed for much more than prayer. In addition to the prayer hall, the mosque comprises social and recreational facilities in a large complex with several different amenities to create a social hub in the city. Officially the Selahattin Eyyubi Camii (Salahaddin Ayyubi Mosque), the Diyarbakır Central Mosque was inaugurated in 2023 after six years of construction. The name Salahaddin Ayyubi honors the famous Muslim Kurdish warrior while also embodying a fusion of Kurdish heritage and Islamic identity.

Designed by an Ankara-based architectural and construction firm, the mosque is the largest in the region—intended to be large enough to host twenty-five thousand people for prayer, with a construction footprint of forty-three thousand square meters. The mosque complex contains a multipurpose room (for about a thousand people), conference and exhibition halls, a playground area, a tea garden, two museums, shops, two libraries, and condolence houses—all of which occupy more space than the prayer hall. As a complex, the new mosque is meant to compete with the famous Kocatepe mosque, the largest mosque in Ankara, which can accommodate up to twenty-four thousand worshippers.

The convergence of Islamic characteristics and urban neoliberal practices was not new for Turkey.[14] Across the country, the AKP in particular adopted a neo-Ottoman-style mosque as a representational tool in fashioning its own version of nation.[15] Strikingly, the Salahaddin Ayyubi Mosque does not simply reproduce neo-Ottoman style. AKP members were aware that simply utilizing the neo-Ottoman mosque template, as they generally do elsewhere in Turkey, would not work for Diyarbakır.

The mosque's website describes the mosque's design as "in harmony with the history and architectural style of our region; a little Mesopotamia, a little Seljuk, a little Ottoman."[16] As is explicit in its own description, the mosque does not cleave to any particular architectural tradition but instead features a mix-and-match style.

Within this eclectic context, the Salahaddin Ayyubi Mosque attempts to create a sense of belonging, tapping into regional architectural references. Conceptually, with its rectangular-plan prayer hall covered by a large octagonal dome, a large courtyard at the front, and four square-shaped minarets, the Salahaddin Ayyubi Mosque evokes early examples of mosques in the region, in particular Aq Qoyunlu mosques (such as Safa Mosque, Sheikh Matar Mosque) in Sur. With its colossal size, the central mosque presents an overgrown version of these structural conceptions, as it attempts to make several other local architectural connections. Dressed with bands of black basalt and white limestone, the façade makes an obvious reference to local architecture that dates back to the fifteenth century. The minarets at each corner are decorated with three rising steps at their base, which along with the stepped, arcaded portico surrounding the courtyard refer to a ziggurat while recalling the culture of Babylon and Assyrian civilizations in the region. The mosque thus makes a pretense as "a little Mesopotamia,"[17] with out-of-proportion representations of a ziggurat temple (figure 31).

While the mosque design appears concerned with adopting vernacular motifs, it also clearly attempts to forge a bond with Anatolian and Turkic origins. In the mosque's use of the eight-pointed star, Anatolian Seljuk features stand out. As the mosque's website points out, the complex is inspired by the "eight-point star," "the symbol of Islamic culture, beginning from Kara-Khanid Khanate [and] sustained by Anatolian Seljuk brought to today."[18] The architectural assimilation whereby the early republic attributed Kurdish monuments and architecture to Turkic dynasties was again in practice; this time the state placed emphasis on the Ottoman and Anatolian Seljuk past. Attributing such a level of Turkish Anatolian identity to Diyarbakır's central mosque openly testifies to the AKP's larger project of making Diyarbakır an Anatolian city, not a Kurdish one.[19] With its massive size, the Salahaddin Ayyubi Mosque is a powerful display of the AKP's city governance. For the AKP, mosque projects represent not only a drastic way to Islamify the city, but also a very strong attempt to imprint the authority of its rule.

FIGURE 31. Salahaddin Ayyubi Mosque (Diyarbakır Central Mosque). *Source:* Author, 2023.

Reconstruction: Municipal Service and City Beautification

While rapidly Islamifying the city, AKP officials knew that replacing the Kurdish memorial landscape with Islamic symbolism would not be sufficient to gain support and legitimacy among residents. Across the country, the AKP had always undertaken grand infrastructure and public landscaping projects to signal a progressive government. Similarly, in Diyarbakır, the party pursued a strategy of urban development that would allow it to gain social and political credibility within various citizen groups. To secure a measure of legitimacy with the urban population and fortify its reputation and authority after the conflict, the AKP needed to conjure up large-scale projects. Thus, in the span of one year, the whole city became a construction site. Between 2017 and 2019, every neighborhood in Diyarbakır had a construction, demolition, or renovation project being conducted by the new administration. Constructing parks and pedestrian bridges, installing new drainage, upgrading roads, paving sidewalks, restoring façades on main streets, landscaping, and road-lighting projects—all were key representations of progress for the AKP's newly appointed government. These initiatives were carried out in accordance with a fresh slogan that appeared on banners in every corner in the city: "When you want it [municipal development], it happens" (figure 32). The slogan, accompanied by images of planned

FIGURE 32. The AKP municipality's advertisement. On the left it reads, "Our work continues for a more beautiful Diyarbakır." In the right upper corner is the slogan "When you want it, it happens."
Source: Author, 2018.

construction works, was clearly a critique of the prior, pro-Kurdish administration—which purportedly failed to bring such a level of development to the city. It also reflected the AKP's accusation against HDP municipalities, according to which the pro-Kurdish party channeled funds to support the PKK instead of developing the city.

City billboards, which used to feature invitations to demonstrations, were now plastered with AKP administration campaigns. These billboards now cited metrics—how many kilometers of asphalted road, how many overpasses built, and so on. But these urban infrastructure and city-beautification projects were about more than urban restoration. With these projects, the AKP sought to signal the end of a twenty-year-long pro-Kurdish party presence in the city.

Indeed, these projects aimed to secure President Erdoğan's conceptualization of "one nation" once again under the umbrella of Islam. Especially after the coup d'état attempt in 2016, new urban projects rode a strong wave of Turkish nationalist sentiment. Directly affiliated with this ideology, the AKP architecture—"millet [nation] parks," "millet mosques," and "millet libraries"—sprawled across the country. In Diyarbakır, government officials regularly expunged Kurdish names from public parks and replaced them with Turkish nationalist titles. Park Orman, one of the largest urban parks opened by the HDP, was renamed July 15 Martyrs Park. Streets were retitled with Arab

Sahaba names, for the companions of the Prophet Muhammad, such as with Iyaz Bin Ganem Street. The newly appointed AKP mayors commissioned artists to produce neighborhood street murals depicting Islamic messages. Construction cranes that previously had hung new Kurdish signs and dismantled symbols of Turkish nationalism were now at work taking down Kurdish signs and replacing them with Islamic symbolism. These landscape projects were inseparable from attempts by the new administration to Islamify the built environment. New urban parks even included small-scale libraries that carried Islamic books and histories of Diyarbakır written by early republican authors who rejected the city's Kurdish identity.

While building new urban parks, the AKP's administration also pointedly neglected the parks previously built by HDP municipalities. The administration selectively stopped landscaping services, watering plants, cutting grass, and painting benches, turning certain public parks into derelict sites. The famous Newroz Park became a ruin. As I discussed in chapter 5, Newroz Park was one of the crucial sites for annual Newroz celebrations, hosting around one million participants every March 21. When I arrived to see the park after the conflict, it was in shambles. The concrete plaza and stage structure were all that remained. Decorations had been disassembled. The stage itself, which used to feature the colors of the Kurdish flag, had been painted black.

The city was changing rapidly. But the public could not be convinced that the AKP's renovation and beautification projects were good-faith efforts. Ciwan, a young shopkeeper in Sur, was excited to reopen his dried-fruit and nuts store when I met with him in 2018 after the conflict in the city. His business had been shut down for almost nine months while the fighting raged, during which time he had sent his family to his village and temporarily worked in a restaurant in Yenişehir. Although his shop now benefited from the renovation projects, he repudiated them. "They [the AKP] always hire their own people [supporters]. They were looking for an excuse to destroy our homes. Now they found it. And the [pro-Kurdish party] organization, by digging the trenches, they played into the state's hands. Look at this street"—he gestured at Melik Ahmet Street in front him. "Who knows whose pockets it is filling? Look at these cobblestones. They say they spent fifty million lira on them. For what? We already had roads. They should return these people's houses instead." I heard similar comments in one-on-one conversations and interviews in 2018 and 2019. Even some of the AKP supporters in the city called the recreational urban projects "eyewash"—insincere developments. Esra (see chapter 4) echoed this point. When I spoke with her in 2018 at her house in Kayapınar, she was bitter: "At least the conflict is over. They planted flowers on the roadside and renovated our roads. They constantly do construction. Sur, Bağlar are still dumps. . . . They only favor their own followers. They spend a lot of money, but they don't resolve our problems. But these are nothing more than an 'eyewash' [göz boyama]. That's all about grass lawns, flowers. . . . Did you see what happened to Tigris Valley? What they did is charlatanry. . . . What a mind!" Her example of "eyewash," the Tigris Valley Recreational Project—at 2,713 acres one of AKP's largest undertakings—was also another case of Islamifying the landscape. The Tigris Valley project had long been a subject of dispute between the pro-Kurdish municipality and the government; indeed, the struggles between the AKP government and the HDP municipality had resulted in several lawsuits and law orders. But at the time the AKP did not have the municipal power to intervene in the area.

In 2013, the state's Ministry of Environment and Urbanization declared the Tigris Valley a preserved site, effectively taking the power away from the municipality to implement its own landscape and recreational projects on the site. That same year, the municipality sought to place Diyarbakır's city walls and its Hevsel Gardens on the UNESCO World Heritage List,[20] and in 2015 the "Diyarbakır Fortress and Hevsel Gardens Cultural Landscape" was registered as a World Heritage Site.

Following the conflict, in 2016, the AKP's administration declared the Hevsel Gardens and Dicle Valley "Special Recreation Areas" and initiated the Tigris Valley Recreational Project. Dubbed a "crazy project" during election campaigns, it was expected to cost over twenty million lira.[21] Despite several appeals by the urban planning chamber in Diyarbakır, and the court's ruling to prevent construction on the Tigris Valley site as a preservation site, landscaping continued in the Hevsel Gardens and Tigris Valley site. Inevitably, one of the first projects the AKP constructed at the site was a mosque. Completed in one year, in 2018, with a shiny copper dome and minaret, the mosque catches the eye right at the entrance of the Tigris Valley by the historic Tigris Bridge (On Gözlü Köprü). Next to it, a blue pathway—recalling an artificial river—runs thorough the site (figure 33). In August 2019, the AKP completed a "Nation's Garden" (Millet bahcesi) with a pond, outdoor activity area, sightseeing, walking paths, children's playgrounds, and cafés and picnic areas.

Such beautification and urban development projects had a dual purpose: they satisfied the AKP's need to legitimize itself in the eyes of Kurdish citizens, while providing lucrative contracts to party members and affiliated businessmen. In almost all instances, the demolisher, the investor, and the redeveloper in such projects were actually the government or a contractor company associated with or supported by the AKP. Unsurprisingly, the AKP's administration contracted the construction of the Tigris Valley project to one of its affiliates, Erkonut Construction, in turn an affiliate company of Erzurum municipality, another city over which the AKP holds power. In fact, most of the time, instead of working with local construction firms, AKP officials contracted urban projects with Ankara- or

FIGURE 33. The Tigris Valley Recreation Area Mosque.
Source: Author, 2018.

Istanbul-based firms that were AKP municipality-affiliated companies, such as Kiptaş Inc. Further, during the military and urban intervention campaign, the AKP's government not only took control of the municipality but also confiscated some major private construction companies, such as Çeysa İnşaat and Birtane İnşaat, within the city. Similar to its procedure for controlling municipalities, after arresting the owners of these companies (on allegations of "aiding and abetting" the PKK), the AKP appointed government officials (*kayyım*) in their place. Further, the AKP's urban intervention was not limited to landscape and recreational projects. It extended its reach into housing and merged with efforts to disarticulate Kurdish blocks.

Turning Sur into a Flat Land

At the end of the conflict, by March 2016, thousands of Sur residents had no home to return to. They were homeless in their own city. Around twenty-four thousand people were displaced, and hundreds of shopkeepers and merchants had to shut down their business during military curfews that lasted several months.[22] Hundreds of homes and registered buildings were destroyed or severely damaged.[23]

The destruction was not limited to individual buildings; it meant the very erasure of the urban fabric. Yet even as obliteration was underway, the image created by the AKP was the inverse. National TV channels broadcast short documentaries on the change in Kurdish cities, while some newspapers known to be close to the AKP printed special issues on the tourism potential of Kurdish cities, with titles such as "The Twenty Pearls of Eastern Tourism," or "On the Move with Culture Tourism,"[24] emphasizing the AKP's beautification of Kurdish cities.

In June 2016, the first morning after I arrived in the city, I attempted to see Sur. Several neighborhoods of Sur, including Hasırlı, Dabanoğlu, Fatih, Cemal Yılmaz, and Savaş—half the size of the whole district—were blockaded by T-walls. Police posts were stationed on almost every corner. I could just manage to get a glimpse of the area from afar by climbing atop the old city walls very early in the morning. From there, I could see that neighborhoods had been completely destroyed. I sought out the Hasırlı neighborhood, where I used to visit the laundry houses and the Free Patriot Association (see chapter 3); but the houses I once visited and roads I had walked along had been razed to the ground (see figure 27).

The debris had already been removed. No trace was left behind. Instead, a long prairie stretched out in front of me where streets and buildings had once stood. Tall yellow grass now covered much of the formerly built-up 230 acres. In the distance, bulldozers and other construction machinery stood in front of four or five newly built two-story white houses. Packs of bricks sat on the ground nearby, waiting for the construction of additional new housing by the AKP government. Later, the sounds of construction machinery broke the silence of the morning. The streets, widened during the fighting for army tanks to pass, and then, after the conflict, widened for the excavators, were gone. The original urban outlines and street plans had been completely obliterated, lost. A large ring road had been built right in front of the historic walls, framing the whole district. Its asphalt was still fresh and shiny, while the land was flattened for redevelopment.

As I discussed in chapter 2, government plans for redevelopment in Sur dated back to 2009, when they were limited to two neighborhoods, Lalebey and Ali Paşa. Later, redevelopment plans extended to almost the entire district. In fact, during the conflict, the government officials' declarations from Ankara hinted at what was to come. In February 2016, the remarks of Prime Minister Ahmet Davutoğlu summed up the government's fifteen-year-old neoliberal urban development plans for Sur. He stated, "Our operations will continue until all cities are cleared. These cities were already crooked and uncontrollably developed since the nineties. Even if these events did not occur, urban transformation needs to be done."[25] Facing heavy criticism for the military destruction of Sur, Davutoğlu announced, during the same meeting, "We'll rebuild Sur so that it is like Toledo [in Spain]: everyone will want to come and appreciate its architectural texture." He added that he himself would like to own a newly built house in Sur—a statement that circulated widely and was heavily derided by Kurdish activists and some intellectuals in the country.[26]

Urgent Expropriation

The destruction that began with heavy artillery, tanks, bombs, and explosives continued after the conflict, with excavations and expulsions in Sur. The government lost no time in resuming its redevelopment plans from 2009. In March 2016, government officials seized 82 percent of the Sur district with an "urgent expropriation decree," a form of eminent domain designed to confiscate properties in case of risk to "public security and order" or a "state of danger" (figure 34).[27]

Expropriation even included neighborhoods not necessarily affected by the fighting. Most striking, even if the district—on paper—did not appear completely annexed, the government had already confiscated the remaining parcels in 2012 under law 6306 concerning the "transformation of areas under disaster risk" (see chapter 2). Thus was the whole district of Sur disposed of and expropriated. For instance, according to the expropriation map prepared by the Ministry of Environment and Urban Planning, the Ali Paşa neighborhood was not included in the government's expropriation plan. In fact, it had been expropriated in 2012.[28]

Recent studies of urbanism from Mumbai to Madrid show how local governments have turned into local developers seeking to boost the city's economy, fostering collaborations with private entities and urban elites. In the case of Diyarbakır, neoliberal urbanism (conducted directly by the state) no longer requires cooperation with urban elites or private agents. This recipe for full dispossession—whereby the AKP serves as demolisher, contractor, developer, and designer—was the case in Sur.[29] While the government hastily expropriated the whole district, Mine Lök Beyaz, the AKP Diyarbakır Parliament member, opened her own private restoration and architectural design firm, Yöre Mimarlik, in Diyarbakır. Her new firm was designated to guide and lead all other architectural firms that would work to restore and reconstruct the damaged buildings in the area. Yöre Architecture operated "in the field as the author [*müellif*] of the Ministry of Environment and Urbanization," Beyaz explained in an interview at a popular Turkish architecture website, adding that they prepared "urban design guidance" for other architectural offices "working in the Sur district to follow."[30]

A couple of weeks after the expropriation act, in April 2016, Prime Minister Davutoğlu arrived in Diyarbakır and delivered a speech in front of the historic

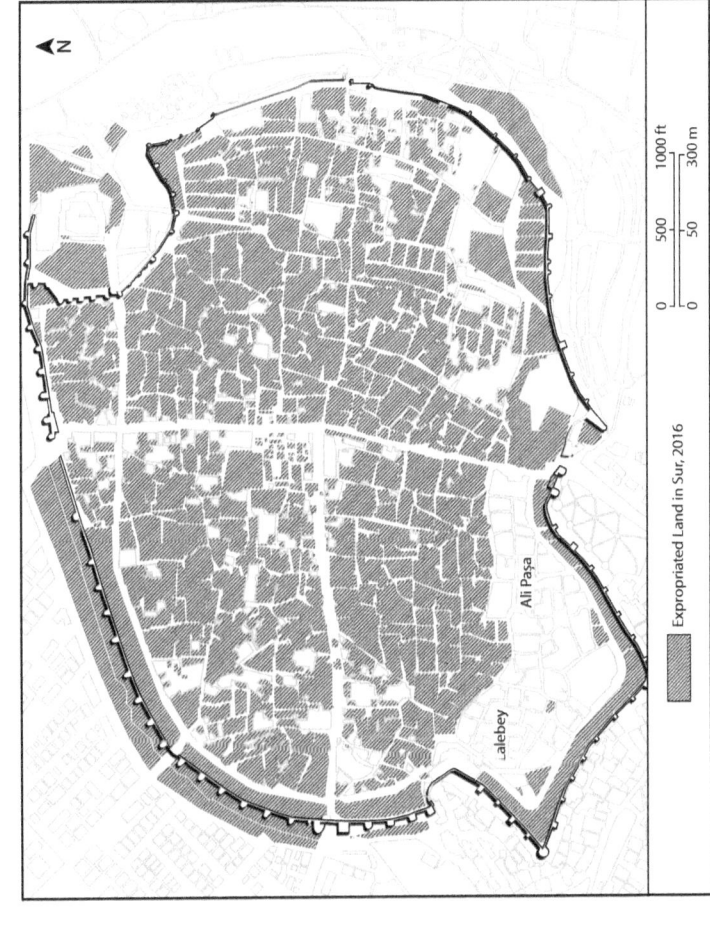

FIGURE 34. The expropriated properties in Sur, before wide-scale destruction, are shaded in gray.
Source: Adapted from Google Earth images and data collected from the Sur municipality.

grand mosque (Ulu Camii) in Sur. His speech stressed the government's project to transform Sur into a tourist destination. Davutoğlu announced that "they will create a city, a miniature city [*biblokent*] in which everyone would freely come and visit." It was not the first time the AKP referred to turning historic cities into *biblokent*—miniature museum cities—to describe its urban development approach across the country. The mention of *biblokent* was a marker of neoliberal urban plans for a historic city, with hotels, motels, and tourist destinations to come. In Diyarbakır, we see not only the coarticulation of neoliberalism and Islamism as often studied in AKP's Turkey, but also a new mode of urban regime dictated by stringent rules. A mode of urban neoliberal governance enacted through surveillance and control of everyday life manifests itself in abrupt urban law changes, sudden expulsions, forced dislocations and evictions, months-long curfews, and arbitrary termination of housing contracts, all of which vigorously feed off what Stephen Graham calls "new military urbanism."[31]

In the summer of 2019, I returned again to Sur. After several attempts to visit the construction site, finally I had found a contact—Hamdi, a civil engineer working at the site—through another acquaintance working at the Sur municipality. This time I was able to visit the Ali Paşa neighborhood. Once again, one of the main contractors of this project was an affiliated AKP municipality elsewhere. Kiptaş Istanbul Residence Development Plan Industry and Trade Inc. is a construction company of Istanbul Metropolitan Municipality, held by the AKP at that time. Kiptaş builds middle-class residential blocks in Istanbul; and yet it was leading the housing projects in Diyarbakır, on the opposite edge of the country.

The walls blocking the site were covered with ads for new construction projects by the Ministry of Environment and Planning. Large banners featured illustrations of housing projects, reading, "Ali Paşa regains its regional texture"; "Diyarbakır architecture"; "Constructing Diyarbakır regional houses"; and "Sur, renovated with its streets, infrastructure, and parks." Each ad conveyed the same message: the government rebuilds Sur "better than before."

In fact, one advertisement boasting satellite photos announced that the houses were built in the form of courtyard housing—a crucial feature of Sur's urban texture. The results were radically different, however.

One morning in August 2019, my municipality acquaintance took me to Ali Paşa; at the gate, Hamdi let me inside the construction site. He advised me not to speak with anyone or ask questions and be quick in my observations. He showed me a two-story house under construction, as an example. As we were walking to the house, I was able to glance at the site briefly. No asphalt or walkways had been laid yet. New developments were constructed in the form of two-story row housing, attached back to back, each with a narrow front yard, approximately nine by twenty-six feet. Each house would receive sunlight only from the back and front. In the development, the "traditional inner courtyard" was transformed into a tiny front yard for each unit, separated from the neighbor's yard with a six-foot-tall concrete wall. The function of privacy and social recreation sustained by the inner courtyard was lost on the new units. When we reached the house, the workers had just completed the stairs, and some were cladding half of the walls with gray limestone, perhaps in an attempt to resemble the city's traditional masonry houses. Behind the new units, construction of a large hotel was advancing, though it was hard for me to imagine such a hotel in close proximity to residential units. My visit was short. I was not allowed to conduct interviews at the construction site or take photos.

Overall, despite civil and political society organizations raising architectural and urban concerns regarding the new housing units in Sur,[32] none of the efforts were adequate to halt the construction projects. Hundreds of historic buildings had been either destroyed or damaged during the conflict, and the street configuration was radically altered. Sur was now unknown to Diyarbakırians. The government's approach to "restoration"—that is, turning Sur into a "tourism jewel"—was erasing the collective memory of the city, formed over thousands of years.[33] The attempt to turn Sur into a tourist destination, moreover, could not be interpreted merely as an eradication of Kurdish spatial memory. Indeed, the reconstruction of Sur as a tourist attraction was not only a matter of building a new memorial landscape but also a project of depopulating Sur of its local residents. As I discussed earlier in this book, Sur, with its networks and residents, has long been a political hub for the Kurdish movement; for that reason alone, the government has wanted to depopulate and dismantle its networks for over fifteen years. The government's depopulation efforts had finally taken shape, in the form of military urban governance.

Having had their land already expropriated, displaced residents, if and when they wanted to return to Sur, were challenged by the difficult conditions the government presented. Depending on their house titles, former residents were given three main options: receive the appreciation fees of their demolished houses, purchase a public housing project, or purchase from the new developments. As for the first option, compensation figures for the residents ranged between 30,000 and 70,000 TL, while new housing prices at the time ran from 130,000 to 300,000 TL.[34]

As I discussed in chapter 3, most Sur residents were already living below the poverty line. Even if they were compensated, buying a new house was almost impossible. As for purchase options in Sur, even if they could somehow afford a purchase, there was no guarantee they would be able to purchase a house in Sur. Houses there were offered through a lottery system to a limited number of residents. Remaining former residents were obligated to take the compensation fee and leave. In fact, by May 2020, the Ministry of Environment and Urbanization unilaterally canceled the housing contracts of around five hundred households waiting to purchase a new house on the land where their former house once stood.[35] These circumstances arose in part because not all demolished houses were replaced with new ones. Previous house numbers were not matched with new numbers. Beside residential projects, Sur's reconstruction plan included hotels, shops, tourist attractions and centers, and recreational spaces. In fact, the new development plans aimed at providing housing for upscale residents rather than relocating former residents (figure 35).

Pushing the Municipality to the Margins

Despite the millions of dollars invested in urban infrastructure and city beautification projects—and after almost three years of tenure backed by state power—the AKP administration lost the 2019 local municipal elections to the HDP in major Kurdish cities. In fact, in those cities, the HDP won by a landslide. The pro-Kurdish party had regained power despite limited campaign resources. The AKP's interventions—military, governmental, and urban—were not adequate to dismantle the HDP's voting base. During the 2019 elections, the first mayoral elections after the conflict, the party even increased its vote by 7 percentage points, to 62 percent for the Diyarbakır Metropolitan Municipality (in 2014, at the peak of Kurdish mobilization, the number was 55 percent). The HDP's 2019 mayoral election campaign slogan was remarkable: "The city is ours." Asserting ownership over cities, the slogan once again illustrates how maintaining control over urban space serves as a crucial tool of the pro-Kurdish movement for enforcing identity politics and mobilization. Reclaiming municipal power was a major success for the HDP; however, this time the HDP's power was very much restricted, and its return was challenging. After the conflict, the creation of new municipal laws and land expropriations, along with coercion from the central government, pushed municipal influence to the margins. Municipalities had their hands tied.

Following the elections, I revisited Sur municipality in July 2019. All elected officials were new to their jobs because, as I mentioned at the beginning of this chapter, previous municipality mayors' staff members were either dismissed by statutory decrees (KHK) or arrested under the state-of-emergency rule. Further, the AKP's administration loomed over them. Despite the HDP's victory

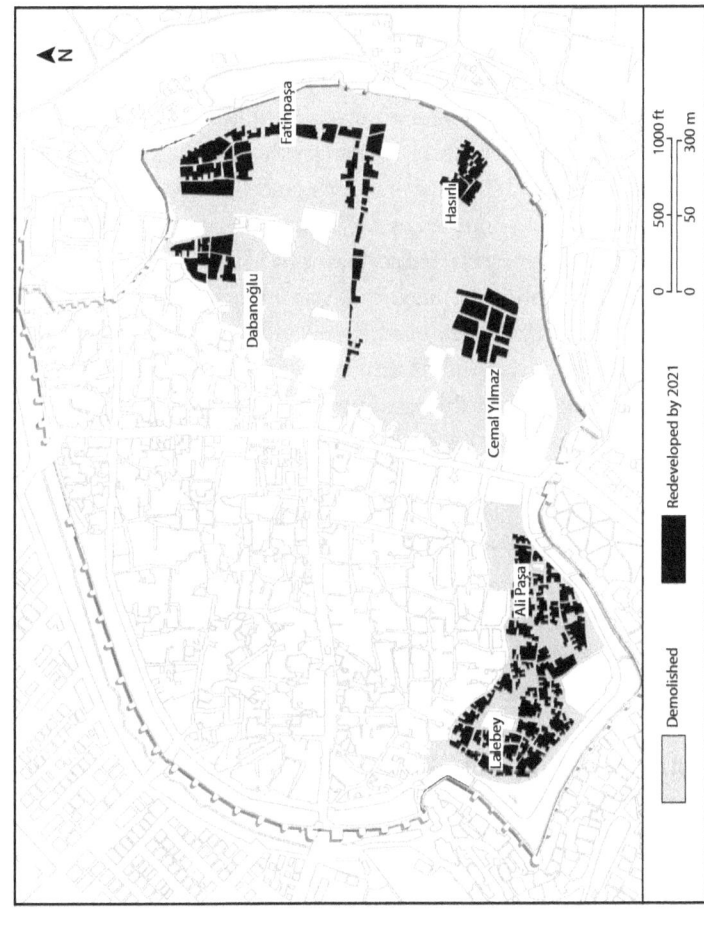

FIGURE 35. Map shows the demolished and redeveloped areas in Sur following the expropriation decree.

Source: Adapted from municipality maps, Google Maps, and Google Images, 2021.

in the elections, the previous AKP mayoral staff remained in the municipality. To understand the new conditions, I interviewed the mayoral leadership at the municipality.

Berzan was one of the new members of the mayoral council. He had a degree in sociology and had previously written for an online Kurdish newspaper. His description of the first day at the municipality after the elections summarizes the tensions between the former municipality staff and the new administration: "As soon as we entered through the municipality gate, we were greeted with a big but silent response. Very few people acknowledged us. Fewer were helpful to us. We were treated like plague. The AKP administration psychology was continuing here." The new mayors' capabilities were greatly constrained in practice because of the land and property transfers and law changes the AKP had effected prior to leaving municipal seats to HDP mayors. Sur's land had been expropriated, and the municipality was still infiltrated by AKP staff members. During my visit, I interviewed Mayor C, the newly elected co-mayor of Sur.

"Now we took back our position [*mevzii*]; it was important for us," Mayor C told me. His use of the military term *mevzii* recalled the words of Mayor Baydemir ten years previously when he depicted Diyarbakır as the "castle of the Kurdish movement." Indeed, that the pro-Kurdish party was holding mayoral power was an important win in its struggle. When I asked about the party's first action plans or projects, Mayor C sounded troubled. "We want to reinstall the Uğur Kaymaz memorial that they destroyed. . . . But they left us a lot of debt, 84 million [TL]. Yet not only the debt; primarily we need to cancel those land allocations." Clearly this time it was different. The new mayors, instead of beginning new projects, first needed to somehow remedy the spatial and bureaucratic damage caused by the previous AKP administration. As soon as the AKP lost elections, in order to maintain control, it transferred major municipality properties—cultural centers, children centers, libraries, and sport centers—to diverse state institutions such as the *kaymakamlık* (district governorship) and the *müftülük* (religious directory).[36] In fact, land and property expropriations and transfers were strategies of the AKP government to seize power from the HDP municipalities. Perhaps taking back the position (*mevzii*), in Mayor C's words, was not enough.

Although it had lost the elections, the AKP aimed to hobble the municipality, limit the local governance practices of the HDP, and cut its sustainable financial resources. Furthermore, the AKP authorities arrogated licensure procedures from the Sur municipality relating to public municipality matters such as building and construction, inspection, licenses, and other permits. In this way the AKP had divided control over the built environment into two main categories: it conferred authority for registered structures to the Regional Board of Cultural

Heritage Conservation of the Ministry of Culture and Tourism and assigned other structures to the Ministry of Environment and Planning.

As a result, for example, the Sur municipality had almost no authority to intervene in Sur's built environment. The expropriation of Sur, as I discussed earlier, was formulated so that no room remained for the municipality to conduct urban planning. According to the new law, the state's Board of Conservation or the Ministry of Environment and Planning had to approve even small-scale construction projects, such as replacing windows. The whole district was in the grip of the central government. The land expropriations had also usurped the municipality's authority over its usual duties—cadastral, building permit, title, and deed work. Only in particular situations did state officials delegate some work to the municipality. The land registry and cadastral surveys were areas in which the government's pressure could be observed. In September 2019, I followed up with Berzan at the municipality. His words highlight the form of urban coercion at work:

> No one is allowed to do anything. Not even hammer a nail to the wall. It would have terrible consequences, like imprisonment. Except in some particular situations. One of the walls of the sixteenth-century Çifte Khan was going to collapse. Both the board and the ministry insisted that we take care of the situation. We closed the narrow street where that wall was located. One or two months later the wall collapsed. They always throw the ball to us in order not to look bad to the public. There were a few shops on that street. The shops remained closed for a while, and we had to convince the shopkeepers about closing the street. We had a similar situation with a house. The house collapsed. They did not allow us to intervene at the building, remove a simple pile that is likely to be demolished. Instead, they just instructed us to close the street.

Such treatment was not unique to Sur municipality; in addition to cutting the financial resources, the AKP arrogated territorial and municipal power in the cities in which the HDP had won the municipal elections. All these actions weakened and impaired HDP municipalities in the region. The Diyarbakır municipality was virtually turned into a subcontractor of the AKP's Regional Board of Cultural Heritage Conservation and the Ministry of Environment and Planning. New municipality members were caught in a dilemma. Even if they were reelected, they worried that the government would dismiss them and appoint their own bureaucrats again. In the face of these threats, the HDP municipalities looked for alternative strategies, developing wiggle room to sustain their projects. Establishing partnerships with chambers, unions, and private organizations were major maneuvers. As Selim, then head of the Culture Department of Diyarbakır Metropolitan Municipality, noted in 2019,

> Under these circumstances, we know that we can be taken from duty and arrested at any time. . . . We learned our lessons from our previous experience; we are getting prepared. . . . We decided to develop several of our cultural projects through private partnerships, so even if they [the state] seize the municipality again, they won't be able to stop our projects. Now we are working on a theater project, but the largest sponsor of this theater will be a private company, with which we are in dialogue.

When I returned to the Sur municipality, I sensed a very similar approach to conducting municipal work. Berzan was working on a pilot street improvement and restoration project that included cleaning and painting the façades of houses on a small street. Even a project that simple was illegal; the municipality had not secured a permit from the preservation board or the Ministry of Environment and Planning in accordance with the new legislation. Berzan noted: "I know they are not going to give us the permission. And the municipality doesn't have the budget. You know, the AKP's administration left us with a lot of debt. We had some friends at one construction firm; they provided the materials and some labor. Soon, the Chamber of Civil Engineers will also participate. Perhaps we can even get some funds from the ministry. If we go ourselves, they would never support us. But the Chamber of Civil Engineers may convince them." For the HDP, developing partnerships with private contractors or other partners would prevent the termination of the urban projects and sustain their construction.

In fact, the party members' wariness was proven justified. The HDP's victory in the Kurdish cities of Turkey was short-lived. HDP mayors were able to stay in power for only two months. As early as August 2019, state authorities once again began to detain newly elected mayors and replace them with their own bureaucrats in 95 of 102 mainly Kurdish municipalities. In December 2019, a couple of months after my visit, Sur municipality was taken over. The mayors of the city, some councilors, and staff members were first dismissed and later arrested for alleged ties to the PKK. In November 2020, Mayor C was imprisoned, only to be released in May 2021. Berzan was not arrested but was dismissed from office following the arrival of the AKP's bureaucrats. Berzan summarized his last day at the municipality: "I learned about the news that an AKP administrator [*kayyım*] was appointed to the municipality at four o'clock in the morning, when the private secretary called me. The next day the co-mayor was taken into custody. A person from the Diyarbakır Chamber of Architects and I worked on the neighborhood renovation project for three hours and delivered letters of approval to the Chamber of Architects and the Chamber of Commerce so that they can continue the project, even when we leave the municipality."

The military and juridical changes created by the AKP arrogated virtually all the powers that had been held by pro-Kurdish municipalities between 1999 and 2015. After the second time the AKP dismissed the elected mayors of Diyarbakır, the seizure of the municipality went to another level. Quickly, the AKP appointed the governor (*vali*) as the metropolitan municipality mayor and district governors (*kaymakams*) as district mayors. The municipality was not only pushed to the margins; this time, the function of the municipality itself was all but eliminated. The AKP's government practically abolished the municipality organs in Diyarbakır; by appointing governors and district governors as mayors, governors would conduct both positions—of governor and mayor—simultaneously. (For the distinct roles of governors and mayors in the city, see chapter 2). In practice, the two institutions merged into one single authority, eliminating the checks and balances that the two institutions working in parallel would provide in cities. Some district governors (*kaymakamlar*) began to manage from their former district offices, further collapsing the distinction between the roles.[37] By 2019, the AKP's rule in the city took on a centralized, disciplinary model looming over Kurdish residents.[38]

(De)Mobilization after the Conflict

In post-conflict Diyarbakır, while imposing an Islamic identity on the city, the AKP's reconstruction sought to refashion collective memory and dismantle Kurdish networks associated with specific sites and neighborhoods. Traces of demobilization in particular were manifestly evident in everyday life. A city known for its Kurdish mobilization and massive protests was silent. There was almost no street action. By 2019, in coffeehouses, the focus of everyday conversation had shifted from Kurdish politics to the economy and unemployment. Even if, from time to time, people did talk about the AKP's appointed mayoral bureaucrats and corruption in the city, they did not talk about the HDP as much as they used to. Between 2016 and 2023, each time I visited the city, I encountered almost no mass demonstrations. In public space, no more HDP flags or party posters appeared. Public billboards, once used to advertise Kurdish festivals and protests, displayed advertisements for household appliances or private schools.

Fear of conducting active politics was palpable among former officials of the HDP municipality and pro-Kurdish party members. For example, Sami (see chapter 5) was one of the top municipality officers who lost his job and position through the emergency decree. Sami was a teacher by training. But because he had been removed through KHK, like hundreds of other municipality staff, he was unable to return to his profession. And because of his ties to the party, Sami was having difficulty finding a job. Since his dismissal in 2016, he had worked in at least five different jobs—three different private schools in a single academic year. At the time of our interview in 2019, Sami was managing a lingerie store. He explained: "Each time they find out I was a member of the HDP, they fire me. Everyone is starving, jobless. You know, people are tired; they don't have the courage to conduct politics or to go out on the streets." In this environment, Sami and others like him began to avoid activism. In 2019, for three months, I regularly visited the municipality in Sur. No one there quoted Abdullah Öcalan while doing political or intellectual work. Between 2007 and 2015, Öcalan had been a standard reference among HDP activists and municipality members. I also learned that several activists whom I used to interview frequently, such as Hasan from the FPA and Saliha and Ahsen from women's organizations, had left Diyarbakır.[39]

The AKP's government was aware of the essential role that local associations and NGOs played in the Kurdish mobilization in the city. As I discussed previously, following the conflict, AKP officials aimed to dismantle the pro-Kurdish organizational network at the local level, with the express purpose of rechanneling the urban poor. They targeted both poverty alleviation associations and cultural associations. Thus, the government either shut down the party's existing neighborhood, financial, and women's associations, or replaced them with its own associations. The AKP wanted to capitalize, if it could, on established networks of the urban poor and refurbish the networks created by the pro-Kurdish party (see chapter 3). In some cases, for instance in Sur, the government did not even change the location of preexisting neighborhood associations; it merely changed their titles and, of course, their program and staff. These newly appropriated associations and organizations, like their HDP predecessors, included women's associations and poverty alleviation organizations. These associations, later placed in every district of Diyarbakır, were tied to the government and overseen by the district governor's office or the governorship. For example, the newly founded "Sur Youth Art Center" was operated by the AKP's Sur municipality, administered by *kayyım*, and coordinated by the Diyarbakır governor. Such a project was supported by the social support program (Sosyal Destek Programı) focused on art and sports classes, and fostered a "citizenship awareness" curriculum financed by the Ministry of Development.

Along with replacing existing organizations with its own, the government formed new groups and affiliations designed to maintain its authority and power over residents. With an aim to dismantle the Kurdish bloc in the city, the AKP supported recognized Islamist groups such as Peygamber Sevdalıları Vakfı

(Foundation of Prophet Lovers), especially their religious meetings and festivals, and even turned a blind eye to networks like Hezbollah, which the AKP did not approve of previously. City-sponsored Quran courses were also visibly expanded. These new organizations were visible on a daily basis, putting on Islamic events even in Newroz Park, a place famously devoted to annual Newroz celebrations. The face of the city changed abruptly—squares were draped with Turkish flags, and invitations to religious events covered neighborhood walls.

Arrests and surveillance generated an atmosphere of fear and apoliticism. During my interviews among activists and the supporters of the pro-Kurdish party, I encountered deep distrust of politics, even by those previously engaged in the issues. Derbas, a forty-year-old schoolteacher and member of the HDP, was living in Kayapınar. Although he and his family were not directly affected by the conflict, his words expressed the disenchantment with party politics: "The destruction of cities and the destruction of houses mean a lot to us. This carries deeper resonance, particularly for Kurds, as the concept of home holds profound meaning in our culture. Even when they thank you in daily life, they say 'malî ava.' This means may your house be built well and solid. Is everything better now? Not at all. . . . The declaration of autonomy radically changed everything, you see; it made it worse." The conflict and its aftermath, as well as the AKP's style of architectural governance and heavy militaristic methods of urbanism, effectively dispersed civil society. Combined, these factors began to weaken the pro-Kurdish party's ties with various support groups. During my fieldwork in the summer of 2019, I closely examined this unraveling. Civil society, even if it supported the party, was very hesitant to engage in street action.

For example, one day in July 2019, after being reelected, Sur's HDP municipality wanted to organize a public meeting with the neighbors to listen to their needs. Organizing public meetings in which mayors hear from the residents has long been common practice for the HDP. The day before the meeting, municipality workers walked through Sur, street by street, and invited residents to the public meeting. As I walked with one of the canvassers, I noted that these municipality members sounded very motivated in their invitation. The next day, when I arrived at the site of the meeting, I only saw empty seats. After a few minutes, a truck arrived, collected the empty chairs, and left. Later, I returned to the municipality to check with the party members. They all looked very disappointed. I learned that the meeting was canceled owing to low participation. Unlike 2000–2015, there was a disconnect between the political party and society. Before, any invitation from the municipality or the party would bring hundreds of residents together. Without much talking, they were all gathered on the top floor next to the mayor's office. I chatted about the incident with Berzan and another council member, Deniz, a young man who had an activist background working for a human rights association in Diyarbakır. "We lost our organization networks here," Deniz said. "But we will rebuild our networks again. We will recover soon." This remark was puzzling; even if votes showed support for the party, civil society was hesitant to participate in any public event. Berzan followed up:

> We cannot obtain the expected response from the neighborhood organizations. Nobody comes to street actions. After all, everyone is going after their bread. Even for a small gathering they record us on camera. They record everyone who attends.... Then they trace, one by one. No one wants to get arrested. They have families to take care of. No one would attend a meeting or a demonstration, but still they would say "I am a Kurd" and vote for the HDP here.

Under the post-conflict conditions, surveillance and control intensified in the city. Indeed, even for a small-scale meeting, police cameras would record each participant, and people could be arrested on the grounds of the new "state of emergency" declared after the coup attempt in 2016. Policing and surveillance measures prevented people from actively participating in campaigns in public space. The result was vanishing engagement not only among activists and party members but also among ordinary supporters. Havin stopped tweeting about politics, stopped seeing his activist friends and attending party meetings and seminars, which did not mean he stopped supporting the party. His withdrawal was partly a response to the atmosphere of fear provoked by the AKP's militaristic practices in the city. When I met with him after the conflict in 2016, his voice had lost its accustomed excitement when he talked about the movement. He was disappointed with the HDP.

When we met outdoors, or at a restaurant, Havin would never mention the AKP and was always careful, lowering his voice if commenting on politics. Wherever we went in the city, Havin would check multiple times who was sitting around us. "You never know," he said; "they [AKP supporters] are everywhere." The most expressive he would get was inside his car, while we were driving from one place to another in the city. The change in him over the years was striking. The Havin who hoped to be part of the future of Kurdistan had completely vanished. His words of admiration for the party and for the movement—words I used to hear each time we were together—had been replaced by expressions of resentment: "I lost my hope for this movement. There was a war here. A war! But no one cared about this war. Also, the party didn't care about us. They made a big mistake." When I asked him why he was angry with the party, he replied,

> Do you know when someone gives up hope on something, right at the moment when it's so close? We were so close! So close. They [the HDP]

made us believe, hope for our victory . . . our independence. But then, because of their terrible strategies, they deprived us from it. They could not develop realistic and correct moves. They took wrong decisions. What does it mean to dig a trench? How stupid that was! Look, I say this, I know I am angry, but I will still vote for the party. Of course, I will still support them. It is our cause! But from now on, I am not going to participate in any event. Nothing. I don't have time for that anymore. Not worth it.

Havin's words exemplified the sentiments of several Diyarbakırians I knew who had lost interest in active politics. In the summer of 2020, Havin left Diyarbakır. He resigned from his position and moved to Izmir, where he began working for a private technology firm. I was stunned, given his passion for Diyarbakır. When I began my fieldwork, I could never have imagined a single factor that would prompt him to move out of the city. He had even persuaded his relatives from Batman to move to Diyarbakır in the early 2000s. I asked him why he decided to move. He justified his decision as a change in his political views. He insisted that it was no longer worth it to stay in Diyarbakır. More interesting than Havin's unexpected move was how politics shaped his relationship with the city. For Havin, Diyarbakır meant Kurdishness and the Kurdish movement. The moment he disengaged from politics, he lost his ties with the city. Yet Havin stayed in Izmir only for one year; in 2021, he returned. He found a new job and moved into a new apartment. When I asked him about his return to Diyarbakır, he said, "Life was not as I expected in Izmir. I was even detained for a tweet that I tweeted years ago; later I was released." Then he added, "There is a saying from where we are: your destiny is the city where you were born. I cannot live outside of Diyarbakır, and there is always hope. Hope for us, for the movement." As Havin's words suggest, what made Diyarbakır the capital of Kurdish nationalism was pro-Kurdish engagement with urban politics.

In the summer of 2023, I once more returned to Diyarbakır. This time, I was able to step into the closed corners of Sur as TOKİ completed the renovation of conflict-impacted streets, now open for business. The AKP's influence persisted everywhere, with President Erdoğan's poster featuring the slogan "Toward the Century of Turkey with Correct Steps" prominently displayed on every street corner. It felt as though TOKİ's urban transformation of Sur had no end in sight.

As I entered the old city through the historic four-legged minaret, the Mar Petyun Keldani Catholic Church stood to my left. Ahead, an extensive, wide street unfolded, a stark contrast to the traditional intertwining byways of Sur. Similar to Baron Haussmann's transformation of Paris in the nineteenth century, the government-led urbanization had erased the accustomed random pattern of streets, replacing them with broad avenues lined with luxury stores, cafés, and restaurants. Behind these were large parking lots, housing units, and boutique hotels. Sur seemed to vanish before my eyes, its former street configurations impossible to trace. It felt like a loss of memory. The once almost impassably narrow streets now accommodated two cars side by side and even more. Among newly placed paving stones and sidewalk tiles, immature trees provided no shade.

Passing by AKP advertisements and franchised cafés like "Espresso Lab," I reached the souvenir shops. The change in the display of Turkish coffee packages reflected the city's transformation. Under the reign of the AKP's neo-Ottoman urban politics, the coffee packages labeled as "Kurdish coffee" during the heyday of Kurdish mobilization (see chapter 4) were now rebranded as "Ottoman coffee," in English and in Arabic script. After walking past the newly located Sur district governorship office (occupying the converted Süleyman Nazif elementary school, as there were no students left in the area) and a luxury clothing store offering brands like Gucci, Armani, and Calvin Klein, I ventured through a string of lavishly decorated restaurants. It took me just ten minutes to reach the other end of Sur, a journey that would normally take forty minutes, weaving through the narrow web of streets and alleys.

What they called the wide avenue I had traversed was the "Diyarbakır Suriçi Açıkhava ve Yaşam Merkezi" (Diyarbakır Suriçi Open-Air Living Center)— I learned this while visiting the TOKİ Real Estate Auction office on the avenue. An architect who was managing tender applications at the office described the area as follows: "Imagine here," she said, "like an open shopping mall, and TOKİ is the owner here, and we are its real estate office managing the lease of these shops." None of the shops or stores were for sale; all were leased by TOKİ for twenty-five years through a tender process. The highest bid above the predetermined reserve price secured the lease. When I inquired if they only leased and never sold, she said that while they leased the stores, some boutique hotels and houses in the Ali Paşa neighborhood would be for sale.

The land expropriated some six years earlier has now become a profit-generating asset for the government. TOKİ, known for its public housing projects, has emerged as a real estate tycoon. Furthermore, the Diyarbakır Surici Open-Air Living Center—an open-air shopping mall—is a prime example of the government's nationwide urban transformation practice. While being transmogrified into a government-designed leisure and tourism landscape, Sur has become devoid of historical value. The old city has been turned into a tourist hub, offering not just visitors but also the residents of Diyarbakır a sense of being tourists, even if it is their own city. Yet this is not solely about erasing the city's memory. Converting Sur's streets into a bustling tourist destination is, in essence, a homogenization, an eradicating of spaces of mobilization while rendering the city no different from any other similarly homogenized "Anatolian" city.

The case of post-2016 Diyarbakır demonstrates how military power and neoliberal urbanization (including creating landscapes of tourism) limit mobilization despite the strength of previous political commitments. As Perry Anderson asserts, even very rigid hegemonic political structures can be straddled and dissolved by war.[40] The AKP's concurrent military, governmental, and urban intervention impacted both civil and political society. To guarantee their rule in the city, the AKP's regime first seized municipalities and later defunctionalized them through amendments to law and expulsions. By the end of 2018, political society was partially tamed—and effectively dispersed from public space. When the fighting was over, the HDP was unable to sustain the active mobilization as it once had. The AKP saw post-conflict conditions as a golden opportunity to re-create Diyarbakır through its vision of "one nation." State officials deployed the tools of urban development and Islamic culture to dismantle the Kurdish bloc in the city. State intervention in the post-2016 period suggests that states can rely on the tools of neoliberal urbanism to perpetuate their rule. New Islamist planning (including making neo-Ottoman tourism landscapes and building great mosques in the city) merged with militarized conditions, supporting the ideals of a neoliberal city designed by government officials.

In fact, the processes of postwar destruction and reconstruction were not only a matter of rebuilding a new memory; they aimed to eviscerate Kurdish networks in the city associated with specific sites and neighborhoods. After the AKP's intervention, Kurdish civil society and political society were almost disarticulated. The AKP's militarized neoliberalism, however, was not adequate to establish hegemonic control over Kurdish society. Even though street action in Diyarbakır had weakened, the link between the party and civil society had not been completely severed. The radical urban interventions of the AKP on different scales merged with the heavy consequences of conflict: exile, mass arrests, and dismissals, creating an atmosphere of fear and a loss of interest in politics that, in effect, led to a decline in mobilization—but not to its end.

CONCLUSION
Wiggle Room

This book is the product of many years of research and writing. The circumstances of Kurdish politics in Turkey when I began my research were completely different from those at the time of this book's completion. Over the course of my sixteen years of research, I witnessed the rise of nationhood, the articulation of political identity, urban mobilization of a political movement, distinct practices of violence and oppression of political and civil society, and an urban struggle to keep the nationness and mobilization alive. During my research, the Diyarbakır Metropolitan Municipality changed mayors six times. Many of the mayors I interviewed were imprisoned and later released. Some escaped to Europe to avoid prison. Some are still being held. After the war in 2016, all top officials of all Diyarbakır municipalities, urban planners, architects, and directors of urban planning and of cultural affairs were dismissed from their positions. According to the KHK emergency decree, they can never be rehired or work in a public sector again. Those who were fortunate were able to open their own business or find a job in a private company; others are likely still unemployed. As I conclude this book, the political momentum may not be very promising for Diyarbakır and the Kurds in Turkey.

Since 2016, each time I have visited Diyarbakır I have seen the destruction of streets I once walked on. I saw the demolition of houses whose courtyards I once sat in and the disappearance of NGOs I used to visit. I watched new construction projects ripping away the city's identity. I witnessed how conflict, unemployment, deep coercion, and fear of arrest caused several activists and party members I know to sit silent, in reserve. I observed the politics and the city change drastically, in good and bad ways. The multiple means by which pro-Kurdish parties used municipal power to articulate Kurdish nationhood, and later the way AKP officials seized the municipalities and urbanization, offer testimony to Peter Marcuse's remark that "neither cities nor places in them are unordered, unplanned; the question is only whose order, whose planning, for what purpose."[1]

Nevertheless, the cities are not hopeless. As I discussed at the beginning of this book, the ways that the pro-Kurdish party deployed urban planning demonstrates that there is a possibility of wiggle room—space in which opposition can struggle, mobilize, at times even achieve social justice and equality.

Studying wiggle room, I suggest, is a way of deciphering the capacities of urban space and urban networks for mobilization. The wiggle room would allow one to explore new alternative ways to turn oppression into opportunity for dissent against political order and to build resilience against unevenly woven landscapes of capitalist and authoritarian urban fabric. Pro-Kurdish party officials were able to open up such an operating space through diverse urban actions such as finding the flaws in existing municipal laws (initially created by the AKP for their own advantage); securing external funding from a European institute when their funds were cut by the central government; establishing grassroots support in the city; contracting with private firms to guarantee completion of their work during a possible municipal occupation or their dismissal by government officials; and creatively turning state oppression into a vehicle for urban mobilization. Such an operating space helped the party battle state coercion and articulate the Kurdish movement. From the ways municipality officials named parks "blank" in protesting the governor's decision, to the ways they creatively exploited urban loopholes to keep informal settlers in the city, the pro-Kurdish party persistently opened up wiggle room to maneuver in the city.

One of the capabilities of wiggle room is demonstrated by the ways the pro-Kurdish party brought both formal and informal organizations together in the city. Party members made women's organizations, cultural centers, youth, and activist networks collaborate, leading to urban mobilization. The connection of urban networks helped the wiggle room expand considerably—and all of these actions required extensive coordination, leadership, and planning by the party.

In this book, I demonstrated how political assertions and struggles take spatial forms amid neoliberalism, oppression, and nationalism. The significance of space—sites of engagement—lies not only in the power of design to challenge authorities but also in the capacity of urban planning and even unplanning to support more inclusive forms of pluralist governance. None of this implies that one specific formula for urban struggle exists; there are multiple ways to find wiggle room, including both the mobilization and immobilization of urban law;

distinct formulations of participatory planning (from neighborhood representatives to associations connecting both formal and informal groups); community organization; confronting the state through the production of art and architecture; the development of urban dissent; powerful mobilization of citizens; and the expansion of urban informal networks—all of which stem from the flexibility and adaptability of urban planning practice instead of blindly following a constitutionally mandated formulation of urban policy. One should consider the moments of planning and unplanning—as the municipality fought to preserve the squatter settlements in Sur, it continued its rapid pace of urban development across the rest of the city. The way the pro-Kurdish party deployed urban planning underscores the significance of spatial analysis if one seeks to understand social and political mobilizations, interrelationships of states and society, alignments with associations and civil society, and identity politics in the city.

One of the most compelling aspects of the pro-Kurdish party is that it manages to persist while being constantly under investigation and on the brink of closure as its members are routinely imprisoned, shut down, taken to court, subject to confiscation, or banned from conducting politics. Such conditions require party members to understand the changing dynamics of both political and civil society and to be creative and develop new strategies for wiggle room. The movement's recent effort to revamp the YSP (Green Left Party, initially founded by the pro-Kurdish movement in 2012) for the 2023 elections, in the face of the HDP's impending closure, is another variation of the wiggle room that the pro-Kurdish movement has practiced over the years in distinct forms. In mid-2021, the chief public prosecutor's office of the Supreme Court of Appeals filed a lawsuit demanding the closure of the HDP on the grounds that it is "the focus of terrorist activities, and HDP members aim to disrupt and destroy the indivisible national integrity of the state."[2] In the 850-page indictment, the prosecutor's office demanded a full political activity ban for some five hundred party members, including the party's cochairs. This ban was intended to prevent the Kurdish movement from repeating its old tactic of establishing another party after the previous one was shut down. By targeting not only the formal party apparatus but also Kurdish politicians on such a wide scale, this new development has serious implications for the movement's ability to survive. In the 2023 parliamentary elections, the YSP secured 8.8 percent of the vote, while the HDP had previously won 11.7 percent in 2018.[3] Later, as the HDP merged with the YSP, the YSP underwent a name change to become the Peoples' Equality and Democracy Party (HEDEP), bearing a closer resemblance to the HDP. By the end of 2023, however, the Peoples' Equality and Democracy Party announced a further alteration of its acronym from HEDEP to DEM Parti, because of the Court of Cassation's objection citing "similarity to closed HADEP." Notably, the

Constitutional Court had closed HADEP in 2003 on the allegation of its being the center of illegal activities.[4]

The Famous Urban Question

The scope of the book has expanded to accommodate the litany of questions and gaps of knowledge I have accumulated over several years. Originally, I wanted to understand what is urban about nationalism and political articulation in the twenty-first century. The scholarship examining the relationship between the nationalism and the built environment has often looked at the articulation of nationhood through modern architecture and planning practices. Yet Diyarbakır has been outside such a framework in two ways. First, Diyarbakır, although a Kurdish nationalist city, has never been a modern city. This is not only because Diyarbakır had associated modernism with the Turkish Republic since the beginning of the twentieth century and developed resistance to modern architectural culture, but also because Diyarbakır has never fully intended to accommodate homogeneous modern architecture and planning. Instead, Diyarbakır accommodated its own plurality. The city produced its own version of postmodernity by welcoming diverse traditions. Diyarbakır has been a postmodern city, with all of the ruptures, fragmentations, and conflicts such a label implies. This book shows the rise of nationalism in a postmodern city. The postmodern Diyarbakır expressed itself through an urban imaginary of Kurdishness, composed of a conglomeration of ideas, memories, exaggerated symbolism, and colorful persuasive messages.

Second, Diyarbakır has never been the official capital of Kurdistan; I examined nationalism in Diyarbakır in the absence of a nation-state. I demonstrated the articulation of nationalism in a postmodern and neoliberal city amid the government's oppressive and coercive practices. I illustrated how urban forms aren't simply the setting of a city, where political struggles unfold; they constitute the very essence of these struggles. Hence, I have aimed to extend recent scholarship by investigating the power of place-making to incite large societal transformations without the backbone of a nation-state.

The pro-Kurdish party and its mayors did not necessarily build Kurdish nationalism via tangible memorial landscapes but more from their ability to reproduce memories of violence embedded in the urban landscape. From housing projects to public demonstrations, party members have actively woven memorial activism into the city and articulated a politicized Kurdish identity. In every single project—the inauguration of a new road, the installation of a memorial, or an art workshop—they effectively orchestrated the forum of national membership in the city. These urban projects invoked Kurdish nationhood by promoting common goals, street mobilization, culture, and historical memories—through which Diyarbakırians can consider themselves members of that nation.[5] Going beyond local circumstances, this book traces the agency of urban space—the built environment and urbanism—for political mobilization and demobilization in the twenty-first-century city.

Over the course of my research, one of the main questions I have wrestled with is how to examine political mobilization in a neoliberal city. Diyarbakır is not a "global" city like Istanbul, London, Dubai, Paris, Madrid, or Mumbai, which exist among the circuits of transnational capital. However, with forceful sites of commodification and consumption, large-scale urban development and well-off housing projects, Diyarbakır is one of thousands of cities across the globe in which neoliberal urbanism is strongly felt in the ways it constantly takes shape.

Scholars of neoliberal urbanism have long focused on the impact of markets on cities.[6] A significant body of scholarship examines how neoliberalism might offer a mode of governance for state control over populations, one that forms new organizations of citizenship and social behavior.[7] More recent scholarship looks at how that state employs modes of urban neoliberalism for control over populations, forming new organizations of citizenship and social behavior.[8]

This book extends this scholarship by demonstrating how neoliberal urbanism, reinforcing its own pattern and order, can be dressed up with urban development and progress to serve identity politics. I study the relationship between identity politics and neoliberal urbanism in two ways: First, I investigate the neoliberal mode of the pro-Kurdish party. I examine how the rise of nationalism and political articulation in Diyarbakır was entangled with—and deployed—neoliberal modes of urbanism.[9] I deliver accounts of the sites of consumption and urban development when they matter to the sense of nationness and how they are symbolically embraced for Kurdish mobilization and the articulation of the Kurdish bloc.

Second, I study urban neoliberalism from the state's practices. I illustrate how neoliberal urbanism and state power coexist and can even correlate, whereby "the nation-state remains fundamentally a territorial organization," regardless of whether it engages with a neoliberal territory.[10] I demonstrate how neoliberal urbanism can be systemically used for government efforts to create desired forms of citizenship, in this case for demobilizing and controlling a minority population. The neoliberal territorial design and the state's territory became practically indistinguishable. I investigated the state's militarized planning approach in order to discuss the emergence of new modes of governmentalities premised on a neoliberal urban treatment of Diyarbakır. Similar to modern planning practices that governments used to shape their societies at the turn of the twentieth century, neoliberal urbanism can be a strong instrument for controlling, repressing, and assimilating minorities in the twenty-first century.

Urbanists have debated "the urban question" since the nineteenth century. More recently, Andy Merrifield, referring to Manuel Castell's famous urban question, asserted that we need a new urban question because "stakes and arenas of struggle have changed markedly since the day Castell wrote the Urban Question."[11] Merrifield cogently argues that the new urban question must be countered by something "much more expansive, something much more far-reaching: by an urban political movement that struggles for generalized democracy."[12] I would defend this position even more vigorously. The twenty-first-century city is more complex, and thus the urban equation might reinvent itself as an ambiguous area, a fluid space in which multiple urban actors can operate. From my point of view, in the face of increasingly dispersed and rapidly transforming urbanization across the world—indeed, in the face of emerging authoritarian forms of urban governance, notwithstanding evolving forms of pro-equality urban governance elsewhere—the urban question must be studied through more detailed and nuanced analysis. This book looks at the urban question as a puzzle, as an equation with multivariate, intersecting gray zones, ambiguous sites, and slippery power relations. Key to this investigation is the "ethnography of urban maneuvers," an approach that speaks to the challenges of investigating versatile power relations in urban space. My field of engagement, an ethnography of urban maneuvers, allowed me to map multiple opposing and intersecting powers in the city and to understand the ways in which urban planning, and sometimes conscious unplanning, creates hubs for conducting opposition and resisting state coercion. Thus, I show how political society (the state, political parties, municipalities, and governors) and civil society (informal networks, women's groups, and cultural and religious associations) align, interact, and confront or evade each other in urban space.

I also provide accounts of urban circumstances that push the boundaries between political and civil societies, between municipality, political party, and grass roots, creating a new form of urban networking. This urban networking and oscillation between grass roots and political parties allowed the pro-Kurdish movement to fill in the blanks between urban institutions, spaces, society, and action. The interconnection of diverse civic organizations not only amalgamated the links between society and party but also led the party to provide alternative forms of self-administration.

The details of these urban circumstances are grounded in the particulars of each case, but the lines of urban analysis are applicable in a wide range of other settings. The diverse accounts of the pro-Kurdish party and its urban activism suggest that the urban equation cannot be formulated with only two variables, as interventions of the state versus the responses of ordinary people in the city. Such complex, floating urban relations are not unique to Diyarbakır but are embedded in the global and transnational transactions of struggle for urban justice and equality, in debates about privileged people, minorities, people of color, disadvantaged populations, as well as in real estate and urbanization decisions, and urban development in relation to all these factors.

In this light, the call of Oren Yiftachel that invited urban theorists to devote their attention to "the question of planning as control" is exigent. The challenge he posed was to consider and broaden our understanding of the "causes, consequences and the use of traditional modernist planning methods to control minority populations."[13] In this light, urban theorists have already recognized that modernist planning does not necessarily make cities better, and that indeed "order and rationality" cannot necessarily replace chaos and irrationality. If modern planning policies have been an attempt to impose order, contemporary urbanism reinforces its own order and pattern, which depends on who governs the city. This book extends this discussion by suggesting two realms of research: "planning as control" and "planning as empowerment."

I sought to show how urban planning is capable of bending rigid political structures and creating political blocs and alliances, and the ways in which urban space allows for optimism and possibility, new and distinct strategic alliances and networks for resistance and opposition even if these alliances and movements are incomplete and contested. But of course all of this can only happen when there is a certain level of democracy. Urban space's capacity for emancipation certainly shrinks, as this book demonstrates, under authoritarian-like practices and military rule.

What this book implies is that understanding the emergent strategies and orchestration of the capacities of the urban space requires more research and further analysis by urbanists as well as architectural historians, geographers, and cultural and political theorists. Such analysis cannot be conducted solely through analytical approaches of socioeconomic and neoliberal consequence, but may be illuminated using distinct and ranging intellectual conceptual tools and research sites that examine the politics of racial, ethnic, and religious minorities and the emergent topographies of identity politics. Examining how various yet legal arrangements constantly change urban laws and policies, state power, regimes of property rights and housing, and political strategies, as well as shape societies, foster inequalities, and endanger minority rights, remains central to the project of critical urban studies.

Along these lines, I have suggested two main analytical frameworks in urban analysis: First is the consideration of the slippery slope of party, state, and society relations in the city, rather than fixed lenses of state or nongovernmental actors.

Second is examination of the creative capacity of planning to shape politics (as an innovative resource to mobilize society, articulate political identity, and endure forces of coercion), as opposed to politics merely shaping urban space. Both of these frameworks of analysis will help us understand new, emerging patterns of inequalities; help us contribute to spatial justices and equities amid new emerging orders and social, political, and spatial processes; and further our effort to discover the possibilities of empowerment and emancipation in the contemporary city.

Notes

INTRODUCTION

1. Bozarslan, "Kurds and the Turkish State." See also Erdem, "Türkiyeli Kürtler Ne Kadar?" Following the 1965 census, the Turkish government outlawed the publication of information about ethnicity and language across the country.
2. Gunter, *Historical Dictionary of the Kurds*, 44.
3. Havin is traditionally a female Kurdish name; however, Havin is a male, and I chose this pseudonym with him.
4. Brubaker, *Ethnicity without Groups*.
5. As I discuss in the first chapter, pro-Kurdish parties in Turkey have repeatedly been closed by constitutional court orders. However, as each party has been closed, another with a new name has been founded by party officials in its place. Even when the party avoids closure, it may opt to change its name. For practical purposes, then, I will use the phrase "pro-Kurdish party" interchangeably with the actual names of pro-Kurdish parties to refer to the succession of parties holding a pro-Kurdish identity.
6. During our conversation, Havin mentioned the trash collection service because during that time trash collection was one of the major problems in Diyarbakır; particularly in Sur, the dump trucks could not get in because of its narrow streets, and some residents would leave their trash in front of their houses.
7. Koz and İşli, *Diyarbakır*.
8. Koz and İşli, *Diyarbakır*.
9. Also known as *beylerbeyliks*, *eyalets* were a primary administrative division of the Ottoman Empire.
10. TUİK (Turkish Statistical Institute), "Population and Demographics."
11. Ayata and Yükseker, "Belated Awakening."
12. Yadirgi, *Political Economy of the Kurds of Turkey*.
13. TUİK, "Regional Results of Income and Living Conditions Survey."
14. For an account of Kurdish nationalism in Diyarbakır at the beginning of the twentieth century see Malmîsanij, *Yirminci Yüzyılın Başında Diyarbekir'de Kürt Ulusçuluğu*.
15. For a detailed examination of the Sheikh Said Rebellion see Olson, *Emergence of Kurdish Nationalism*.
16. See Vale in his argument on the expression of political power: "I seek to explore the ways that a variety of national regimes have used architecture and urban design to express political power and control and to investigate how designers have manipulated the urban built environment to promote a version of identity that would support and legitimize this rule." Vale, *Architecture, Power and National Identity*, xii.
17. See, for example, Bozdoğan, *Modernism and Nation Building*; Kusno, *Behind the Postcolonial*; Kezer, *Building Modern Turkey*; Vale, *Architecture, Power and National Identity*.
18. See, for instance, Ghirardo, *Architecture after Modernism*; Lane, *Architecture and Politics in Germany*.
19. Holston, *Modernist City*.
20. See, for example, Wedeen, *Peripheral Visions*; Brubaker, *Nationalism Reframed*; Brubaker, *Ethnicity without Groups*.

21. Brubaker, *Nationalism Reframed*, 21.
22. Brubaker, 21.
23. Brubaker, 21.
24. Brubaker, *Ethnicity without Groups*.
25. Laclau and Mouffe, *Hegemony and Socialist Strategy*, 105.
26. De Leon, Desai, and Tuğal, *Building Blocs,* 3–5.
27. De Leon, Desai, and Tuğal, 3–5.
28. De Leon, Desai, and Tuğal, 94–95.
29. It is important to note that, during this time, the PKK and its civic networks transferred their experience of mass mobilization from rural conditions to an urban context with a particular organizational and networking dynamism.
30. See, for instance, Davis, *Cities and Sovereignty*.
31. Brenner, Marcuse, and Mayer, *Cities for People, Not for Profit*.
32. Roy, "21st-Century Metropolis"; Yiftachel, "From Displacement to Displaceability"; Watson, "Shifting Approaches to Planning Theory"; Miraftab, "Insurgent Planning."
33. Brenner, Madden, and Wachsmuth, "Assemblages, Actor-Networks"; Jessop, *State Power*; Simone, *Jakarta, Drawing the City Near*; Bayat, *Life as Politics*; Bou Akar, *For the War Yet to Come*.
34. For instance, in her work on Yemen, Lisa Wedeen demonstrates that experiences of national belonging and identity can be generated by everyday practices of collective vulnerability rather than by state institutions and their representations, or through industrialization. She argues that national solidarities and identities are not necessarily formed through top-down interventions, because they are not made once and for all. More particularly, she remarks that "national identity is not given by, nor are people born with, national attachment; rather, it can be made and remade through different sets of practices." Wedeen, *Peripheral Visions*, 92–93. See also Agnew and Corbridge, *Mastering Space*; Brenner, *New State Spaces*.
35. See Migdal, *State in Society*; Mitchell, "Society, Economy, and the State Effect"; and Jessop, *State Power*.
36. Tuğal, "Urban Dynamism of Islamic Hegemony."
37. Migdal, *State in Society*; de Leon, *Party and Society*.
38. See, for instance, Davis, *Cities and Sovereignty*.
39. Burawoy, "Extended Case Method"; Burawoy, "Revisits."
40. Burawoy, "Extended Case Method"; Burawoy, "Revisits."
41. Brubaker, *Nationalist Politics*, 11.

1. WHOSE CITY?

1. In the Ottoman era, *mutasarrıf* was an administrative authority of certain sanjacks (administrative divisions of the Ottoman Empire) who were appointed directly by the sultan. The last name of Said Paşa appears as "Diyarbekirli," which means "from Diyarbekir." Said Paşa was originally from Diyarbekir. He was the governor of Mardin, which at that time was a town within the Diyarbekir region. The name of the city was changed from "Diyarbekir" to "Diyarbakır" under orders by Atatürk in 1938.
2. Said Paşa, *Diyarbekir vilâyetinin tarihçesi*, 2.
3. Said Paşa, 14.
4. Günkut, *Diyarbekir Tarihi*, 22–23.
5. By the early 1930s Atatürk introduced the "Turkish History Thesis" in a series of official conferences and publications, arguing that many civilizations had come from Turkish origins, including the Medes, whom Kurds consider their ancestors. For further discussion see Cagaptay, "Race, Assimilation and Kemalism."

6. Günkut, *Diyarbekir Tarihi*, 22–23.
7. Günkut, 22–23.
8. It is worth noting that the discourse of "Turkish nationalism" was not new to the republic. Indeed, it emerged as a cultural movement in the late nineteenth century during the Ottoman period, particularly under the "Young Turk" movement. See Üngör, *Making of Modern Turkey*.
9. Konyar, *Diyarbekir*, 5.
10. Scott, *Seeing like a State*, 82.
11. Although the state recognized the existence of diverse minorities, it would no longer recognize the cultural rights of the minorities. Further, all non-Turkish residents of the country (other than Armenians, Greeks, and Jews) now had to become Turkish. Following this approach, by the 1930s any resistance movement was perceived and managed as a social problem under the influence of bandits, sheikhs, landlords, and tribes in the region.
12. Gellner, *Nations and Nationalism*, 1.
13. Özerdim, *Atatürk devrimi Kronolojisi*, 93. It is important to note that during this early period of the republic, non-Muslim citizens of Turkey were also subject to several types of discrimination. For instance, the State Employee Law, endorsed in 1926, made Turkishness a necessary condition to becoming a state employee. Similarly, the Wealth Tax Law, enacted in 1942, aimed to seize an important part of the wealth owned by non-Muslims in Turkey. For further discussion see Oran, *Türkiye'de azınlıklar*; Yeğen, "'Prospective-Turks' or 'Pseudo-Citizens'"; Cagaptay, "Race, Assimilation and Kemalism."
14. Üngör, *Making of Modern Turkey*, 64.
15. Weber, *Politics as a Vocation*; Herb and Kaplan, *Nested Identities*, 10.
16. Jongerden, *Settlement Issue in Turkey*, 2.
17. Açikyildiz, "Ideology, Nationalism, and Architecture."
18. The name of the city in 1932, Diyarbekir, literally means the land of "bekir," which is believed to come from the word "bakır," meaning "copper." Atatürk's statement was given before he changed the name of the city from "Diyarbekir" to "Diyarbakır."
19. Diyarbakır Üniversitesi, *Atatürk ve Diyarbakir*, 99.
20. Kezer, *Building Modern Turkey*.
21. Çınar, "Imagined Community as Urban Reality," 151.
22. Turam, *Between Islam and the State*.
23. Gambetti, "Decolonizing Diyarbakır."
24. Gambetti, "Decolonizing Diyarbakır"; Diyarbakır Valiliği, *Cumhuriyetin 15inci yılında Diyarbakır*, 96.
25. Üngör, "Creative Destruction."
26. Diken, *Sırrını Surlarına Fısıldayan Şehir*, 40–42, 87–93. Also see Beysanoğlu, *Anıtları ve kitâbeleri ile Diyarbakır tarihi*, 3:1033–37.
27. Diyarbakır Valiliği, *Cumhuriyetin 15inci yılında Diyarbakır*, 25–27.
28. Kezer, *Building Modern Turkey*, 168.
29. Jongerden, *Settlement Issue in Turkey*.
30. These institutions included boarding schools, the National Schools (Millet Mektepleri) (1928), the Public Orators' Institution of the Republican People's Party (CHP Halk Hatipleri Teşkilatı) (1931), the Turkish Historical Society (Türk Tarih Kurumu) (1931), People's Houses (Halkevleri) (1932), the Turkish Language Society (Türk Dil Kurumu) (1932), the Faculty of Language History and Geography (Dil Tarih Coğrafya Fakültesi) (1936), and People's Rooms (Halkodaları) (1939–1940).
31. Mustafa Kemal Paşa (Ataturk's name at the time) first arrived in the Diyarbekir (now Diyarbakır) region in March 1916. He was appointed brigadier general, head of the Sixteenth Corps of the Ottoman army.

32. Mustafa Kemal references the music of the People's House band.
33. Diyarbakır Üniversitesi, *Atatürk ve Diyarbakır*, 26.
34. When the Diyarbakır People's House first opened, it initially used the building of the Diyarbakır Turk Ocağı (Turkish Hearth). It is also argued that People's Houses were built on the political base of Turkish Hearts (Türk Ocakları), an organization disseminating Turkishness and Turkish nationalism, founded in 1912. For further discussion see Karaömerlioğlu, "People's Houses"; Ozer, "Türk Modernleşmesinde Halkevleri ve Diyarbakır Halkevi Örneği." More information on Turkish Hearts can be found in Üstel, *İmparatorluktan ulus-devlete Türk milliyetçiligi*; and Karaer, *Türk Ocaklari*.
35. Yeşilkaya, *Halkevleri*, 125.
36. Özer, "Türk Modernleşmesinde Halkevleri ve Diyarbakır Halkevi Örneği."
37. By the end of 1930s there were around 160 People's Houses in the country.
38. *Diyarbekire bir bakış; Cumhuruyetin büyük eserlerinden olan tren Diyarbekire yeni bir hayat getirdi*, 7.
39. Özer, "Türk Modernleşmesinde Halkevleri ve Diyarbakır Halkevi Örneği," 680.
40. Özer, 680.
41. Diken, *Sırrını Surlarına Fısıldayan Şehir*, 172.
42. Diken, *Diyarbekir Diyarım, Yitirmişem Yanarım*, 71.
43. In 1925, Kurds, led by the religious leader Sheikh Said, revolted against the Turkish Republic. It took three months for government forces to suppress the rebellion, during which the rebels seized control of several towns in the East. For an assessment of the rebellion see Olson, *Kurdish Nationalist Movement*, 19. These reports were kept secret but became available with Mehmet Bayrak's book *Kurdology Documents (Kürdoloji Belgeleri)*, which includes a collection of secret governmental documents. To date, few scholars have discussed them, with the exception of Mesut Yeğen, "'Prospective-Turks' or 'Pseudo-Citizens.'"
44. Bayrak, *Açık-Gizli, Resmi-Gayrıresmi Kürdoloji Belgeleri*, 253–55.
45. Bayrak, 255. It is also important to note that, as Uğur Ümit Üngör argues, the Young Turk government's deportation of natives from the city actually began before the foundation of the republic. First, there was the 1915 deportation of Armenians, which was followed by the deportations of Kurds in 1916. For local accounts see Çelik and Dinç, *Yüz yıllık Ah*.
46. These forced evacuations, settlements, and resettlements of the early republican period were not the last massive displacement of populations within the borders of Turkey. By the late 1980s and 1990s, the Republic of Turkey orchestrated another massive wave of forced displacement, which I discuss in the following section.
47. Öktem, "Nation's Imprint," 67.
48. It is widely accepted that the emergence and development of the Kurdish national movement dates back to Sheikh Ubaydallah's rebellions in 1879–1881, which included Kurds of the Ottoman Empire. Right before the foundation of the republic, the first serious revolt was the Koçgiri uprising against the assembly of Turkey. See also Jwaideh, *Kurdish National Movement*; Bruinessen, *Kurdish Ethno-Nationalism versus Nation-Building States*; and Heper, *State and Kurds in Turkey*.
49. For various descriptions of "decades of silence" see McDowall, *Modern History of the Kurds*; White, *Primitive Rebels or Revolutionary Modernisers?*, 200; Ahmed and Gunter, *Evolution of Kurdish Nationalism*.
50. Jongerden, *Settlement Issue in Turkey*.
51. See Burkay, *Anılar, belgeler*; Tezcür, "Violence and Nationalist Mobilization."
52. Nicole Watts, "Silence and Voice."
53. "Minister Elçi Spoke: There Are Kurds in Turkey and I Am a Kurd Too," *Hürriyet* newspaper, April 19, 1979.

54. Bozarslan, *Doğu'nun Sorunları*, 15.
55. For a similar discussion see Yavuz, "Five Stages."
56. Tilly, *Contentious Performances*.
57. Diken, *Amidalılar*, 57.
58. Aren, *TİP Olayı, 1961–1971*, 70–71.
59. Ballı, *Kürt Dosyası*, 189.
60. Kaya, *Mapping Kurdistan*, 148.
61. For further discussion on Eastern questions see Kaya, *Mapping Kurdistan*, 148.
62. Ekinci, *Sol siyaset sorunları*, 306.
63. Bozarslan, "Kurdish Nationalism."
64. Güneş, *Kurdish National Movement in Turkey*.
65. During this period, the PKK announced a unilateral cease-fire on multiple occasions, in 1993, 1995, 1998, 1999, 2006, 2009, and finally in 2013, which ended in 2015. See also Tezcür, "Violence and Nationalist Mobilization"; Jongerden and Akkaya, "Born from the Left"; and Güneş, *Kurdish National Movement in Turkey*.
66. İmset, *PKK*.
67. Jongerden and Akkaya, "Born from the Left."
68. PKK (Türkiye), *Kürdistan devriminin yolu*, 39, 60.
69. Güneş, *Kurdish National Movement in Turkey*.
70. PKK (Türkiye), *Kürdistan devriminin yolu*, 20.
71. PKK (Türkiye), 100–101.
72. In the rural areas the village guard system was composed of local Kurds fighting on the side of the government against the PKK and secret gendarme units of the state's "anti-terror struggle," called Jitem. Also, the liberalization of the economy after 1980 reduced state support for agriculture and led to the upsurge in rural-to-urban migration. Keyder and Yenal, "Agrarian Change under Globalization."
73. See PKK (Türkiye), *Kürdistan devriminin yolu*, 39, 60.
74. See also Watts, *Activists in Office*.
75. Demirel said, "We acknowledge the Kurdish reality": *Milliyet*, 1992. It is also important to note that President Turgut Özal, before Demirel, had a more liberal approach to the Kurdish question than any other politician during the 1990s.
76. See, for instance, White, *Primitive Rebels or Revolutionary Modernisers?*, 218.
77. For a discussion of the "creativity" of political parties see de Leon et al., *Building Blocs*, 1–35.
78. Even the HEP and its successors frequently sustained a link with the PKK (the Kurdistan Workers Party). Turkey's first pro-Kurdish parties cannot be simply considered a front for the PKK. See Somer, "Turkey's Kurdish Conflict"; Watts, "Re-considering State Society Dynamics."
79. Demokrat Haber, "HDK yerel Seçim strajesini açıkladı."
80. Watts, "Re-considering State-Society Dynamics."
81. Watts, *Activists in Office*, 143.
82. Watts, 143.
83. For further discussion of Kurdish symbolism see chapter 5.
84. The Democratic opening process aimed "to improve standards of democracy, freedom, and respect for human rights in Turkey." Some aspects of this initiative that sought to expand Kurdish rights for those living in the country included opening TV station broadcasting in Kurdish and giving approval for universities to teach the Kurdish and Zazaki languages among other "living" languages. However, and at the same time, the country witnessed the imprisonment of pro-Kurdish politicians, mayors, activists, and community leaders as a result of their "pro-PKK" separatist activities in the city. In fact, because of the country's rapidly changing political environment, in the span of two

years some of my interviewees were detained and released again, while others remain in prison.

85. Tuğal, *Passive Revolution*, 33.
86. De Leon, Desai, and Tuğal, *Building Blocs*, 27.
87. For further discussion of the roles of governors and mayors in Turkish cities see chapter 2.
88. See introduction.

2. BUILDING THE FRONTIER

1. Enson Haber, "Diyarbakır'da Olaylar Çıktı," 2012.
2. As scholars have stressed, we should also pay attention to systemic powers shaping urban societies beyond capitalist urbanization. See, for instance, Yiftachel, "From Displacement to Displaceability."
3. Yiftachel, "Planning and Social Control," 396–400; see also Yiftachel, "From Displacement to Displaceability," 6.
4. These divisions are based on geographical features, economic conditions, and public service requirements (City Administration Law accepted in 1949, no. 5442).
5. According to City Administration Law accepted in 1949, no. 5442.
6. According to 1982 Constitution Article No. 127.
7. However, the first municipality practices of the Ottoman Empire began in Istanbul's Beyoğlu District in 1876.
8. Tekeli, *Cumhuriyetin belediyecilik öyküsü*, 186–87; Danielson and Keleş, *Politics of Rapid Urbanization*.
9. Finkel, "Municipal Politics and the State."
10. The first democratization practices of municipalities began in 1945 with the founding of the Turkish Municipality Association (Türk Belediyecilik Derneği). Andrew Finkel, "Municipal Politics and the State in Contemporary Turkey," in *Turkish State, Turkish Society*, ed. Andrew Finkel and Nükhet Sirman (London: Routledge, 1990), 185–218.
11. Tezcür, *Oxford Handbook of Turkish Politics*.
12. Finkel, "Municipal Politics and the State."
13. During the same period, municipalities became legally responsible for such municipal services as "transportation, urban development, urban renovation and restoration, infrastructure, city information systems, environment and environmental health, and the renovation and development of public parks, as well as social services and aid, such as marriage services, vocational and skill development training." Heper, *Dilemmas of Decentralization*; İncioğlu, "Local Elections," 73–90. For independence of municipalities see Koçak, "Legislative Reforms in Turkey," 9–18. It is important to note, however, that even this independence had its limitations; for example, all city plans required approval by the Ministry of Planning, with the exception of the master plans.
14. İncioğlu, "Local Elections," 73–90.
15. Tuğal, *Passive Revolution*, 49–53.
16. See Cihan Tuğal, *Passive Revolution*, 147–50.
17. Dorronsoro and Watts, "Toward Kurdish Distinctiveness," 457–78.
18. Mehdi Zana, interview by Maşallah Dekak, "Mehdi Zana: Kararı Leyla ile birlikte aldık."
19. Dorronsoro and Watts, "Toward Kurdish Distinctiveness," 457–78.
20. Watts, *Activists in Office*.
21. Dorronsoro and Watts, "Toward Kurdish Distinctiveness." It is also important to note that Zana was unable to expand his power over Diyarbakır or in the Kurdish movement owing to severe political and financial constraints from the central government.

Moreover, he did not have the clear political party patronage of the TİP. For further discussion on this topic see Dorronsoro and Watts, "Toward Kurdish Distinctiveness."

22. Yavuz, "Five Stages of the Construction of Kurdish Nationalism in Turkey."

23. As a response to such limitations, in the 1994 local elections the Kurdish movement called for a general boycott—or, if the citizens had to vote, they should spoil the vote, which is one reason that the Islamist Welfare party won the local elections in 1994. That same year, the Constitutional Court of the Republic of Turkey shut down the People's Labor Party (HEP). Those who had been active in the party moved to the HADEP. See also chapter 1, for the party closures.

24. Erzurum, "Hadep: PKK'yla Ortak Yanlarımız Var."

25. Finkel and Sirman, *Turkish State*.

26. In 2004 the pro-Kurdish candidates ran for local election under the SHP because the HADEP was closed, and the SHP was the only left-wing party with which they could align. In 2009 they ran for election under the DTP, and in 2014 under the BDP (because the DTP was shut down by the government); in 2019, they ran under the HDP, with mayor Adnan Selçuk Mızraklı. In 2019, even pro-Kurdish politicians were elected to mayoral seats in the city; in a span of months, they were either arrested, ousted, or dismissed by the state. See chapter 6 for more information.

27. Watts, *Activists in Office*, 85.

28. Watts, 143–44; see also Gambetti, "Conflictual (Trans)formation of Public Sphere."

29. Kuyucu, "Politics of Urban Regeneration," 1152–76.

30. Bozdoğan and Akcan, "Illegal City and New Residential Segregation."

31. The first official acknowledgment of these settlements in Turkey came with the *Gecekondu* law (775) in 1966, which referred to these settlements as "unauthorized constructions built on land or plots that do not belong to the owner, without adhering to the regulations and general provisions governing zoning and construction activities."

32. Further, the colossal destruction caused by the 1999 Izmit earthquake, which killed over seventeen thousand people in the northwest of the country and destroyed thousands of residential buildings, validated the need for new housing and urban development policy.

33. For instance, approval of municipal assembly decisions and budgets by the central government was eliminated. However, although some of the centrally held powers were delegated to the municipalities, their resources remained relatively limited because of the central government's control of their aid. Likewise, most income for the provincial budgets comes directly from state aid, with the remainder from rents, payments for services, fines, and a 1 percent share of national tax revenues. Despite more independence to municipalities under the new law, the funds and aid are still controlled by the state's central government.

34. See for example TOKİ, "TOKİ yaptığı yatırımlarla "geleceğin Kocaelisi'ni" inşa ediyor."

35. TOKİ, "Alt Gelir Grubu Basvuru Sartlari" (Lower income application requirements).

36. Bozdoğan and Akcan, "Illegal City."

37. Karaman, "Urban Neoliberalism."

38. TUİK, "Population and Demographics."

39. Orueta and Fainstein, "New Mega-projects," 770.

40. Turkun, "Urban Regeneration"; Çavuşoğlu and Strutz, "Producing Force and Consent."

41. TUİK, "Construction and Housing Statistics."

42. Demiralp, "Making Winners"; Sert and Kuruüzüm, "Alienated Imagination."

43. Kumral, "Globalization, Crisis and Right-Wing Populists"; Tuğal, "Politicized Megaprojects."

44. Gülhan, "Neoliberalism and Neo-dirigisme in Action"; Tuğal, "Politicized Megaprojects."
45. Brenner and Theodore, *Spaces of Neoliberalism*.
46. The year 2009 was not the first time the term "castle" was used to describe the state of pro-Kurdish politics at the local level by the pro-Kurdish movement. The analogy of "castle" by the pro-Kurdish movement was first used in 1977 during the election of independent candidate Mehdi Zana. See also Watts, *Activists in Office*, 47.
47. It is important to note that squatter settlements in Diyarbakır were not limited to Sur but also included the Bağlar and Ben-u Sen neighborhoods.
48. The word *sur* in Turkish literally translates as "city walls."
49. During the Ottoman period, Sur, or the old city, was a central province of the southeast, which largely housed Armenian, Syrian Orthodox, Jewish, and Muslim communities. Particularly by the late nineteenth century, under the Ottomans and later beginning in the republican period, the same homogenization and assimilation practices experienced elsewhere in Turkey began to decrease the multicultural fabric of Sur.
50. This is a rough estimate. Government figures say around three hundred thousand people, while domestic and international human rights organizations estimate the number of Kurdish forced migrants as high as high as four million. See Jongerden, "Village Evacuation"; Ayata and Yükseker, "Belated Awakening."
51. Ten thousand TL approximately equaled eight thousand US dollars in 2009.
52. Urfa is a neighboring city to Diyarbakır, its municipalities run by the AKP (the governing party) at that time.
53. Brenner, Marcuse, and Mayer, *Cities for People*, 5.
54. Yetiskul, Kayasü, and Ozdemir, "Local Responses to Urban Redevelopment Projects"; Lovering and Türkmen, "Bulldozer Neo-liberalism in Istanbul."
55. See chapter 3 for further discussion of the informal economy of the Sur residents.
56. Based on an interview with a governorship official, April 2011.
57. See chapter 1 for further discussion.
58. Berlage Institute, *After Displacement*, 26–30.
59. Berlage Institute, 23.
60. Les Ateliers, *Ben U Sen in Diyarbakir*.
61. Les Ateliers, 23.
62. Elicin, "Neoliberal Transformation," 154; see also Kuyucu and Ünsal, "'Urban Transformation.'"
63. The Ministry of Public Works and Housing was established in 1983 and was reorganized under the name of Ministry of Environment and Urban Planning in 2011.
64. All authorizations of the Ministry of Public Works and Housing in the *gecekondu* areas were transferred to TOKİ by an amendment in the *Resmî Gazete*, *Gecekondu* Law No. 775 and Law No. 5069, enacted in 2007.
65. With the decision of the Council of Ministers, an urgent expropriation decision was taken for the Lalebey and Ali Paşa neighborhoods based on *Resmî Gazete* Article 27 of the Expropriation Law No. 2942, enacted in 2013.
66. Aslan et al., "Sur'da Yıkımın İki Yüzü: Kentsel Dönüşüm ve Abluka İlişkisi," 8.
67. After the urban conflict ended, not only Lalebey and Ali Paşa but the entire Sur district was classified as a "disaster zone" and confiscated with "urgent expropriation." Over a span of ten years, the AKP's urban projection in Diyarbakır shifted from urban development to disaster zone to "urgent expropriation" under extraordinary law changes. Simultaneously, the mayors of Diyarbakır were detained and governors were appointed instead of the mayors. See chapter 6.
68. See, for instance, Mitchell, *Right to the City*; Herlambang et al., "Jakarta's Great Land Transformation"; Leitner and Sheppard, "From Kampungs to Condos?"

69. Smith, "New Globalism"; see also Porter and Shaw, *Whose Urban Renaissance?*
70. Sabah, "Kentsel dönüşümü tamamlayamazsak terörü de bitiremeyiz."
71. For further discussion see chapter 3.
72. Laclau and Mouffe, *Hegemony and Socialist Strategy*, 135–36.
73. Brubaker et al., *Nationalist Politics*, 14; Wedeen, *Peripheral Visions*, 167.
74. Bianet, "AKP Mitingi Öncesi Diyarbakır'da Protesto Gösterileri."
75. Brubaker, *Nationalism Reframed*, 7; Wedeen, *Peripheral Visions*, 98.
76. Hobsbawm, *Nations and Nationalism*; Tilly, *Coercion, Capital, and European States*; Wedeen, *Peripheral Visions*.

3. SEEING LIKE A MOVEMENT, ACTING LIKE A STATE

1. As discussed earlier, the concept of political articulation draws on the work de Leon, Desai, and Tuğal, *Building Blocs*.
2. For example, see the works of Perlman, *Myth of Marginality*; Castells, *City and the Grassroots*.
3. AlSayyad, "Squatting and Culture"; Bayat, "From 'Dangerous Classes' to 'Quiet Rebels.'"
4. Roy and AlSayyad, *Urban Informality*, 5.
5. Roy and AlSayyad, 5.
6. On the interaction between the Islamist movement and the civil society in the city, Cihan Tuğal has developed a similar perspective and argues how Islamism gives squatter settlements a new sense of identity. He shows how Islamism shaped the city through its own interpretation of immigrant agency and how immigrants develop their agency under Islamist leadership. See Tuğal, "Urban Dynamism of Islamic Hegemony," 429.
7. For further discussion see chapter 2.
8. The title of this chapter is beholden to James Scott's *Seeing Like a State*. By "state" I mean here the pro-Kurdish party holding municipal power. By "social movement" I mean the pro-Kurdish party as a social movement establishing networks of activism against the central government's order in the city.
9. Watts, *Activists in Office*.
10. Watts, *Activists in Office*.
11. De Leon, Desai, and Tuğal, *Building Blocs*.
12. As Jenny White elaborates, similar strategies of cell-to-cell and house-to-house engagement with local communities were used in Islamist movements in Turkey in the 1990s. See White, *Islamist Mobilization*, 178.
13. White, 178.
14. Ayata and Yükseker, "Belated Awakening."
15. Yadirgi, *Political Economy of the Kurds*, 245–50.
16. See Burtan Doğan and Celik, "Diyarbakır'daki Kentsel Yoksullugun Ana Bilesen Analizi Dahilinde Degerlendirilmesi (Assessment of Urban Poverty in Diyarbakır within Principal Component Analysis)"; Ersoy, "Kente Göç ve Yoksulluk—Diyarbakır Örneği (Urban Migration and Poverty: Diyarbakır Case)."
17. In the Kurdish movement, Abdullah Öcalan is also referred to as "Apo," short for Abdullah. In Kurdish, Apo also means uncle.
18. For the conceptualization of politicized Kurds I would like to thank Cihan Tuğal. See also Tuğal, *Passive Revolution*.
19. Wacquant, "Territorial Stigmatization."
20. Castells, *City and the Grassroots*.
21. Bayat, "Globalization and the Politics," 90–91.
22. Bayat, 90–91.

23. "Went to the "mountains" is a euphemism for fighting on behalf of the PKK in the mountains. PKK militants frequently camp in the mountains in the southeast of Turkey and in northern Iraq.

24. In the *Historical Dictionary of the Kurds*, Michael Gunter describes the KCK (Koma Civakên Kurdistanê, Kurdistan Democratic Confederation or Kurdistan Communities Union) as an umbrella organization bringing together the Kurdistan Workers Party (PKK) and the Kurdistan Free Life Party (PJAK) of Iran with much smaller PKK allies, such as the Democratic Union Party (PYD) in Syria and the Kurdistan Democratic Solution Party (PCDK) in Iraq. According to the Turkish state, the KCK is an urban-based civil arm of the PKK inciting violence against the Turkish state and helping coordinate PKK activities in cities. Further, Gunter points out that Abdullah Öcalan has described the KCK as an armed, illegal organization in the rural and urban areas of Turkey and Europe. See Gunter, *Historical Dictionary*.

25. The Turkish government militarily intervened there in 2015. The neighborhood of Hasırlı, in which the association was located, was one of the first targets of the Turkish military during urban warfare in Sur. During the clashes between the PKK and the Turkish military forces, the FCA and the neighborhood were virtually razed, to the point that currently one cannot recognize the street lines. See chapter 6.

26. Both Cihan Deniz and Hüsnü Albay were released in 2004, after ten years of imprisonment for their PKK membership.

27. Öcalan, "Democratic Confederalism," 21.

28. Gambetti, "Decolonizing Diyarbakır," 97–129.

29. Social worker, interview with the author, Sur municipality, March 2011.

30. For further discussion on *dengbej* see Scalbert-Yücel, "Invention of a Tradition."

31. Scalbert-Yücel, "Invention of a Tradition."

32. Hamelink and Barış, "Dengbêjs on Borderlands."

33. For the way similarly intertwined activities are discussed in informal settlements see Simone, *For the City Yet to Come*.

34. See, for instance, Bianet, "Dehap Kadın Adayları Amaçlarını Açıkladı."

35. Drechselová, *Local Power and Female Political Pathways*, 61.

36. Biehl, "Bookchin, Öcalan, and the Dialectics of Democracy."

37. Biehl, "Bookchin, Öcalan, and the Dialectics of Democracy."

38. Öcalan, "Democratic Confederalism."

39. Öcalan, "Democratic Confederalism," 21–24. See also Akkaya and Jongerden, "Reassembling the Political," for further discussion.

40. Öcalan, "War and Peace in Kurdistan."

41. Öcalan, "Democratic Confederalism." For further reference on the Kurdish movement's ideological development in society see Kurdistan, *Democratic Autonomy in North Kurdistan*.

42. For further discussion see Küçük, "Burden of Sisyphus," 760.

43. Abdullah Demirbaş, interview with the author, Diyarbakır, April 2011.

44. Yesil, *Media in New Turkey*, 126.

45. See Brubaker, *Nationalism Reframed*, 21. For further discussion see this book's introduction.

46. Tuğal, *Passive Revolution*, 61.

47. Here I am inspired by the theoretical discussion of Rogers Brubaker "on nationhood as a political claim, rather than an ethno-cultural fact." See Brubaker, "In the Name of the Nation."

48. Anderson, *Imagined Communities*, 35–36.

49. Sarigil, *Ethnic Boundaries in Turkish Politics*; Türkmen, *Under the Banner of Islam*.

50. It is important to note that generally Mazlum-Der in Diyarbakır was more sensitive to Kurdish rights and justice than it was at its other branches in the rest of the country.
51. See chapter 5 for further discussion on Civil Friday Prayers in Diyarbakır
52. See Tezcür, *Century of Kurdish Politics*, for further discussion on this topic.
53. See, for example, Ismail, *Political Life*, xvii–xxxv.
54. Ismail, xvii–xxxv.
55. See, for example, Bou Akar, *For the War Yet to Come*; Ismail, *Political Life*; Simone, *For the City Yet to Come*; Soliman, Roy, and AlSayyad, "Tilting at Sphinxes"; Bayat, *Street Politics*.
56. In fact, by the end of 2015, partial relocation happened in Sur in the aftermath of severe bombardment and urban warfare between the Kurdish guerrillas and the state army. Until then, the party and civil society networks resisted in order to stay in Sur. See chapter 6 for further discussion.
57. Here I am referring to Wedeen's analysis of alternative public spaces for collective debate on politics, particularly her analysis of qat chews in Yemen. Wedeen, *Peripheral Visions*, 103–48.
58. Arendt, *Human Condition*.
59. Arendt, 200–204.
60. De Leon, *Party and Society*, 158. For example, for Islamist movements' provision of public services and their engagements with civil society see Roy, *Hamas and Civil Society in Gaza*, and White, *Islamic Mobilization*.
61. See de Leon, Desai, and Tuğal, *Building Blocs*, 26–27. For further discussion of the influence of preexisting intellectual formations on parties see the introduction to this book.

4. BRANDING THE CITY

1. Molnár, "Mythical Power of Everyday Objects," 168.
2. See, for instance, Vale, "Temptations of Nationalism," 199.
3. Brenner and Theodore, *Spaces of Neoliberalism*.
4. Molnár, "Mythical Power of Everyday Objects," 168.
5. Brubaker et al., *Nationalist Politics and Everyday Ethnicity in a Transylvanian Town*.
6. For detailed discussion on the demonstrations in Diyarbakır resonating with the Arab Spring see chapter 5.
7. See, for example, Hürriyet, "Diyarbakır'da arsa fiyatları çıldırdı"; Sabah, "Diyarbakır'da arsa fiyatları çıldırdı."
8. Hürriyet, "Diyarbakır'da arsa fiyatları çıldırdı."
9. Hürriyet, "Diyarbakır'da arsa fiyatları çıldırdı."
10. See chapter 5.
11. *Evrensel Gazetesi*, "Baydemir: Tarım arazileri imara açılmayacak."
12. Habertürk, "Diyarbakır'da 'arsa balonu' patladı!"
13. Yüksel, "Rescaled Localities."
14. Yüksel, "Rescaled Localities."
15. Diyarbakır Chamber of Commerce and Industry, annual report, 2013.
16. Diyarbakır Büyükşehir Belediyesi, Faaliyet Raporu, 2008.
17. Diyarbakır Büyükşehir Belediyesi, Faaliyet Raporu, 2008.
18. Diyarbakır Büyükşehir Belediyesi, Faaliyet Raporu, 2008.
19. According to the Diyarbakır Association of Real Estate Agents and Advisers.
20. For a detailed discussion on Diyarbakır's construction economy see Genç, "Politics in Concrete."
21. Adalet, *Hotels and Highways*.

22. Kusno, *Behind the Postcolonial*, 97.
23. Söz, "Yollar asfaltlanıyor!"
24. See chapter 5.
25. Although "Başkan" translates into English as "president," in this context it refers to the "municipality mayor" or "mayor."
26. See Wedeen, *Peripheral Visions*, 131, on the ways in which Wedeen examines khat chew gatherings in Yemen facilitating nationness among the society.
27. Anderson, *Imagined Communities*, 2006.
28. Hurriyet, "Belediye'nin yaptığı 5 km'lik çevre yolu ulaşıma açıldı."
29. Hurriyet, "Belediye'nin yaptığı 5 km'lik çevre yolu ulaşıma açıldı."
30. Anderson, *Imagined Communities*, 2006.
31. Haber 3, "Diyarbakır'da Kamışlı Bulvarı Açıldı." "Zoxê" is the Kurdish word referring to the Turkish city of Cizre, in Şırnak Province.
32. See Diyarbakır Büyükşehir Belediyesi, 2004–2008 Activities, 174.
33. Diyarbakır Büyükşehir Belediyesi, 2004–2008 Activities, 27.
34. *Betonlaşma* is the word used to criticize the concrete urbanization—mushrooming of concrete buildings in cities in Turkey.
35. Atlı, "Kürt Orta Sınıfların Mekânsal Teşekkülü."
36. Until the late 1990s, vast farmlands at the peripheries of Diyarbakır had been in the possession of a few large families in Diyarbakır. See also see Genç, "Politics in Concrete."
37. Kayapınar District was only established within the boundaries of the Metropolitan Municipality with Law No. 5747, published in the Repeating Official Gazette No. 26824, March 22, 2008.
38. After the validation of the 1/25,000 scale zoning plan by the municipal council in 2006, 1/5,000 scale zoning plans and 1/1000 scale application plans were prepared in a span of two years.
39. Kayapınar Municipality Activity Report, 2006.
40. TUİK, "Population and Demographics."
41. Küçük, "Burden of Sisyphus."
42. Yüksel, "Rescaled Localities and Redefined Class Relations."
43. Low, "Edge and the Center."
44. Particularly during and after the urban warfare in 2015, the abstention of working middle and upper classes, mostly residents of Kayapınar, from collective struggle against state violence was denounced among activist circles. However, this criticism was never strong enough to draw a line between the residents of Diyarbakır. See also Küçük, "Burden of Sisyphus."
45. See chapter 6.
46. See chapter 1 for the discussion of "eastern" concept.
47. For Havin's account see introduction.
48. For the peace process see chapter 1.
49. Sümer Park was restored and reconstructed for the Diyarbakır municipality for 4.3 million euros.
50. Genç, "Politics in Concrete."
51. See chapter 5.
52. Gunter, *Out of Nowhere*.
53. The use of the double-headed eagle is not unique to Diyarbakır. It can be traced in diverse Mesopotamian, Anatolian, and Asian civilizations' lusterware and structures, particularly beginning in the ninth century. For example, diverse adaptations of the double-headed eagle can be seen across Anatolia and in Anatolian Seljuk art as well. Otto-Dorn, "Figural Stone Reliefs."

54. There are several records on the importance of Nineveh for Kurdish history. As for early records see Driver, "Studies in Kurdish History."
55. De Soto, *Mystery of Capital*.
56. The first quote is from an auto gallery owner, in an interview with the author, Diyarbakır, October 2012. The second quote is from a local businessman, in an interview with the author, Diyarbakır, June 2009.
57. The government shut down the organization in 2016 because it contained the word "Kurdistan" in its title. Kurdistan24, "KÜRSİAD'a kapatılma, yöneticisine ceza."
58. Brubaker, *Nationalism Reframed*, 6–7.
59. Mukerji, "Space and Political Pedagogy."
60. Brubaker, *Nationalism Reframed*.
61. Hobsbawm, *Nations and Nationalism*.
62. I did not go to Sülüklü Khan only with Havin. During my stay in Diyarbakır I would sometimes go with Esra and his fourteen-year-old son, Serkan, and conduct some of my interviews there.
63. Sülüklü Khan means "khan with the leech" in Turkish. Rumors suggested that herbalists used leech therapy in this type of inn, called a "khan," which typically featured a large courtyard functioning as both a trading center and hostel. The name "Sülüklü Khan" itself was said to have originated from this practice.
64. Billig, *Banal Nationalism*.
65. Molnár, "Mythical Power of Everyday Objects," 151. See also Palmer, "From Theory to Practice"; Johannes, *Nourishing the Nation*.
66. Caldwell, "Taste of Nationalism."
67. Caldwell, "Taste of Nationalism."
68. Romano, *Kurdish Nationalist Movement*.
69. Molnár, *Building the State*.
70. Molnár, "Mythical Power of Everyday Objects," 168.
71. See, for instance, Harvey, *Brief History of Neoliberalism*; Gilpin, *Challenge of Global Capitalism*.
72. See, for instance, Lueck, Due, and Augoustinos, "Neoliberalism and Nationalism."
73. Here my discussion is inspired by Adam Harmes's argument on the dependent relationship between neoliberalism and nationalism. Harmes, "Rise of Neoliberal Nationalism."
74. Desai and Sanyal, *Urbanizing Citizenship*.
75. Harmes, "Rise of Neoliberal Nationalism."
76. Tuğal, "Politicized Megaprojects"; Madra and Yılmaz, "Turkey's Decline into (Civil) War Economy."
77. Gülhan, "Neoliberalism and Neo-dirigisme in Action"; Erensü and Madra, "Neoliberal Politics in Turkey"; Tuğal, "Politicized Megaprojects."
78. Gellner, *Nations and Nationalism*, 48.
79. Anderson, *Imagined Communities*, 2006.
80. Wedeen, *Peripheral Visions*.
81. Kezer, *Building Modern Turkey*, 195.
82. Yüksel, "Rescaled Localities and Redefined Class Relations."
83. De Leon, Desai, and Tuğal, "Political Articulation."

5. SCULPTING VIOLENCE, ACTIVATING THE STREET

1. It was only eight months after the PKK's declaration of a cease-fire in March 2013.
2. In Turkish popular culture, it is common practice to promote one city, particularly an Anatolian city, through its famous produce or fruit.

3. Güvenç, "Constructing Narratives of Kurdish Nationalism." See also Watts, *Activists in Office*, and Kezer, *Building Modern Turkey*.
4. Gambetti, "Decolonizing Diyarbakır."
5. See how Carol Duncan defines museums as places where "rituals of citizenship" are played out. Duncan, *Civilizing Rituals*.
6. Brubaker, *Nationalism Reframed*, 16.
7. Özyürek, *Politics of Public Memory*. See also Tuğal, "Islamism in Turkey."
8. Özyürek, *Politics of Public Memory*; Boyarin, *Storm from Paradise*; Gillis, *Commemorations*.
9. Vale, *Architecture, Power and National Identity* (2008); Kusno, *Behind the Postcolonial*; Bozdoğan, *Modernism and Nation Building*.
10. Kusno, *Behind the Postcolonial*, 26.
11. Sodaro, *Exhibiting Atrocity*, 17.
12. See, for example, cases and discussion in Sodaro, *Exhibiting Atrocity*, and Neumann and Thompson, *Historical Justice and Memory*.
13. Balibar, *Race, Nation, Class*, 93.
14. For another example see Wedeen, *Peripheral Visions*, 92–93.
15. Savage, *Monument Wars*, 198.
16. Diken, *Sırrını surlarına fısıldayan şehir*, 123.
17. For vandalism at Koşuyolu Park see chapter 6.
18. According to the myth, Medes are acknowledged as the ancestors of Kurds who were enslaved by the Assyrian king Dehak and lived under his tyranny. Kurdish youth rebelled against the king under the leadership of Kawa the blacksmith. Particularly since the 1960s, the myth of Kawa has been symbolically important for the discourse of Kurdish rebellion and resistance. See Çağlayan, "From Kawa the Blacksmith."
19. The installation of the Kawa sculpture never happened because of the events of 2015.
20. This phrase has always been common and emerged as a theme during my interviews.
21. See Baydemir's speech at Haber7, "Diyarbakır Yasam Hakki Aniti Acildi."
22. Bernstein, "Review of Prosthetic Memory."
23. See, for instance, the opinion piece by Gürsel, "Arab Spring."
24. AlSayyad and Güvenç, "Virtual Uprisings."
25. AlSayyad and Güvenç, "Virtual Uprisings."
26. For the conceptualization of spectacle in this case see Güvenç, "Propositions for the Emancipatory Potential."
27. Güvenç, "Constructing Narratives of Kurdish Nationalism," 29.
28. See chapter 2 for more information on Saliha, Hasan, and Ahsen.
29. Salahaddin Ayyubi (1138–1193), known in the West as Saladin, was a famous Muslim Kurdish warrior and founder of the Islamic Ayyubid dynasty. His sultanate included Egypt, Syria, Mesopotamia, the Hejaz, and Yemen. He was a devout Islamic figure and a successful commander who led the Muslim military campaign against the Crusaders in the Middle East in the twelfth century.
30. See Hürriyet, "Civil Disobedient Prayer;" Milliyet, "Alternative Friday;" and NTV Haber, "Friday Prayer with the Apo Poster."
31. Arendt, *Human Condition*, 198–99.
32. Arendt, *Between Past and Future*, 95–96.
33. Arendt, *Human Condition*, 198–99.
34. The Uğur Kaymaz memorial was removed following the state's intervention in 2015; for further discussion see chapter 6.
35. An official investigation concluded that Ceylan Önkol had detonated an unexploded device left in the area at a previous time. Local groups and human rights

organizations, however, blaming state officials, asserted that such a mortar had to be fired from nearby and therefore must have purposefully targeted her. The opening ceremony for the park thus once again merged two different events—the death of Ceylan Önkol and the arrests of politicians—into the narratives of collective violence, death, and tyranny.

36. Volk, *Memorials and Martyrs in Modern Lebanon*, 136.
37. See chapter 4 for more discussion of the Meds/Medes.
38. See chapter 4.
39. Kayapinar Belediyesi, December 2008.
40. See chapter 6 for the removal of Lamassu reliefs from the municipality.
41. For a further discussion on Dengbej culture see chapter 3.
42. De Leon, Desai, and Tuğal, "Political Articulation," 194.
43. See Haber Diyarbakir, "Ayşe Şan'ın İsmi Parka Verildi."
44. The Kurdish word *newroz* actually stems from the Persian *nowruz*, meaning "new year," which signifies the arrival of spring.
45. Aydın, "Mobilizing the Kurds in Turkey."
46. Güneş, *Kurdish National Movement in Turkey*.
47. PJAK, the Kurdistan Free Life Party, or Partiya Jiyana Azad a Kurdistanê in Kurdish, is a militant anti-Iranian-government group affiliated with the PKK through the Kurdistan Communities Union.
48. One of the highlights of the 2013 Newroz celebrations was the delivery of Abdullah Öcalan's famous letter from prison announcing the withdrawal of the PKK's military forces from Turkey. Weeks before Newroz day, the upcoming reading of the letter was announced by pro-Kurdish officials, without revealing its contents. Then, on Newroz day, several national TV channels interrupted their broadcasts to feature a live transmission from the festival site. Öcalan's message was then read out, in both Kurdish and Turkish, by two members of Parliament from the pro-Kurdish Peace and Democracy Party (BDP) amid the chanting of a crowd in front of the podium. Following the live broadcast, commentators debated the meaning of Öcalan's message. The next day, the mainstream Turkish press reported it as a historical "farewell to arms," with photographs of tens of thousands of people celebrating Newroz at Diyarbakır. Newspaper commentators across the Middle East allocated their column space to interpretations of Öcalan's message and discussions of the future of the Kurdish movement in Turkey. See also Cengiz Çandar's article "Ocalan's Message Is Much More Than a Cease-Fire," *Al-Monitor*, March 24, 2013.
49. See, for example, Bozdoğan, *Modernism and Nation Building*; Vale, *Architecture, Power and National Identity* (2008); Kusno, *Behind the Postcolonial*.
50. Crysler, "Violence and Empathy." For a discussion of nationalism and the museum identity see, for example, Aslı Gür, "Stories in Three Dimensions."
51. Crysler, "Violence and Empathy."
52. Sodaro, *Exhibiting Atrocity*.
53. Sodaro, *Exhibiting Atrocity*; Crysler, "Violence and Empathy."
54. Malmîsanj, *Yirminci Yüzyılın Başında Diyarbekir'de Kürt Ulusçuluğu (1900–1920)*.
55. Bianet, "Diyarbekirli Cemilpaşa Ailesi."
56. Diken, *Diyarbekirli Udi Yervant Bostancı*.
57. As of this writing, these two museum projects have not been realized because of the conflict that erupted in December 2015, followed by the state's intervention in the city. See chapter 6.
58. See chapter 6.
59. Haberler.com, "Diyarbakır Kent Müzesi Hizmete Girdi."
60. Duncan, *Civilizing Rituals*; Sirefman, "Formed and Forming."

61. I am indebted here to Lisa Wedeen's discussion of the production and the manipulation of the symbolic world, in Wedeen, *Ambiguities of Domination*, 32. See also Mbembe, "Domaines de la nuit et autorité onirique."
62. Anderson, *Imagined Communities*, 145.
63. Anderson, 35.

6. DISMANTLING THE KURDISH LANDSCAPE

1. See Ghandour and Fawaz, "Spatial Erasure"; Herscher, *Violence Taking Place*; Smith, "Leviathan's Architect."
2. Graham, *Cities under Siege*.
3. See also Thomas Smith's article discussing the initial phases of Sur's reconstruction as the deliberate erasure of social and political space. Smith, "Leviathan's Architect."
4. Hürriyet, "Diyarbakır, Ortadoğu'ya açılan önemli bir kapı olacak."
5. It is also important to note that on July 15, 2016, a faction within the Turkish armed forces that called itself the Peace at Home Council attempted a coup d'état against state institutions, including the government and President Recep Tayyip Erdoğan.
6. Ghandour and Fawaz, "Spatial Erasure"; Bevan, *Destruction of Memory*.
7. Merrifield, *Politics of the Encounter*.
8. For comparisons of images with their previous condition see chapter 5.
9. Batuman, *New Islamist Architecture and Urbanism*, 3.
10. White, *Muslim Nationalism and the New Turks*.
11. For example, the newly appointed administration at Kayapınar municipality changed the Kurdish name of the Kompleksa Werzîşê Ya Amedê facility to Martyr Police Halit Gülser Sports Complex (after a police officer who died in another city during the July 15 coup attempt). See the Sendika.org, "Kayyum, Park Orman'ın ismini değiştirdi." Frequently, citizens and activists reacted to these name changes with street protests in an attempt to get the AKP officials to repeal the changes.
12. Mbembe, *On the Postcolony*, 110.
13. Anadolu Ajansı, "Cumhurbaşkanı Erdoğan, Diyarbakır Merkez Camisi'nin Temelini Attı."
14. Karaman, "Urban Neoliberalism with Islamic Characteristics."
15. Batuman, *New Islamist Architecture and Urbanism*, 46.
16. "Diyarbakır Merkez Cami—Yaptırma Derneği."
17. "Diyarbakır Merkez Cami—Yaptırma Derneği."
18. "Diyarbakır Merkez Cami—Yaptırma Derneği."
19. In fact, it is worth mentioning that the emphasis on Anatolian Seljuk appears in almost every architectural style the AKP has employed in the last five to ten years. For further discussion on the AKP's mosques see Batuman, *New Islamist Architecture and Urbanism*.
20. During the application process, the municipality collaborated closely with the Ministry of Culture and Tourism.
21. *Evrensel Gazetesi*, "İstinaf Mahkemesi Dicle Vadisi'ndeki iptal kararını onayladı."
22. Amnesty.org, "Turkey: Displaced and Dispossessed."
23. According to the assessment report prepared by the archaeologist and former coordinator of the Cultural Landscape Area Administration Nevin Soyukaya, by 2017 a total of 1,519 structures had been destroyed, including 89 registered sites destroyed completely and 40 destroyed partially. For example, as the assessment report shows, the historic Hasırlı Mosque, the Armenian Catholic Church (which had been restored in 2014), and the Mehmet Uzun House (a famous Kurdish author's home) were completely destroyed,

the debris removed without a trace. Soyukaya, "Sur—the Walled City of Diyarbakır Conflict, Dispossession and Destruction Damage Assessment Report."

24. Sabah, "Diyarbakır Kultur Turizmi ile atakta."

25. Sözcü, "'Sur'u Toledo gibi yapacağız.'"

26. The city of Toledo is the capital of the province of Toledo of the autonomous community of Castilla–La Mancha, Spain, known for its resistance to fascist forces during the Spanish Civil War. See also Gümüş, "Toledo Benzetmesinin Arkasındaki Sorunlar," February 8, 2016.

27. On March 21, 2016, with the decision of the Council of Ministers, expropriation was decreed (urgent expropriation decree no. 2016/8659) for 6,292 of 7,714 parcels that included the Hasırlı, Dabanoğlu, Fatih, Cevatpaşa, Cemal Yılmaz, and Savaş neighborhoods.

28. See chapter 2.

29. Zerrin Biner offers an interesting discussion of "the practices of dispossession and experiences of being dispossessed" and how "the loss of life, property, and means of livelihood are at the core of the present histories of dispossession" through everyday experiences in the Kurdish region of Turkey. Biner, *States of Dispossession*, 5.

30. According to an interview with Ms. Lök Beyaz, in Yüksel, "Suriçi'nde Neler Oluyor."

31. Graham, *Cities under Siege*, 14–16; Liu and Yuan, "Making a Safer Space?"

32. For example, the Diyarbakır Chamber of Architects organized multiple press releases and demonstrations and applied for court appeals. In one press release, they likened the new front gardens to prison cells. Kayar, "Mimarlar Odası Diyarbakır Şube Başkanı."

33. Yıldız, "Diyarbakır's Objects of Memory," 55.

34. TOKİ, "Updated Sale List for Çölgüzeli."

35. T24, "Sur'un Eski Sakinleri: 'Yeni Evleri Bize Parayla Bile Vermiyorlar.'"

36. *Evrensel Gazetesi*, "Kayapınar Belediyesi kayyumu kaymakamlığı belediyeye taşıyor."

37. For example, the photograph competition organized by the municipalities was broadcast on the governor's website.

38. For discussion of the emergence of new types of colonial relations see Yiftachel, "Theoretical Notes on 'Gray Cities.'"

39. For more on Hasan, Saliha, and Ahsen see chapter 3.

40. Anderson, *H-Word*.

CONCLUSION

1. Marcuse, "Not Chaos, but Walls," 244.

2. BBC News Türkçe, "HDP'ye kapatma davasının iddianamesinde neler var, süreç bundan sonra nasıl işleyecek?"

3. In the presidential and parliamentary elections held in May 2023, the HDP leaders provided unconditional support to the opposition candidate and CHP leader Kemal Kılıçdaroğlu in Turkey's presidential race. However, this unwavering support did not yield any advantages for the pro-Kurdish party.

4. Dri, "Turkey's Pro-Kurdish HEDEP to Change Acronym on Court Objection."

5. Smith, *National Identity*, 14.

6. Brenner, Marcuse, and Mayer, *Cities for People*; Brenner and Theodore, *Spaces of Neoliberalism*.

7. Davies, "Rethinking Urban Power"; Tuğal, *Passive Revolution*; Springer, "Neoliberalism as Discourse"; Brown, "American Nightmare."

8. See, for example, Karaman, "Urban Neoliberalism with Islamic Characteristics"; Low, "Security at Home"; Lovering and Türkmen, "Bulldozer Neo-liberalism in Istanbul"; Davies, "Rethinking Urban Power"; Tuğal, *Passive Revolution*; Springer, "Neoliberalism as Discourse"; Brown, "American Nightmare."
9. Molnár, "Mythical Power of Everyday Objects," 168.
10. Brubaker, *Grounds for Difference*, 144.
11. Merrifield, *New Urban Question*, xi.
12. Merrifield, 69.
13. Yiftachel, "Dark Side of Modernism," 236.

Bibliography

Açikyildiz, Birgül. "Ideology, Nationalism, and Architecture: Representations of Kurdish Sites in Turkish Art Historiography." *International Journal of Islamic Architecture* 11, no. 2 (2022): 323–53. https://doi.org/10.1386/ijia_00082_1.
Adalet, Begüm. *Hotels and Highways: The Construction of Modernization Theory in Cold War Turkey.* Stanford, CA: Stanford University Press, 2018.
Agnew, John A., and Stuart Corbridge. *Mastering Space: Hegemony, Territory and International Political Economy.* London: Routledge, 1995.
Ahmed, Mohammed M. A., and Michael M. Gunter. *The Evolution of Kurdish Nationalism.* Costa Mesa, CA: Mazda, 2006.
Akkaya, Ahmet Hamdi, and Joost Jongerden. "Reassembling the Political: The PKK and the Project of Radical Democracy." *European Journal of Turkish Studies: Social Sciences on Contemporary Turkey*, no. 14 (June 1, 2012). https://doi.org/10.4000/ejts.4615.
AlSayyad, Nezar. "Squatting and Culture: A Comparative Analysis of Informal Developments in Latin America and the Middle East." *Habitat International* 17, no. 1 (January 1, 1993): 33–44. https://doi.org/10.1016/0197-3975(93)90044-D.
AlSayyad, Nezar, and Muna Güvenç. "Virtual Uprisings: On the Interaction of New Social Media, Traditional Media Coverage and Urban Space during the 'Arab Spring.'" *Urban Studies* 52, no. 11 (August 1, 2015): 2018–34. https://doi.org/10.1177/0042098013505881.
Amnesty.org. "Turkey: Displaced and Dispossessed." https://www.amnesty.org/en/latest/campaigns/2016/12/sur-displaced-and-dispossessed/.
Anadolu Ajansi, "Cumhurbaşkanı Erdoğan, Diyarbakır Merkez Camisi'nin Temelini Attı." April 1, 2017. https://www.aa.com.tr/tr/turkiye/cumhurbaskani-erdogan-diyarbakir-merkez-camisinin-temelini-atti/785759.
Anderson, Benedict R. O'G. *Imagined Communities: Reflections on the Origin and Spread of Nationalism.* Rev. ed. London: Verso, 2006.
Anderson, Perry. *The H-Word: The Peripeteia of Hegemony.* New York: Verso, 2017.
Aren, Sadun. *TİP Olayı, 1961–1971.* Istanbul: Cem Yayınevi, 1993.
Arendt, Hannah. *Between Past and Future: Eight Exercises in Political Thought.* New York: Viking, 1968.
———. *The Human Condition.* Chicago: University of Chicago Press, 1998.
Aslan, Serhat, Derya Aydın, Hakan Sandal, and Güllistan Yarkın. "Sur'da Yıkımın İki Yüzü: Kentsel Dönüşüm ve Abluka İlişkisi." Analysis Report. Zan Institute, March 30, 2016. http://zanenstitu.org/uploads/dosyalar/Sur-Rapor.pdf.
Atlı, Mehmet. "Kürt Orta Sınıfların Mekânsal Teşekkülü: Diyarbakır Diclekent'in Dönüşümü Örneği: Ortaokuldan Terklerin Orta Sınıf Çocukları." *Birikim Orta Sınıf*, no. 306 (2014): 83–86. Istanbul: Birikim Yayınları.
Ayata, Bilgin, and Deniz Yükseker. "A Belated Awakening: National and International Responses to the Internal Displacement of Kurds in Turkey." *New Perspectives on Turkey* 32 (2005): 5–42. https://doi.org/10.1017/S089663460000409X.
Aydın, Delal. "Mobilizing the Kurds in Turkey: Newroz as a Myth." In *The Kurdish Question in Turkey: New Perspectives on Violence, Representation and*

Reconciliation, edited by Cengiz Gunes and Welat Zeydanlioglu, 68–88. Exeter Studies in Ethno Politics. London: Routledge, 2014. https://doi.org/10.4324/9780203796450.

Balibar, Étienne. *Race, Nation, Class: Ambiguous Identities*. London: Routledge, Chapman & Hall, 1991.

Ballı, Rafet. *Kürt Dosyası*. Istanbul: Cem Yayınevi, 1991.

Batuman, Bülent. *New Islamist Architecture and Urbanism: Negotiating Nation and Islam through Built Environment in Turkey*. Architext Series. Milton: Routledge, Taylor & Francis Group, 2018. https://doi.org/10.4324/9781315667409.

Bayat, Asef. "From 'Dangerous Classes' to 'Quiet Rebels': Politics of the Urban Subaltern in the Global South." *International Sociology* 15, no. 3 (September 1, 2000): 533–57. https://doi.org/10.1177/026858000015003005.

———. "Globalization and the Politics of the Informals in the Global South." In *Urban Informality: Transnational Perspectives from the Middle East, Latin America, and South Asia*, edited by Ananya Roy and Nezar AlSayyad, 67–78. Oxford: Lexington Books, 2004.

———. *Life as Politics: How Ordinary People Change the Middle East*. 2nd ed. Stanford, CA: Stanford University Press, 2013.

———. *Street Politics: Poor People's Movements in Iran*. New York: Columbia University Press, 1997.

Bayrak, Mehmet. *Açık-Gizli, Resmi-Gayrıresmi Kürdoloji Belgeleri*. Ankara: Öz-Ge Yayınları, 1994.

BBC News Türkçe. "HDP'ye kapatma davasının iddianamesinde neler var, süreç bundan sonra nasıl işleyecek?" March 18, 2021. https://www.bbc.com/turkce/haberler-turkiye-56445871.

Berlage Institute. *Accommodating the Displaced: A New Municipal Housing Service in Diyarbakır*. Berlage Institute Research Report, 2010.

———. *After Displacement: Large-Scale Housing Solutions for Diyarbakir*. Berlage Institute Research Report, 2010.

Bernstein, Lee. "Review of *Prosthetic Memory: The Transformation of American Remembrance in the Age of Mass Culture* by Alison Landsberg." *History Teacher* 39, no. 1 (November 1, 2005): 126–28. https://doi.org/10.2307/30036756.

Bevan, Robert. *The Destruction of Memory: Architecture at War*. Vol. 55423. Reaktion Books, 2016.

Beysanoğlu, Şevket. *Anıtları ve kitâbeleri ile Diyarbakır tarihi*. Vol. 3. Diyarbakır, Turkey: Diyarbakır Belediyesi, 1987.

Bianet—Bağımsız İletişim Ağı. "AKP Mitingi Öncesi Diyarbakır'da Protesto Gösterileri." June 1, 2011. https://bianet.org/haber/akp-mitingi-oncesi-diyarbakir-da-protesto-gosterileri-130421.

———. "Dehap Kadın Adayları Amaçlarını Açıkladı." October 7, 2002. https://bianet.org/haber/dehap-kadin-adaylari-amaclarini-acikladi-13728.

———. "Diyarbekirli Cemilpaşa Ailesi." https://www.bianet.org/bianet/toplum/55164-diyarbekirli-cemilpasa-ailesi.

Biehl, Janet. "Bookchin, Öcalan, and the Dialectics of Democracy | New Compass." New Compass. http://new-compass.net/articles/bookchin-%C3%B6calan-and-dialectics-democracy.

Billig, Michael. *Banal Nationalism*. Thousand Oaks, CA: Sage, 1995.

Biner, Zerrin Özlem. *States of Dispossession: Violence and Precarious Coexistence in Southeast Turkey*. Ethnography of Political Violence. Philadelphia: University of Pennsylvania Press, 2020.

Bou Akar, Hiba. *For the War Yet to Come: Planning Beirut's Frontiers*. Stanford, CA: Stanford University Press, 2018.
Boyarin, Jonathan. *Storm from Paradise: The Politics of Jewish Memory*. Minneapolis: University of Minnesota Press, 1992.
Bozarslan, Hamit. "Kurdish Nationalism under the Kemalist Republic: Some Hypotheses." In *The Evolution of Kurdish Nationalism*, edited by Mohammed M. A. Ahmed and Michael M. Gunter, 36–51. Costa Mesa, CA: Mazda, 2007.
———. "Kurds and the Turkish State." In *The Cambridge History of Turkey*, vol. 4, *Turkey in the Modern World*, edited by Reşat Kasaba, 333–35. Cambridge: Cambridge University Press, 2008.
Bozarslan, M. Emîn. *Doğu'nun Sorunları*. Istanbul: Avesta, 2002.
Bozdoğan, Sibel. *Modernism and Nation Building: Turkish Architectural Culture in the Early Republic*. Studies in Modernity and National Identity. Seattle: University of Washington Press, 2001.
Bozdoğan, Sibel, and Esra Akcan. "The Illegal City and New Residential Segregation." In *Turkey: Modern Architectures in History*. London: Reaktion Books, 2012.
Brenner, Neil. *New State Spaces: Urban Governance and the Rescaling of Statehood*. Oxford: Oxford University Press, 2004. http://site.ebrary.com/id/10263694.
Brenner, Neil, David J. Madden, and David Wachsmuth. "Assemblages, Actor-Networks, and the Challenges of Critical Urban Theory." In *Cities for People, Not for Profit: Critical Urban Theory and the Right to the City*, edited by Neil Brenner, Peter Marcuse, and Margit Mayer, 118–19. London: Routledge, 2012.
Brenner, Neil, Peter Marcuse, and Margit Mayer, eds. *Cities for People, Not for Profit: Critical Urban Theory and the Right to the City*. London: Routledge, 2012.
Brenner, Neil, and Nik Theodore. *Spaces of Neoliberalism: Urban Restructuring in North America and Western Europe*. Malden, MA: Wiley-Blackwell, 2003.
Brown, Wendy. "American Nightmare: Neoliberalism, Neoconservatism, and De-democratization." *Political Theory* 34, no. 6 (2006): 690–714.
Brubaker, Rogers. *Ethnicity without Groups*. Cambridge, MA: Harvard University Press, 2004.
———. *Grounds for Difference*. Cambridge, MA: Harvard University Press, 2015. https://doi.org/10.4159/9780674425293.
———. "In the Name of the Nation: Reflections on Nationalism and Patriotism." *Citizenship Studies* 8, no. 2 (June 2004): 115–27.
———. *Nationalism Reframed: Nationhood and the National Question in the New Europe*. Cambridge: Cambridge University Press, 1996.
Brubaker, Rogers, Margit Feischmidt, Jon Fox, and Liana Grancia. *Nationalist Politics and Everyday Ethnicity in a Transylvanian Town*. Princeton, NJ: Princeton University Press, 2006.
Bruinessen, Martin Van. *Kurdish Ethno-Nationalism versus Nation-Building States: Collected Articles*. Istanbul: Isis, 2000.
Burawoy, Michael. "The Extended Case Method." *Sociological Theory* 16, no. 1 (1998).
———. "Revisits: An Outline of a Theory of Reflexive Ethnography." *American Sociological Review* 68, no. 5 (2003).
Burkay, Kemal. *Anılar, belgeler*. Istanbul: Deng Yayınları, 2002.
Burtan Doğan, Bahar, and Yusuf Celik. "Diyarbakır'daki Kentsel Yoksullugun Ana Bilesen Analizi Dahilinde Degerlendirilmesi." Suleyman Demirel University, *Journal of Faculty of Economics and Administrative Sciences* 17, no. 3 (2012): 129–62.

Cagaptay, Soner. "Race, Assimilation and Kemalism: Turkish Nationalism and the Minorities in the 1930s." *Middle Eastern Studies* 40, no. 3 (2004): 86–101. https://doi.org/10.1080/0026320042000213474.

Çağlayan, Handan. "From Kawa the Blacksmith to Ishtar the Goddess: Gender Constructions in Ideological-Political Discourses of the Kurdish Movement in Post-1980 Turkey; Possibilities and Limits." *European Journal of Turkish Studies: Social Sciences on Contemporary Turkey*, no. 14 (June 1, 2012). https://doi.org/10.4000/ejts.4657.

Caldwell, Melissa L. "The Taste of Nationalism: Food Politics in Postsocialist Moscow." *Ethnos* 67, no. 3 (2002): 295–319. https://doi.org/10.1080/0014184022000031185.

Çandar, Cengiz. "Ocalan's Message Is Much More Than a Cease-Fire." *Al-Monitor*, March 24, 2013. http://www.al-monitor.com/pulse/originals/2013/03/ocalan-ceasefire-newroz-speech-farewell-to-arms.html#ixzz4D4Afor65.

Çınar, Alev. "The Imagined Community as Urban Reality: The Making of Ankara." In *Urban Imaginaries: Locating the Modern City*, edited by Alev Çınar and Thomas Bender. Minneapolis: University of Minnesota Press, 2007.

Castells, Manuel. *The City and the Grassroots: A Cross-Cultural Theory of Urban Social Movements*. Berkeley: University of California Press, 1984.

Çavuşoğlu, Erbatur, and Julia Strutz. "Producing Force and Consent: Urban Transformation and Corporatism in Turkey." *City (London, England)* 18, no. 2 (2014): 134–48. https://doi.org/10.1080/13604813.2014.896643.

Çelik, Adnan, and Namık Kemal Dinç. *Yüz yıllık Ah: Toplumsal hafızanın izinde 1915 Diyarbekir*. Istanbul: İsmail Beşikçi Vakfı, 2015.

Crysler, C. Greig. "Violence and Empathy: National Museums and the Spectacle of Society." *Traditional Dwellings and Settlements Review* 17, no. 2 (Spring 2006): 19–38.

Danielson, Michael N., and Ruşen Keleş. *The Politics of Rapid Urbanization: Government and Growth in Modern Turkey*. New York: Holmes & Meier, 1985.

Davies, Jonathan. "Rethinking Urban Power and the Local State: Hegemony, Domination and Resistance in Neoliberal Cities." *Urban Studies* 51, no. 15 (November 1, 2014): 3215–32. https://doi.org/10.1177/0042098013505158.

Davis, Diane E., and Libertun de Duren. *Cities and Sovereignty: Identity Politics in Urban Spaces*. Bloomington: Indiana University Press, 2011. http://site.ebrary.com/id/10448613.

De Leon, Cedric. *Party and Society: Reconstructing a Sociology of Democratic Party Politics*. Political Sociology Series. Cambridge: Polity, 2014.

De Leon, Cedric, Manali Desai, and Cihan Tuğal. *Building Blocs: How Parties Organize Society*. Palo Alto, CA: Stanford University Press, 2015.

———. "Political Articulation: Parties and the Constitution of Cleavages in the United States, India, and Turkey." *Sociological Theory* 27, no. 3 (2009): 193–219.

Demiralp, Seda. "Making Winners: Urban Transformation and Neoliberal Populism in Turkey." *Middle East Journal* 72, no. 1 (2018): 89–108. https://doi.org/10.3751/72.1.15.

Desai, Renu, and Romola Sanyal, eds. *Urbanizing Citizenship: Contested Spaces in Indian Cities*. Thousand Oaks, CA: Sage, 2011.

De Soto, Hernando. *The Mystery of Capital: Why Capitalism Triumphs in the West and Fails Everywhere Else*. Repr. ed. New York: Basic Books, 2003.

Diken, Şeyhmus. *Amidalılar: Sürgündeki Diyarbekirliler*. Istanbul: İletişim, 2007.

———. *Diyarbekir Diyarım, Yitirmişem Yanarım*. Istanbul: Iletisim Yayinevi, 2013.

———. *Diyarbekirli Udi Yervant Bostancı: "Ulla Fille Hosgeldin."* Istanbul: İletişim Yayınları, 2015.

———. *Sırrını Surlarına Fısıldayan Şehir: Diyarbakır*. Istanbul: İletişim Yayınları, 2002.
Diyarbekire bir bakış; Cumhuruyetin büyük eserlerinden olan tren Diyarbekire yeni bir hayat getirdi. Diyarbakır, Turkey: Diyarbekir Basimevi, 1935.
Diyarbakır Büyükşehir Belediyesi Faaliyet Raporu (Diyarbakır Metropolitan Municipality Activity Report). 2008.
Diyarbakır Chamber of Commerce and Industry. Annual report, 2013.
Diyarbakır Merkez Camii. "Diyarbakır Merkez Cami—Yaptırma Derneği." http://diyarbakirmerkezcami.org.tr/.
Diyarbakır Üniversitesi. *Atatürk ve Diyarbakır: Diyarbakır Üniversitesi 100. yıl yayını 1981*. Diyarbakır, Turkey: Diyarbakır Üniversitesi Basimevi Müdürlüğü, 1981.
Diyarbakır Valiliği. *Cumhuriyetin 15inci yılında Diyarbakır*. Diyarbakır Matbaası, 1938.
Dorronsoro, Gilles, and Nicole F. Watts. "Toward Kurdish Distinctiveness in Electoral Politics: The 1977 Local Elections in Diyarbakir." *International Journal of Middle East Studies* 41, no. 3 (2009): 457–78. http://www.jstor.org/stable/40389257.
Drechselová, Lucie G. *Local Power and Female Political Pathways in Turkey: Cycles of Exclusion*. Cham, Switzerland: Palgrave Macmillan, 2020.
Dri, Karwan Faidhi. "Turkey's Pro-Kurdish HEDEP to Change Acronym on Court Objection." Rudaw, November 24, 2023. https://www.rudaw.net/english/middleeast/turkey/24112023.
Driver, G. R. "Studies in Kurdish History." *Bulletin of the School of Oriental Studies, University of London* 2, no. 3 (1922): 491–511. http://www.jstor.org/stable/606996.
Duncan, Carol. *Civilizing Rituals: Inside Public Art Museums*. London: Routledge, Taylor & Francis Group, 1995. https://doi.org/10.4324/9780203978719.
Ekinci, Tarık Ziya. *Sol siyaset sorunları: Türkiye İşçi Partisi ve Kürt aydınlanması*. Istanbul: Cem yayınevi, 2004.
Elicin, Yeseren. "Neoliberal Transformation of the Turkish City through the Urban Transformation Act." *Habitat International* 41 (2014): 150–55. https://doi.org/10.1016/j.habitatint.2013.07.006.
Enson Haber. "Diyarbakır'da Olaylar Çıktı." November 3, 2012. https://www.ensonhaber.com/gundem/diyarbakirda-olaylar-cikti-2012-11-03.
Erdem, Tarhan. "Türkiyeli Kürtler Ne Kadar?" *Radikal Gazetesi*, September 11, 2013. http://www.radikal.com.tr/yazarlar/tarhan_erdem/turkiyeli_kurtler_ne_kadar-1130023.
Erensü, Sinan, and Yahya M. Madra. "Neoliberal Politics in Turkey." In *The Oxford Handbook of Turkish Politics*, edited by Güneş Murat Tezcür, 158–86. New York: Oxford University Press, 2022. https://doi.org/10.1093/oxfordhb/9780190064891.013.17.
Ersoy, Melih. "Kente Göç ve Yoksulluk—Diyarbakır Örneği." Orta Doğu Teknik Üniversitesi Kentsel Politika Planlaması ve Yerel Yönetimler Anabilim Dalı 2001 Yılı Stüdyo Çalışması. Ankara: ODTÜ (METU), 2002.
Erzurum, Orhan Bozkurt. "Hadep: PKK'yla Ortak Yanlarımız Var." *Milliyet*, October 4, 1999. https://www.milliyet.com.tr/the-others/hadep-pkkyla-ortak-yanlarimiz-var-5252339.
Evrensel Gazetesi. "Baydemir: Tarım arazileri imara açılmayacak." Evrensel.net, March 9, 2011. https://www.evrensel.net/haber/1678/baydemir-tarim-arazileri-imara-acilmayacak.
———. "İstinaf Mahkemesi Dicle Vadisi'ndeki iptal kararını onayladı." Evrensel.net, June 9, 2020. https://www.evrensel.net/haber/406706/istinaf-mahkemesi-dicle-vadisindeki-iptal-kararini-onayladi.

——. "Kayapınar Belediyesi kayyumu kaymakamlığı belediyeye taşıyor." Evrensel.net, February 2020. https://www.evrensel.net/haber/397782/kayapinar-belediyesi-kayyumu-kaymakamligi-belediyeye-tasiyor.
Finkel, Andrew. "Municipal Politics and the State in Contemporary Turkey." In *Turkish State, Turkish Society*, edited by Andrew Finkel and Nükhet Sirman, 185–218. London: Routledge, 1990.
Finkel, Andrew, and Nükhet Sirman, eds. *Turkish State, Turkish Society*. London: Routledge, 1990.
Fırat, M. Şerif. *Doğu İlleri ve Varto Tarihi*. 2nd ed. Ankara: Millî Eğitim Basımevi, 1961.
Gambetti, Zeynep. "The Conflictual (Trans)Formation of the Public Sphere in Urban Space: The Case of Diyarbakır." *New Perspectives on Turkey* 32 (2005): 43–71. https://doi.org/10.1017/S0896634600004106.
——. "Decolonizing Diyarbakır: Culture, Identity and the Struggle to Appropriate Urban Space." In *Comparing Cities: The Middle East and South Asia*, edited by Kamran Asdar Ali and Martina Rieker, 97–129. Oxford: Oxford University Press, 2009.
Gellner, Ernest. *Nations and Nationalism*. Ithaca, NY: Cornell University Press, 1983.
Genç, Fırat. "Politics in Concrete: Social Production of Space in Diyarbakır, 1999–2014." PhD diss., Atatürk Institute for Modern Turkish History, Boğaziçi University, 2014.
Ghandour, Marwan, and Mona Fawaz. "Spatial Erasure: Reconstruction Projects in Beirut." *ArteEast Quaterly* (Spring 2010). http://arteeast.org/quarterly/spatial-erasure-reconstruction-projects-in-beirut/.
Ghirardo, Diane. *Architecture after Modernism*. New York: Thames & Hudson, 1996.
Gillis, John R. *Commemorations: The Politics of National Identity*. Princeton, NJ: Princeton University Press, 1994.
Gilpin, Robert. *The Challenge of Global Capitalism: The World Economy in the 21st Century*. Princeton, NJ: Princeton University Press, 2018.
Graham, Stephen. *Cities under Siege: The New Military Urbanism*. London: Verso, 2011.
Gülhan, Sinan Tankut. "Neoliberalism and Neo-dirigisme in Action: The State-Corporate Alliance and the Great Housing Rush of the 2000s in Istanbul, Turkey." *Urban Studies (Edinburgh, Scotland)* 59, no. 7 (2022): 1443–58. https://doi.org/10.1177/00420980211012618.
Gümüş, Korhan, "Toledo Benzetmesinin Arkasındaki Sorunlar." Mimdap, February 8, 2016. http://mimdap.org/2016/02/toledo-benzetmesinin-arkasyndaki-sorunlar-korhan-gumuth/.
Gündoğan, Azat Zana. "Space, State-Making and Contentious Kurdish Politics in the East of Turkey: The Case of Eastern Meetings, 1967." *Journal of Balkan and Near Eastern Studies* 13, no. 4 (2011): 389–416.
Güneş, Cengiz. *The Kurdish National Movement in Turkey: From Protest to Resistance*. New York: Routledge, 2012.
Günkut, Bedri. *Diyarbekir Tarihi*. Diyarbekir Halkevi neşriyatından 3. Diyarbakır, Turkey: Diyarbakır Basimevi, 1936.
Gunter, Michael M. *Historical Dictionary of the Kurds*. Lanham, MD: Scarecrow, 2010.
——. *The Kurds in Turkey: A Political Dilemma*. Westview Special Studies on the Middle East. Boulder, CO: Westview, 1990.
——. *Out of Nowhere: The Kurds of Syria in Peace and War*. London: Hurst, 2014.
Gür, Aslı. "Stories in Three Dimensions: Narratives of the Nation and the Anatolian Civilizations Museum." In *The Politics of Public Memory in Turkey*, edited by Esra Özyürek, 40–69. Modern Intellectual and Political History of the Middle East. Syracuse, NY: Syracuse University Press, 2007.

Gürsel, Kadri. "The Arab Spring, the Kurdish Summer." *Hurriyet Daily News*, April 11, 2011. http://www.hurriyetdailynews.com/default. aspx?pageid=438&n=the-arab-spring-the-kurdish-summer-2011-04-11.

Güvenç, Muna. "Constructing Narratives of Kurdish Nationalism in the Urban Space of Diyarbakir, Turkey." *Traditional Dwellings and Settlements Review* 23, no. 1 (2011): 25–40.

———. "Propositions for the Emancipatory Potential of Urban Spectacle." *City* 23, no. 3 (May 4, 2019): 342–65. https://doi.org/10.1080/13604813.2019.1648037.

Haber3. "Diyarbakır'da Kamışlı Bulvarı Açıldı." November 12, 2013. https://www.haber3.com/guncel/diyarbakirda-kamisli-bulvari-acildi-haberi-2255792.

Haber7. "Diyarbakir Yasam Hakki Aniti Acildi." September 12, 2008. http://www.haber7.com/haber/20080912/Diyarbak1r- Yasam-Hakki-Aniti-acildi.php.

Haber Diyarbakır. "Ayşe Şan'ın İsmi Parka Verildi." http://www.haberdiyarbakir.com/ayse-sanin-ismi-parka-verildi-15528h/.

Haberler.com. "Diyarbakır Kent Müzesi Hizmete Girdi." May 28, 2015. https://www.haberler.com/diyarbakir-kent-muzesi-hizmete-girdi-7358553-haberi/.

Habertürk. "Diyarbakır'da 'arsa balonu' patladı!" March 4, 2011. https://www.haberturk.com/ekonomi/emlak/haber/616881-diyarbakirda-arsa-balonu-patladi.

Hamelink, Wendelmoet, and Hanifi Barış. "Dengbêjs on Borderlands: Borders and the State as Seen through the Eyes of Kurdish Singer-Poets." *Kurdish Studies* 2, no. 1 (May 17, 2014): 34–60. https://doi.org/10.33182/ks.v2i1.378.

Harmes, Adam. "The Rise of Neoliberal Nationalism." *Review of International Political Economy* 19, no. 1 (February 2012): 59–86. https://doi.org/10.1080/09692290.2010.507132.

Harvey, David. *A Brief History of Neoliberalism*. Oxford: Oxford University Press, 2007.

Heper, Metin. *Dilemmas of Decentralization: Municipal Government in Turkey*. Bonn: Friedrich Ebert Stiftung, 1986.

———. *The State and Kurds in Turkey: The Question of Assimilation*. Basingstoke, UK: Palgrave Macmillan, 2007.

Herb, Guntram Henrik, and David H. Kaplan. *Nested Identities: Nationalism, Territory, and Scale*. Lanham, MD: Rowman & Littlefield, 1999.

Herlambang, Suryono, Helga Leitner, Liong Ju Tjung, Eric Sheppard, and Dimitar Anguelov. "Jakarta's Great Land Transformation: Hybrid Neoliberalisation and Informality." *Urban Studies* 56, no. 4 (2019): 627–48. https://doi.org/10.1177/0042098018756556.

Herscher, Andrew. *Violence Taking Place: The Architecture of the Kosovo Conflict*. Vol. 440. Cultural Memory in the Present. Redwood City, CA: Stanford University Press, 2010.

Hobsbawm, E. J. *Nations and Nationalism since 1780: Programme, Myth, Reality*. Cambridge: Cambridge University Press, 1990.

Holston, James. *The Modernist City: An Anthropological Critique of Brasilia*. Chicago: University of Chicago Press, 1989.

hthayat.haberturk.com. "Diyarbakır'da 'arsa balonu' patladı!" April 3, 2011. https://www.haberturk.com/ekonomi/emlak/haber/616881-diyarbakirda-arsa-balonu-patladi.

Hürriyet. "Belediye'nin yaptığı 5 km'lik çevre yolu ulaşıma açıldı." January 23, 2009. https://www.hurriyet.com.tr/gundem/belediyenin-yaptigi-5-kmlik-cevre-yolu-ulasima-acildi-10842916.

———. "Civil Disobedient Prayer." May 6, 2011. https://www.hurriyet.com.tr/gundem/sivil-itaatsizlik-namazi-17724782.

———. "Diyarbakır'da arsa fiyatları çıldırdı." March 3, 2011. https://www.hurriyet.com.tr/ekonomi/diyarbakirda-arsa-fiyatlari-cildirdi-17162486.

———. "Diyarbakır, Ortadoğu'ya açılan önemli bir kapı olacak." June 4, 2005. https://www.hurriyet.com.tr/gundem/diyarbakir-ortadogu-ya-acilan-onemli-kapi-olacak-38736352.

İmset, İsmet G. *The PKK: A Report on Separatist Violence in Turkey, 1973–1992*. Ankara: Turkish Daily News, 1992.

İncioğlu, Nihal. "Local Elections and Electoral Behavior." In *Politics, Parties, and Elections in Turkey*, edited by Sabri Sayari and Yilmaz R. Esmer, 73–90. Boulder, CO: Lynne Rienner, 2002.

Ismail, Salwa. *Political Life in Cairo's New Quarters: Encountering the Everyday State*. Minneapolis: University of Minnesota Press, 2006.

Jessop, Bob. *State Power: A Strategic-Relational Approach*. Cambridge: Polity, 2007.

Johannes, Venetia. *Nourishing the Nation: Food as National Identity in Catalonia*. New Directions in Anthropology, vol. 44. New York: Berghahn Books, 2019.

Jongerden, Joost. *The Settlement Issue in Turkey and the Kurds: An Analysis of Spatial Policies, Modernity and War*. Social, Economic, and Political Studies of the Middle East and Asia, vol. 102. Leiden: Brill, 2007.

———. "Village Evacuation and Reconstruction in Kurdistan (1993–2002)." *Études Rurales* 186, no. 186 (2010): 77–100. https://doi.org/10.4000/etudesrurales.9241.

Jongerden, Joost, and Ahmet Hamdi Akkaya. "Born from the Left: The Making of the PKK." In *Nationalisms and Politics in Turkey: Political Islam, Kemalism, and the Kurdish Issue*, edited by Marlies Casier and Joost Jongerden, 123–42. New York: Routledge, 2011.

Jwaideh, Wadie. *The Kurdish National Movement: Its Origins and Development*. Contemporary Issues in the Middle East. Syracuse, NY: Syracuse University Press, 2006.

Karaer, Ibrahim. *Türk Ocaklari: 1912–1931*. Ankara: Türk Yurdu, 1992.

Karaman, Ozan. "Urban Neoliberalism with Islamic Characteristics." *Urban Studies* 50, no. 16 (December 1, 2013): 3412–27. https://doi.org/10.1177/0042098013482505.

Karaömerlioğlu, M. Asim. "The People's Houses and the Cult of the Peasant in Turkey." *Middle Eastern Studies* 34, no. 4 (October 1, 1998): 67–91. https://doi.org/10.2307/4283970.

Kaya, Zeynep N. *Mapping Kurdistan: Territory, Self-Determination and Nationalism*. Cambridge: Cambridge University Press, 2020. https://doi.org/10.1017/9781108629805.

Kayapinar Belediyesi. December 12, 2008. http://www.Diyarbakırkayapinar.bel.tr/index.php?option=com_content&task=vie w&id=298&Itemid=2.

Kayapınar Municipality Activity Report. Kayapınar Municipality, Diyarbakır. 2006.

Kayar, Sertaç. "Mimarlar Odası Diyarbakır Şube Başkanı: Sur'daki evleri yapan mimarın proje çizme ehliyeti yok, evler cezaevine benzedi." *Sputnik*, April 12, 2019. https://tr.sputniknews.com/turkiye/201912041040760517.

Keyder, Çağlar, and Zafer Yenal. "Agrarian Change under Globalization: Markets and Insecurity in Turkish Agriculture." *Journal of Agrarian Change* 11, no. 1 (2011): 60–86. https://doi.org/10.1111/j.1471-0366.2010.00294.x.

Kezer, Zeynep. *Building Modern Turkey: State, Space, and Ideology in the Early Republic*. Pittsburgh: University of Pittsburgh Press, 2016.

Koçak, Süleyman Yaman. "Legislative Reforms in Turkey: The Case of Public Administration." *Reformele Legislative În Turcia: Cazul Administrației Publice* 62, no. 1 (June 2010): 9–18.

Konyar, Basri. *Diyarbekir*. Ankara: Ulus Basımevi, 1936.
Koz, M. Sabri, and E. Nedret İşli, eds. *Diyarbakır: Müze Şehir*. Istanbul: YKY, 1999.
Küçük, Bülent. "The Burden of Sisyphus: A Sociological Inventory of the Kurdish Question in Turkey." *British Journal of Middle Eastern Studies* 46, no. 5 (October 20, 2019): 752–66. https://doi.org/10.1080/13530194.2019.1634394.
Kumral, Şefika. "Globalization, Crisis and Right-Wing Populists in the Global South: The Cases of India and Turkey." *Globalizations*, February 2, 2022, 1–30. https://doi.org/10.1080/14747731.2021.2025294.
Kurdistan24. "KÜRDSİAD'a kapatılma, yöneticisine ceza." February 2, 2017. https://www.kurdistan24.net/tr/news/7750c170-a1da-41c0-a372-c7053ddc3153/-KÜRDSİAD-kapatılma--yöneticisine-ceza.
Kurdistan, Tatort. *Democratic Autonomy in North Kurdistan: The Council Movement, Gender Liberation, and Ecology*. Translated by Janet Biehl. Translation edition. Porsgrunn, Norway: New Compass, 2013.
Kusno, Abidin. *Behind the Postcolonial: Architecture, Urban Space and Political Cultures in Indonesia*. London: Routledge, 2000.
Kuyucu, Tuna. "Politics of Urban Regeneration in Turkey: Possibilities and Limits of Municipal Regeneration Initiatives in a Highly Centralized Country." *Urban Geography* 39, no. 8 (2018): 1152–76. https://doi.org/10.1080/02723638.2018.1440125.
Kuyucu, Tuna, and Özlem Ünsal. "'Urban Transformation' as State-Led Property Transfer: An Analysis of Two Cases of Urban Renewal in Istanbul." *Urban Studies* 47, no. 7 (2010): 1479–99. https://doi.org/10.1177/0042098009353629.
Laclau, Ernesto, and Chantal Mouffe. *Hegemony and Socialist Strategy: Towards a Radical Democratic Politics*. London: Verso, 1985.
Lane, Barbara Miller. *Architecture and Politics in Germany, 1918–1945*. Cambridge, MA: Harvard University Press, 1968.
Leitner, Helga, and Eric Sheppard. "From Kampungs to Condos? Contested Accumulations through Displacement in Jakarta." *Environment and Planning A: Economy and Space* 50, no. 2 (2018): 437–56. https://doi.org/10.1177/0308518X17709279.
Les Ateliers. *Ben U Sen in Diyarbakir: Potentials of Evolution of a Self-Made District*. May 13, 2011. https://www.ateliers.org/media/workshop/documents/topic_atelier_diyarbakir.pdf.
Liu, Tianyang, and Zhenjie Yuan. "Making a Safer Space? Rethinking Space and Securitization in the Old Town Redevelopment Project of Kashgar, China." *Political Geography* 69 (2019): 30–42. https://doi.org/10.1016/j.polgeo.2018.12.001.
Lovering, John, and Hade Türkmen. "Bulldozer Neo-liberalism in Istanbul: The State-Led Construction of Property Markets, and the Displacement of the Urban Poor." *International Planning Studies* 16, no. 1 (2011): 73–96. https://doi.org/10.1080/13563475.2011.552477.
Low, Setha M. "The Edge and the Center: Gated Communities and the Discourse of Urban Fear." *American Anthropologist*, n.s., 103, no. 1 (2001): 45–58.
———. "Security at Home: How Private Securitization Practices Increase State and Capitalist Control." *Anthropological Theory* 17, no. 3 (September 1, 2017): 365–81. https://doi.org/10.1177/1463499617729297.
Lueck, Kerstin, Clemence Due, and Martha Augoustinos. "Neoliberalism and Nationalism: Representations of Asylum Seekers in the Australian Mainstream News Media." *Discourse & Society* 26, no. 5 (September 2015): 608–29. https://doi.org/10.1177/0957926515581159.

Madra, Yahya M., and Sedat Yılmaz. "Turkey's Decline into (Civil) War Economy: From Neoliberal Populism to Corporate Nationalism." *South Atlantic Quarterly* 118, no. 1 (2019): 41–59. https://doi.org/10.1215/00382876-7281588.

Malmîsanij. *Yirminci Yüzyılın Başında Diyarbekir'de Kürt Ulusçuluğu, 1900–1920*. Araştırma-İnceleme 8. Istanbul: Vate Yayınevi, 2010.

Marcuse, Peter. "Not Chaos, but Walls: Postmodernism and the Partitioned City." In *Postmodern Cities and Spaces*, edited by Sophie Watson and Katherine Gibson, 243–54. Oxford: Blackwell, 1995.

Mbembe, Achille. "Domaines de la nuit et autorité onirique dans les maquis su sud-Cameroun (1955–1958)." *Journal of African History* 32, no. 1 (1991): 89–121.

———. *On the Postcolony*. Berkeley: University of California Press, 2001.

McDowall, David. *A Modern History of the Kurds*. London: I. B. Tauris, 2000.

Merrifield, Andy. *The New Urban Question*. London: Pluto, 2014.

———. *The Politics of the Encounter: Urban Theory and Protest under Planetary Urbanization*. Athens: University of Georgia Press, 2013.

Migdal, Joel S. *State in Society: Studying How States and Societies Transform and Constitute One Another*. Cambridge: Cambridge University Press, 2001.

Milliyet. "Alternative Friday." April 9, 2011. https://www.milliyet.com.tr/siyaset/alternatif-cuma-1375352.

Miraftab, Faranak. "Insurgent Planning: Situating Radical Planning in the Global South." *Planning Theory (London, England)* 8, no. 1 (2009): 32–50. https://doi.org/10.1177/1473095208099297.

Mitchell, Don. *The Right to the City: Social Justice and the Fight for Public Space*. New York: Guilford, 2003.

Mitchell, Timothy. "Society, Economy, and the State Effect." In *State/Culture: State Formation after the Cultural Turn*, edited by George Steinmetz, 76–98. Ithaca, NY: Cornell University Press, 1999.

Molnár, Virág. *Building the State: Architecture, Politics, and State Formation in Postwar Central Europe*. Architext. London: Routledge, 2013. https://doi.org/10.4324/9781315811734.

———. "The Mythical Power of Everyday Objects: The Material Culture of Radical Nationalism in Postsocialist Hungary." In *National Matters: Materiality, Culture, and Nationalism*, edited by Geneviève Zubrzycki 147–72. Stanford, CA: Stanford University Press, 2017.

Mukerji, Chandra. "Space and Political Pedagogy at the Gardens of Versailles." *Public Culture* 24, no. 3 68 (2012): 509–34. https://doi.org/10.1215/08992363-1630663.

Neumann, Klaus, and Janna Thompson. *Historical Justice and Memory*. Madison: University of Wisconsin Press, 2015.

NTV Haber. "The Friday Prayer with the Apo Poster." April 15, 2011. https://www.ntv.com.tr/turkiye/apo-posterli-cuma-namazi,bm7O9YvDzEa8IiRef9oWOg.

Öcalan, Abdullah. "Democratic Confederalism." International Initiative edition. London: Transmedia, 2011.

———. "War and Peace in Kurdistan: Perspectives for a Political Solution of the Kurdish Question." Cologne International Initiative "Freedom for Abdullah Öcalan—Peace in Kurdistan," 2008. www.freedom-for-ocalan.com.

Öktem, Kerem. "The Nation's Imprint: Demographic Engineering and the Change of Toponyms in Republican Turkey." *European Journal of Turkish Studies: Social Sciences on Contemporary Turkey*, no. 7 (November 18, 2009). http://ejts.revues.org/2243.

Olson, Robert W. *The Emergence of Kurdish Nationalism and the Sheikh Said Rebellion, 1880–1925*. Austin: University of Texas Press, 1989.

——. *The Kurdish Nationalist Movement in the 1990s: Its Impact on Turkey and the Middle East*. Lexington: University Press of Kentucky, 1996.
Oran, Baskın. *Türkiye'de azınlıklar: Kavramlar, teori, Lozan, iç mevzuat, içtihat, uygulama*. Istanbul: İletişim, 2004.
Orueta, Fernando Diaz, and Susan S. Fainstein. "The New Mega-projects: Genesis and Impacts." *International Journal of Urban & Regional Research* 32, no. 4 (December 2008): 759–67. https://doi.org/10.1111/j.1468-2427.2008.00829.x.
Otto-Dorn, Katharina. "Figural Stone Reliefs on Seljuk Sacred Architecture in Anatolia." *Kunst des Orients* 12, no. 1/2 (1978): 103–49.
Özer, Ismail. "Türk Modernleşmesinde Halkevleri ve Diyarbakır Halkevi Örneği." PhD diss., Gazi Üniversitesi, Ankara, 2010.
Özerdim, Sami N. *Atatürk devrimi Kronolojisi*. Istanbul: Varlik, 1963.
Özyürek, Esra. *The Politics of Public Memory in Turkey*. Modern Intellectual and Political History of the Middle East. Syracuse, NY: Syracuse University Press, 2007.
Palmer, Catherine. "From Theory to Practice: Experiencing the Nation in Everyday Life." *Journal of Material Culture* 3, no. 2 (1998): 175–99. https://doi.org/10.1177/135918359800300203.
Perlman, Janice E. *The Myth of Marginality: Urban Poverty and Politics in Rio de Janeiro*. Berkeley: University of California Press, 1979.
PKK (Türkiye). *Kürdistan devriminin yolu: (Manifesto)*. Cologne: Serxwebûn, 1984.
Porter, Libby, and Kate Shaw. *Whose Urban Renaissance? An International Comparison of Urban Regeneration Strategies*. London: Routledge, 2009.
Romano, David. *The Kurdish Nationalist Movement: Opportunity, Mobilization and Identity*. Cambridge: Cambridge University Press, 2006.
Roy, Ananya. "The 21st-Century Metropolis: New Geographies of Theory." *Regional Studies* 43, no. 6 (2009).
Roy, Ananya, and Nezar AlSayyad, eds. *Urban Informality: Transnational Perspectives from the Middle East, Latin America, and South Asia*. Transnational Perspectives on Space and Place. Lanham, MD: Lexington Books, 2004.
Roy, Sara M. *Hamas and Civil Society in Gaza: Engaging the Islamist Social Sector*. Princeton Studies in Muslim Politics. Princeton, NJ: Princeton University Press, 2014. https://doi.org/10.1515/9781400848942.
Sabah. "Diyarbakır'da arsa fiyatları çıldırdı." March 3, 2011. https://www.sabah.com.tr/ekonomi/2011/03/03/diyarbakirda_arsa_fiyatlari_cildirdi.
——. "Diyarbakır Kultur Turizmi ile atakta." June 30, 2018. https://www.sabah.com.tr/ekonomi/2018/06/30/diyarbakir-kultur-turizmi-ile-atakta.
——. "Kentsel dönüşümü tamamlayamazsak terörü de bitiremeyiz." November 13, 2007. http://arsiv.sabah.com.tr/2007/11/13/haber,4AA4DF6AB979476B878FDF60B19BD9F0.html.
Said Paşa, Diyarbekirli. *Diyarbekir vilâyetinin tarihçesi*. Diyarbekir, Turkey: Vilâyet Matbaasi, 1884.
Sarigil, Zeki. *Ethnic Boundaries in Turkish Politics: The Secular Kurdish Movement and Islam*. New York: NYU Press, 2018.
Savage, Kirk. *Monument Wars: Washington, D.C., the National Mall, and the Transformation of the Memorial Landscape*. Berkeley: University of California Press, 2011.
Scalbert-Yücel, Clémence. "The Invention of a Tradition: Diyarbakır's Dengbêj Project." *European Journal of Turkish Studies: Social Sciences on Contemporary Turkey*, no. 10 (December 29, 2009). http://ejts.revues.org/4055.
Scott, James C. *Seeing Like a State: How Certain Schemes to Improve the Human Condition Have Failed*. Yale Agrarian Studies. New Haven, CT: Yale University Press, 1998.

Sendika.org. "Kayyum, Park Orman'ın ismini değiştirdi: '15 Temmuz Şehitler Parkı.'" Accessed July 14, 2017. https://sendika64.org/2017/07/kayyum-park-ormanin-ismini-degistirdi-15-temmuz-sehitler-parki-433314/.

Sert, Deniz S., and Umut Kuruüzüm. "Alienated Imagination through a Mega Development Project in Turkey: The Case of the Osman Gazi Bridge." *New Perspectives on Turkey* 66 (2022): 160–79. https://doi.org/10.1017/npt.2022.2.

Simone, AbdouMaliq. *For the City Yet to Come: Changing African Life in Four Cities*. Illustrated ed. Durham, NC: Duke University Press, 2004.

———. *Jakarta, Drawing the City Near*. Minneapolis: University of Minnesota Press, 2014. https://doi.org/10.5749/j.ctt7zw6g5.

———. *Transforming South Africa: The Role of the State and Community in Development*. Dakar: Codesria, 1999.

Sirefman, Susanna. "Formed and Forming: Contemporary Museum Architecture." *Daedalus* 128, no. 3 (1999): 297–320.

Smith, Anthony D. *National Identity*. Reno: University of Nevada Press, 1991.

Smith, Neil. "New Globalism, New Urbanism: Gentrification as Global Urban Strategy." *Antipode* 34, no. 3 (July 1, 2002): 427–50. https://doi.org/10.1111/1467-8330.00249.

Smith, Thomas W. "Leviathan's Architect: Urbicide, Urban Renewal, and the Right to the City in Turkish Kurdistan." *Human Rights Quarterly* 44, no. 2 (2022): 387–416. https://doi.org/10.1353/hrq.2022.0014.

Sodaro, Amy. *Exhibiting Atrocity: Memorial Museums and the Politics of Past Violence*. New Brunswick, NJ: Rutgers University Press, 2018.

Soliman, Ahmed M., Ananya Roy, and Nezar AlSayyad. "Tilting at Sphinxes: Locating Urban Informality in Egyptian Cities." In *Urban Informality: Transnational Perspectives from the Middle East, Latin America, and South Asia*, edited by Ananya Roy and Nezar AlSayyad, 171–208. Lanham, MD: Lexington Books, 2003.

Somer, Murat. "Turkey's Kurdish Conflict: Changing Context, and Domestic and Regional Implications." *Middle East Journal* 58, no. 2 (April 1, 2004): 235–53.

Soyukaya, Nevin. "Sur—the Walled City of Diyarbakir: Conflict, Dispossession and Destruction Damage Assessment Report." August 1, 2017, 20.

Söz, Diyarbakır. "Yollar asfaltlanıyor!" Diyarbakır Söz, 11:56:27Z. https://www.diyarbakirsoz.com/Diyarbakir/Yollar-asfaltlaniyor--diyarbakir-soz-71120.

Sözcü. "'Sur'u Toledo gibi yapacağız.'" February 1, 2016. https://www.sozcu.com.tr/2016/gundem/suru-toledo-gibi-yapacagiz-1069462/.

Springer, Simon. "Neoliberalism as Discourse: Between Foucauldian Political Economy and Marxian Poststructuralism." *Critical Discourse Studies* 9, no. 2 (May 1, 2012): 133–47. https://doi.org/10.1080/17405904.2012.656375.

Tekeli, İlhan. *Cumhuriyetin belediyecilik öyküsü, 1923–1990*. Istanbul: Tarih Vakfı Yurt Yayınları, 2009.

Tezcür, Güneş Murat. *A Century of Kurdish Politics: Citizenship, Statehood and Diplomacy*. London: Routledge, 2020.

———. *The Oxford Handbook of Turkish Politics*. New York: Oxford University Press, 2020.

———. "Violence and Nationalist Mobilization: The Onset of the Kurdish Insurgency in Turkey." *Nationalities Papers* 43, no. 2 (2015): 248–66. https://doi.org/10.1080/00905992.2014.970527.

Tilly, Charles. *Coercion, Capital, and European States, AD 990–1990*. Cambridge, MA: Blackwell, 1990.

——. *Contentious Performances*. Cambridge: Cambridge University Press, 2008.
T24. "Sur'un Eski Sakinleri: 'Yeni Evleri Bize Parayla Bile Vermiyorlar.'" https://t24.com.tr/haber/sur-un-eski-sakinleri-yeni-evleri-bize-parayla-bile-vermiyorlar,877925.
TOKİ. "Alt Gelir Grubu Başvuru Şartları." https://www.toki.gov.tr/basvuru-sartlari.
——. "TOKİ | Toplu Konut İdaresi Başkanlığı." https://www.toki.gov.tr/.
——. "TOKİ yaptığı yatırımlarla 'geleceğin Kocaelisi'ni' inşa ediyor." https://a.toki.gov.tr/haber/toki-yaptigi-yatirimlarla-gelecegin-kocaelisini-insa-ediyor.
——. "Updated Sale List for Çölgüzeli." https://www.toki.gov.tr/Projeler/projeler/diyarbakir.html.
Tuğal, Cihan Z. "Islamism in Turkey: Beyond Instrument and Meaning." *Economy and Society* 31, no. 1 (2002): 85–111. https://doi.org/10.1080/03085140120109268.
——. *Passive Revolution: Absorbing the Islamic Challenge to Capitalism*. Stanford, CA: Stanford University Press, 2009.
——. "Politicized Megaprojects and Public Sector Interventions: Mass Consent under Neoliberal Statism." *Critical Sociology* 49, no. 3 (2022): 089692052210862. https://doi.org/10.1177/08969205221086284.
——. "The Urban Dynamism of Islamic Hegemony: Absorbing Squatter Creativity in Istanbul." *Comparative Studies of South Asia, Africa and the Middle East* 29, no. 3 (2009): 423–37.
TUİK (Turkish Statistical Institute). "Construction and Housing Statistics." https://data.tuik.gov.tr/Kategori/GetKategori?p=insaat-ve-konut-116&dil=2.
——. "Population and Demographics," 2011. https://data.tuik.gov.tr/Kategori/GetKategori?p=Nufus-ve-Demografi-109.
——. "Regional Results of Income and Living Conditions Survey," 2019. https://data.tuik.gov.tr/Bulten/Index?p=Gelir-ve-Yasam-Kosullari-Arastirmasi-Bolgesel-Sonuclari-2019-33821.
Turam, Berna. *Between Islam and the State: The Politics of Engagement*. Stanford, CA: Stanford University Press, 2007.
Türkmen, Gülay. *Under the Banner of Islam: Turks, Kurds, and the Limits of Religious Unity*. New York: Oxford University Press, 2021.
Turkun, Asuman. "Urban Regeneration and Hegemonic Power Relationships." *International Planning Studies* 16, no. 1 (2011): 61–72.
Üngör, Uğur Ümit. "Creative Destruction: Shaping a High-Modernist City in Interwar Turkey." *Journal of Urban History* 39, no. 2 (2013): 297–314. https://doi.org/10.1177/0096144212439473.
——. *The Making of Modern Turkey: Nation and State in Eastern Anatolia, 1913–1950*. Oxford: Oxford University Press, 2011.
Üstel, Füsun. *İmparatorluktan ulus-devlete Türk milliyetçiligi: Türk Ocaklari, 1912–1931*. Istanbul: İletişim, 1997.
Vale, Lawrence J. *Architecture, Power and National Identity*. 2nd ed. London: Routledge, 2008.
——. "The Temptations of Nationalism in Modern Capital Cities." In *Cities and Sovereignty: Identity Politics in Urban Spaces*, edited by Diane E. Davis and Libertun de Duren, 196–209. Bloomington: Indiana University Press, 2011.
Volk, Lucia. *Memorials and Martyrs in Modern Lebanon*. Bloomington: Indiana University Press, 2010.
Wacquant, Loïc. "Territorial Stigmatization in the Age of Advanced Marginality." *Thesis Eleven* 91, no. 1 (November 1, 2007): 66–77. https://doi.org/10.1177/0725513607082003.

Watson, Vanessa. "Shifting Approaches to Planning Theory: Global North and South." *Urban Planning* 1, no. 4 (December 2016): 32–41.
Watts, Nicole F. *Activists in Office: Kurdish Politics and Protest in Turkey*. Seattle: University of Washington Press, 2010.
———. "Re-considering State-Society Dynamics in Turkey's Kurdish Southeast." *European Journal of Turkish Studies: Social Sciences on Contemporary Turkey*, no. 10 (December 29, 2009). http://ejts.revues.org/4196.
———. "Silence and Voice." In *The Evolution of Kurdish Nationalism*, edited by Mohammed M. A. Ahmed and Michael M. Gunter, 52–77. Costa Mesa, CA: Mazda, 2006.
Weber, Max. *Politics as a Vocation*. Philadelphia: Fortress, 1965.
Wedeen, Lisa. *Ambiguities of Domination: Politics, Rhetoric, and Symbols in Contemporary Syria*. Chicago: University of Chicago Press, 1999.
———. *Peripheral Visions: Publics, Power, and Performance in Yemen*. Chicago: University of Chicago Press, 2008.
White, Jenny B. *Islamist Mobilization in Turkey: A Study in Vernacular Politics*. Studies in Modernity and National Identity. Seattle: University of Washington Press, 2002.
———. *Muslim Nationalism and the New Turks*. Princeton Studies in Muslim Politics. Princeton, NJ: Princeton University Press, 2014.
White, Paul J. *Primitive Rebels or Revolutionary Modernisers? The Kurdish Nationalist Movement in Turkey*. London: Zed Books, 2000.
Yadirgi, Veli. *The Political Economy of the Kurds of Turkey: From the Ottoman Empire to the Turkish Republic*. Cambridge: Cambridge University Press, 2017.
Yavuz, M. Hakan. "Five Stages of the Construction of Kurdish Nationalism in Turkey." *Nationalism & Ethnic Politics* 7, no. 3 (September 2001): 1.
Yeğen, Mesut. "'Prospective-Turks' or 'Pseudo-Citizens': Kurds in Turkey." *ESQ* 63, no. 4 (2009): 597.
Yesil, Bilge. *Media in New Turkey: The Origins of an Authoritarian Neoliberal State*. Geopolitics of Information, vol. 9. Champaign: University of Illinois Press, 2016. https://doi.org/10.5406/j.ctt18j8x8p.
Yeşilkaya, Neşe Gurallar. *Halkevleri: İdeoloji ve mimarlık*. Istanbul: İletişim, 1999.
Yetiskul, Emine, Serap Kayasü, and Suna Yaşar Ozdemir. "Local Responses to Urban Redevelopment Projects: The Case of Beyoğlu, Istanbul." *Habitat International* 51 (2016): 159–67. https://doi.org/10.1016/j.habitatint.2015.10.019.
Yiftachel, Oren. "The Dark Side of Modernism: Planning as Control of an Ethnic Minority." In *Postmodern Cities and Spaces*, edited by Sophie Watson and Katherine Gibson, 216–39. Oxford: Blackwell, 1995.
———. "From Displacement to Displaceability: A Southeastern Perspective on the New Metropolis." *City (London, England)* 24, no. 1–2 (2020): 151–65. https://doi.org/10.1080/13604813.2020.1739933.
———. "Planning and Social Control: Exploring the Dark Side." *Journal of Planning Literature* 12, no. 4 (1998): 395–406. https://doi.org/10.1177/088541229801200401.
———. "Theoretical Notes on 'Gray Cities': The Coming of Urban Apartheid?" *Planning Theory* 8, no. 1 (February 1, 2009): 88–100. https://doi.org/10.1177/1473095208099300.

Yıldız, Ceylan Begüm. "Diyarbakır's Objects of Memory: 'Restoration' of the Kurdish City into a Biblokent." *London Journal of Critical Thought* 1, no. 1 (2018): 51–61.

Yüksel, Ayse Seda. "Rescaled Localities and Redefined Class Relations: Neoliberal Experience in South-East Turkey." *Journal of Balkan and Near Eastern Studies* 13, no. 4 (2011): 433–55.

Yüksel, Heval Zeliha. "Suriçi'nde Neler Oluyor." Arkitera, March 22, 2018. https://www.arkitera.com/soylesi/suricinde-neler-oluyor/.

Zana, Mehdi. Interview by Maşallah Dekak. Rudaw, November 2, 2019. https://www.rudaw.net/turkish/interview/02112019.

Index

Page numbers in *italics* refer to figures and tables.

Adana, 33
Adıyaman, 45
Afran (local author), 81–82
Ağrı rebellion, 29
Ahmet (informant), 67, 113–14
Ahsen (informant), 87, 138, 186
AKP (Justice and Development Party), 64, 100, 107, 110, 121, 180, 208n67, 216n19; political competition with pro-Kurdish party, 42, 90, 92; post-conflict reconstruction in Diyarbakır, 159–91, *171*, 193; urban development, 47–51, 54, 58–59, 67–68
Albay, Hüsnü, 78, 148, 210n26
Ali Paşa neighborhood, 54–60, *57*, 64–66, *65*, 68, 151–56, 175–76, 178–79, 190, 208n65, 208n67
Alkan, Zekiye, 148
AlSayyad, Nezar, 71
Amida (Amid or Amed, now Diyarbakır), 5, 102
An Yapı, 110, 112
ANAP (Motherland Party), 36
Anderson, Benedict, 88, 121, 157
Anderson, Perry, 191
Ankara, 9, 30, 42–43, 106, 112, 122, 168, 173
Anlı, Fırat, 46, 162
Anter, Musa, 31, 118
Arab Spring, 97, 133–34, 136
Aras (sculptor), 141–42
architecture: Anatolian Seljuk style, 169, 216n19; Artuqids, 53; modern, 26, 106, 195 (*see also* public housing); museums, 150–52; nationalism and, 8–11; neo-Ottoman, 169; political power and, 201n16; in post-conflict reconstruction, 170–79. *See also* Sur
Arda (informant), 108–10
Arendt, Hannah, 92, 139
Arif, Ahmet, 115
Armenians, 19, 156, 203n11, 204n45, 208n49, 216n23
articulation: defined, 10. *See also* political articulation
assimilation, 1, 20–21, 197

Assyrians, 20, 169
Atatürk, Mustafa Kemal, 5, 22–27, 53, 118, 124, 126, 136–37, 202n5, 203n31
Atilla, Cumali, 162–63
autonomy, Kurdish, 32, 34, 85–86, 119, 131, 160, 164
Ayşe Şan Park, 145–46
Aziziye neighborhood, 79

Bağıvar neighborhood, 87–88
Bağlar, 5, 45, *107*, 143, 147, 172, 208n47
Balibar, Étienne, 128
Barzani, Mesut, 118
Barzani, Molla Mustafa, 118, *119*
Barzani rebellion (Iraq), 30
Batman, 7, 32, 44–45
Batuman, Bülent, 166
Bayat, Asef, 75
Baydemir, Osman, 3–4, 46, 51, 59–60, 62, 71, 97–102, 107–8, 125, 131–33, 146, 182
BDP (Peace and Democracy Party), 35–36, 39, 58, 63, 68, 71–72, 76, 82, 88, 90–91, 93, 98–100, *107*, 133–39, 141, 148, 207n26, 215n48
Ben-u Sen neighborhood, 5, 62–63, 79, 208n47
Berlage Institute, 61–62
Berzan (Sur municipality council member), 182–84, 187–88
Beyaz, Mine Lök, 176
biblokent (miniature city), 178
Biehl, Janet, 85
billboards, 51, 63, 103, *104*, 148, 171, *171*, 185
Billig, Michael, 116
Biner, Zerrin, 217n29
Bingöl, 7, 45
Birtane İnşaat, 174
Bitlis, 45
Board of Conservation, 183
Bookchin, Murray, 85
Bozarslan, Mehmet Emin, 30
Brenner, Neil, 56, 95
Brubaker, Rogers, 10, 69, 114, 127, 210n47
budgets, 46, 89, 182–84, 193, 207n33

235

INDEX

built environment: destruction and reconstruction of, 160 (*see also* reconstruction, post-conflict); nationalism and, 3, 8–11, 13, 16, 76, 195–96. *See also* architecture; Diyarbakır; housing; memorial landscape; parks; urban development
Burawoy, Michael, 14
Burkay, Kemal, 31
business sector, 112–14, 173. *See also* commerce

cafés and coffeehouses, 114–18, 151, 157, 185, 190
capitalism, 4, 12, 66, 121, 193; nationalism and, 112–14. *See also* neoliberal urbanism
Castell, Manuel, 197
Çekül Foundation, 151
Çelik, Feridun, 46
Cemil (informant), 95–97
Cemil Paşa Mansion, 151–56, *152*
central government, 206n21, 207n33; authority over urban planning, 64–66, 180–85; infrastructure support, 100–101; local control and, 41–43. *See also* AKP; governorship
Ceylan Karavil Park Mall, 106, 112
Ceylan Önkol Park, 140–41, 147
Çeysa İnşaat, 174
CHP (Republican People's Party), 25–27, 217n3
city-beautification projects, 160, 170–74, *171*
civil disobedience, 133–39
Civil Friday Prayers, 135–39, *137*
civilization, 22, 25; "backwardness," 23, 29, 31–32
civil society organizations, 7, 11–13, 45; demobilization of, 186–88; events in public parks, 138; Kurdish mobilization and, 72, 77–93, 145; political society and, 12–13, 191, 197–99; urban renewal and, 54–55, 63
Ciwan (informant), 172
Cizre, 159
coffee, *117*, 117–18, 190
Çölgüzeli neighborhood, 56–57, *57*, 66, 105
collective memory, 127, 133, 150–58, 179, 185; erasure of, 160, 162–64, 179, 185–91. *See also* memorial landscape
commerce, 49, 56, 62, 86–87. *See also* business sector; consumer culture; informal economy
Commission of Peoples and Beliefs, 90
condolence houses, 89, 92
conservative associations, 89–91
construction firms, 49–50, 95, 97, 106, 112–14, 173–74; post-conflict projects, 170–79, 192

consumer culture, 94, 112, 114–19, *120*, 122, 160, 196
Costa, Lucia, 9
cultural centers, 145, 160, 166–67, 193. *See also* Kurdish culture

Dağkapı Square, 26–27, 136–37
Davutoğlu, Ahmet, 175–78
Dehak (Assyrian king), 131, 214n18
DEHAP (Democratic People's Party), 35
de Leon, Cedric, 10–11
Demirbaş, Abdullah, 53–55, 59, 71, 76–77, 80–82, 86, 140
Demirel, Rahşan, 148
Demirel, Süleyman, 34, 205n75
Demirtaş, Selahattin, 40, 71, 118, 162
democracy, 34–35, 198
democratic confederalism, 85–86, 90
"Democratic Initiative" project, 38, 205n84
"Democratic Solution Tent," 133–39
demonstrations and protests, 7, 33, 39, 51, 68, 74, 147, 216n11; demobilization of, 185; at parks and memorials, 126, 128–29, 133–39, 157
DEM Parti, 194
Dengbej House, 151
dengbej music, 9, 81–82, 89, 145, 150
Deniz (informant), 187–88
Deniz, Cihan, 78, 148, 210n26
DEP (Democracy Party), 35, 45
Department of Dwelling Affairs, 64
Derbas (informant), 187
Dersim rebellion, 29
Desai, Manali, 11
De Soto, Hernando, 113
DİAY-DER (Religious Scholars Assistance Solidarity Foundation), 90–91
Dicle University, 2, 59, 108, 114, 141, 148
Dicle Valley, 173
Dildar, "Ey Reqib," 111
DİP (Revolutionary Workers' Party), 35
Directorate of Religious Affairs, 135–36, 168
disasters, 49, 64, 207n32, 208n67
discrimination, 31, 34–35, 54, 87, 101, 203n13
displacement, 7, 21, 33, 40, 51–52, 54, 66, 73, 75, 161, 174, 179, 204n46, 208n50
dispossession, 176, 217n29
dissent, 193–94
district governors, 185
districts, 41
Diyarbakır: branding of, 122; as center for Kurdish nationalism and capital-to-be, 1, 9, 21, 32, 94, 101–3, 153, 189, 195; expansion,

6, 94, 97, 105; history of, 5–7, 19–21, *24*, 43–47, 203n18; metropolitan municipality status, 43; ownership claims, 4, 22, 59–60, 69, 180; as postmodern city, 9–10, 195; as site of urban contestation, 7, 39–41, 46–69, 120, 143–44, 157; size of, 4–5; spatial layout, 23–25; Turkification of, 7, 20–29, 203n30; watermelon as symbol of, 28, 124–26, *125*. *See also* Kayapınar; memorial landscape; political mobilization; Sur (inner city of Diyarbakır)
Diyarbakır Central Mosque (Salahaddin Ayyubi Mosque), 167–69, *170*
Diyarbakır Chamber of Architects, 104, 217n32
Diyarbakır City Museum, 151–56, *152*
Diyarbakır Fortress, 63, 173
Diyarbakır Halkevi (Diyarbakır People's House), 25–27, *26*, 204n34
Diyarbakır Metropolitan Municipality, 3–4, 6, 7–8, 54; activity reports (2004–2008), 103; after 2019 election, 180–85; cultural affairs, 135; history of, 43–47; memorials and, 145, 153 (*see also* memorial landscape); post-conflict reconstruction, 159–80; public meetings, 128, 187; structure and responsibilities of, 41–43, 206n10, 206n13, 207n33; Sur preservation efforts, 59–63. *See also* mayors; pro-Kurdish party
Diyarbakır Municipality Guest House, 89
Diyarbakır–Urfa road, 105
Dora, Şilan, 146
DP (Democratic Party), 27
DTK (Democratic Society Congress), 85, 134
DTP (Democratic Society Party), 3, 35–36, 51, 58, 100, *107*, 207n26

earthquakes, 49, 64, 207n32
East Anatolia Region, 28–29
Eastern Meetings, 32, 44
"Eastern" question, 28–32
ecological society, 84–85
economy, 5–7. *See also* business sector; commerce; consumer culture; informal economy; neoliberal urbanism; poverty alleviation projects; unemployment
Edi Bese memorial, 143
Egypt, Tahrir Square demonstrations, 133–34, 136
Elçi, Şerafettin, 30
elections: local, 42–43, 207n23; national, 36, 47, 97, 133–34, 159, 217n3; pro-Kurdish party and, 3, 45–46, 51, 122, 159, 180, 207n26, 217n3
Elif (Mehmet's wife), 110
elites, Kurdish, 30, 37, 43, 63, 66, 71, 97, 122, 176
Elvan (informant), 155
emergency decree (KHK), 162–63, 185–86, 192
eminent domain. *See* urgent expropriation
Erdoğan, Recep Tayyip, 50, 92, 107, 162, 166–68, 171, 189, 216n5
Erhan (informant), 155
Erzurum municipality, 173
Esma Ocak House, 151
Esra (informant), 99–100, 109, 172
ethnography of urban maneuvers, 13–16, 197. *See also* wiggle room
"Every Night One Story, Every House Is a School" project, 81–82
Eylo (sculptor), 131–32, 139

Fatih Paşa neighborhood, *161*, 217n27
FCA (Free Compatriot Association), 77–79, *78*, 92–93, 138, 175, 186, 210n25
Feras (sculptor), 131–32
Forum Diyarbakır (shopping mall), 106

gated communities *(site)*, *104*, 104–12, *111*, 122
Gazi (Veteran) Street, 23
Gecekondu law (1966), 207n31. *See also* squatter settlements
Gellner, Ernest, 121
General Directorate of Highways, 168
gentrification, 49, 56, 66, 121
Geveri, Adem, 90
Gezmiş, Deniz, 118, *119*
Global South, 11–12, 66
Governor H, 55–56, 58
governorship: conflicts with municipalities, 7, 39–41, 46–47, 54–56; post-conflict control over Diyarbakır, 185; structure and responsibilities of, 41–43
Graham, Stephen, 178
grassroots community-building, 37, 44, 46, 81–87, 90–91, 133, 160, 193, 197
Güney, Yılmaz, 118, *119*
Günkut, Bedri, 19–20
Gunter, Michael, 210n24
Gürsel, Cemal, 29

HADEP (People's Democracy Party), 35, 45, *107*, 194–95, 207n23, 207n26
Hakkari, 7, 45
Hamdi (informant), 178

Harmes, Adam, 213n73
Hasan (informant), 77–79, 138, 186
Hasan Paşa Khan, 118, *119*, 141
Hasırlı neighborhood, 77–79, *161*, 210n25, 217n27
Havin (informant), 2–3, 68, 109, 114–16, 141, 151, 188–89
Hawler, Iraq, 102
Hawler Boulevard, 102
HDP (Peoples' Democratic Party), 3–4, 35–37, 90, 106–9, *107*, 121, 162, 171, 180–85, 188–89, 194, 207n26, 217n3
HEDEP (Peoples' Equality and Democracy Party), 36, 194
HEP (People's Labor Party), 35, 205n78, 207n23
Hevsel Gardens, 63, 173
Hezbollah, 187
highways. *See* road construction
Holtay, Arif Hikmet, 26
Holzmeister, Clemens, 9
home-based projects, 81–82, 84–87
housing: crisis in Diyarbakır, 50–58 (*see also* squatter settlements); historic, 151–56; projects by TOKİ, 48–51, 54–68, 105, 189–90; reconstruction of, 160, 178–79
Hulu, Şirin Elem, 148
human rights, 72, 129, 140–41, 157

İç Kale, 60
identity politics, 13, 58, 60, 180, 198; neoliberal urbanism and, 196. *See also* Kurdish identity; Turkish national identity
imprisonment of pro-Kurdish politicians, 44, 46, 80, 87, 134, 153, 162, 180, 184, 187, 191–92, 194, 205n84, 210n26
informal economy, 54, 57, 60, 73, 82–87, 113
infrastructure projects: megaprojects, 50; post-conflict reconstruction, 160, 170–74; by pro-Kurdish party, 98–104, 113, 121–22; road construction, 98–104; in squatter settlements, 47
İnönü, İsmet, 27, 53
Iran, 1, 102, 113, 210n24
Iraq, 1, 30, 102, 111, 113, 135, 210n24
İskenderpaşa neighborhood, 75, 81
Islamification of public space, 160, 166–69, 172, 185, 191
Islamist groups, 43, 89–91, 186–87, 208n49, 209n6, 209n11. *See also* RP (Welfare Party)
Istanbul, 30, 33, 42–43, 56, 90, 106, 109, 112–13, 122, 178
Izmir, 30, 42–43, 90, 109, 189

KADEM (Women's Support Houses), 83–87, 93, 138
Karatekin, Zülküf, 144
Kars, 31
Kawa (mythological figure), 131, 147, 214n18
Kaya, Ahmet, 118, *119*
Kayapınar, 5, 56, 95–96, 99, *104*, 104–6, *107*, 110–12, *111*, 141–44, 172, 212n44, 216n11
Kaymaz, Uğur, 139–40, *140*, 157, 214n34
KCK (Kurdistan Democratic Communities Union), 76, 160, 210n24, 215n47
Kemalist doctrine, 22, 26–27, 136–37
Kezer, Zeynep, 25, 122
Kiptaş, 48, 174, 178
Kılıçdaroğlu, Kemal, 217n3
Kışanak, Gültan, 36, 46, 153, 162
Koçgiri uprising, 204n48
Konyar, Basri, 20
Koşuyolu Park: destruction of memorials in, 162–65; memorials in, 128–33; protests and demonstrations in, 128–29, 133–39
Kurdish bloc, 3, 18, 40, 66–72, 92–93, 122, 167, 186–91, 196
Kurdish culture, 9, 107, 145; cuisine, 116–18; festivals, 146–49, 185; historical narratives, 99; house meetings, 81–82. *See also* cultural centers; museums
Kurdish flag, 107, 111, 134–35
Kurdish identity, 1–2; control over urban space and, 180; development of, 10–11; everyday expressions of, *21*, 114–22, *117*, *119*; gated communities and, 107; housing and, 68–69; international urban planning and, 63–64; leftist politics and, 30; as political category, 10; state action to outlaw public expression of, 160; symbols of, 110–12, 122, 143–44, 162; Turkish state's rejection of, 20–29. *See also* memorial landscape
Kurdish intelligentsia, 30–31, 33
Kurdish language, 20, 37–38; bans on use of, 44, 53, 109, 143–44, 157; Islamic prayers in, 90; in museums, 153; political mobilization and, 88–89; projects for expansion of, 72, 76, 80–82; in Sur's squatter settlements, 73; teaching of, 134, 166, 205n84
Kurdish mobilization, 1–14, 34, 43–46, 58, 68–77, 93, 146, 158–60; demobilization in post-conflict Diyarbakır, 185–91
Kurdish nationalism: collective imagination of, 102–3; emergence of, 204n48; heroes and martyrs, 147–48; political parties and (*see* pro-Kurdish party); rebellions, 26, 29 (*see also* Sheikh Said Rebellion); rights

and freedom, 38, 87, 101, 148, 205n84; in twentieth century Diyarbakır, 29–38
Kurdistan Revolutionaries movement, 33. *See also* PKK
Kurds: ban on use of term, 21, 30; "Kurdish" question, 28–32; population size, 1, 28
Kurmanji (dialect), 73
Kutlay, Naci, 31

Laclau, Ernesto, 10, 67
Lalebey neighborhood, 54–60, 57, 64–66, 65, 68, 175, 208n65, 208n67
Lamassu reliefs, 145, 163
land speculation, 95–98
languages: multilingual municipality services, 53–54, 80–81. *See also* Kurdish language; Turkish language
Les Ateliers (organization), 62
Levon (Turkish Armenian author), 81–82
local politics, 37–38; as site of contestation, 7, 39–41, 46–69, 120, 143–44, 157

Mahabad Boulevard, 99–102, 110
Malatya, 31
Marcuse, Peter, 56, 193
Mardin, 45
martial law, 45–46
martyrs, 147–48
Marwani Bridge, 102
Marwanids, 21
material culture, 94, 107, 114–19, 120, 122
Matra Project, 61–62
Mayer, Margit, 56
Mayor C (mayor), 182, 184
mayors: pro-Kurdish, 7, 39–46, 53–55, 59, 180–85, 192; responsibilities of, 41–43; state-appointed *(kayyım)*, 162–63, 174, 186
MAZLUM-DER (Association for Human Rights and Solidarity for the Oppressed), 90, 211n50
Mbembe, Achille, 156, 167
Med City Mahabad, 110–12, 111, 143
Medes, 20, 111, 143, 202n5, 214n18
media: traditional, 88, 96, 139. *See also* social media
Medya Park, 143
Mehmet (Kurdish intellectual), 110
Mehmet Uzun House, 216n23
Melih (informant), 77
memorial activism, 127, 156, 195
memorial landscape, 124–58; festivals, 146–49; as form of protest, 143–46; Kurdish mobilization and, 195–96; monuments registering state oppression and violence, 127–33, 138–43; museums, 150–56, 158, 160, 168, 214n5 152; Turkish remaking of, 124–26; vandalized and demolished, 157–58, 162–64, 164–65. *See also* collective memory
Merrifield, Andy, 163, 197
Mersin, 33
Meryem (informant), 138
Mesopotamia Boulevard, 108
metropolitan municipalities: establishment of, 43. *See also* Diyarbakır Metropolitan Municipality
micro-entrepreneurship projects, 8, 84–87, 92–93
middle class. *See* upper and middle classes
Ministry of Environment and Urbanization, 49, 64–65, 168, 173, 176, 178, 180, 183–84, 208n63
Ministry of Public Works and Housing, 64, 208nn63–64
Ministry of Urbanization, 206n13
minority groups, 20–21, 81, 91, 197–98, 203n11
Miraftab, Faranak, 12
Miran (informant), 99–100, 107, 109
Mızraklı, Adnan Selçuk, 46, 207n26
modernity, 22–23, 195; republican modernism, 9–10, 20, 22–27; urban development and, 103
mosques, 26, 49, 81, 136–37, 160, 167–69, 170, 173, 174, 178, 191, 216n23
Mouffe, Chantal, 10, 67
multilingual municipality services, 53–54, 80–81
municipalities, pro-Kurdish. *See* Diyarbakır Metropolitan Municipality
municipal laws, 40, 42; disaster risk level, 64; *Gecekondu* law (1966), 207n31; on historic preservation, 58–60; limiting municipal influence, 180, 191; wiggle room and, 193
Murat (informant), 138
Muş, 7, 45
museums, 150–56, 158, 160, 168, 214n5 152

national belonging, 69, 114, 116, 119, 121–22, 149, 154, 157, 202n34
nationalism: built environment and, 3, 8–11, 13, 16, 76, 195–96; capitalism and, 112–14; economic, 121; ordinary citizens and, 38, 72, 74, 95, 100, 147, 157; territorial aspects, 98
nationhood, 10–16, 37–38, 99, 114, 122, 127, 150, 157, 192–96
nationness, 10, 14, 69, 100, 114, 122, 127, 160, 192

neighborhood associations, 72–73, 77, 186; women's income-generating activities and, 83–87

neoliberal urbanism: housing construction and, 49–50; identity politics and, 196; Islamism and, 169, 178; municipal reform and, 42; nationalism and, 94–95, 119–22; political mobilization and, 191, 196; relocation and, 56; rise of, 9; speculation and, 97; state power and, 196–97; struggles for control and, 40–41; urban development and, 66; urgent expropriation and, 176

Newroz celebrations (Persian New Year), 146–49, 172, 187, 215n48

Newroz Park, 105, 131, 147–48, 172, 187

NGOs (nongovernmental organizations), 7, 11, 71, 83–87, 92, 110, 145, 186, 192

Nidar (informant), 68

Ninova Mall, 106, 112

Nur (informant), 90

Nursi, Said-i, *119*

Nusaybin, 159

Öcalan, Abdullah, 33–34, 74, *75*, 78–79, 84–86, 90, 148, *149*, 186, 209n17, 210n24, 215n48

Ofis neighborhood, 5, 116

Okçuoğlu, Ahmet Zeki, 32

Önkol, Ceylan, 140–41, 147, 157, 214n35

Onur (informant), 138

Ottoman Empire: architectural styles, 169; Diyarbakır and, 5, 23, 208n49; end of, 21; governance, 201n9, 202n1, 206n7; Kurds in, 204n48; Turkish nationalism in, 203n8

Özal, Turgut, 205n75

parks, 105, 110, 126, 128–48, *144*, 157, 171–72, 187, 212n49

Parliament, 3–4, 31, 36, 39–40, 133–34

Paşa, Cemil, 151–56

Peace at Home Council, 216n5

Peace Mothers Initiative, 133, 142

People's Houses, 25–27, *26*, 58, 204n34, 204n37

Perwer, Şivan, 118

Peyas village, 105

pious associations, 89–91

PJAK (Kurdistan Free Life Party), 148, 210n24, 215n47

PKK (Kurdistan Workers' Party): formation and growth of, 32–34; HDP and, 171; HEP and, 205n78; KCK and, 210n24; local leaders and, 88; Roboski incident, 141; supporters of, 74, 75, 77–79, 111, 148, 171, 174, 184; village guard system and, 205n72

PKK-Turkish military conflict, 89, 92, 131, 134, 156; forced migration and displacement, 7, 33, 51–52, 54, 66, 73, 208n50; in Hasırlı, 210n25; "in the mountains," 74, 76, 81, 88, 92, 210n23; peace process, 109, 125, 159, 205n65; PKK withdrawal from Turkey, 215n48; in Sur, 211n56; urban warfare (2015–2016), 158–62, 212n44, 216n23

planning policies. *See* urban planning

political articulation, 14, 17–18, 40, 193–96; defined, 10–11; destruction of, 159–60; urban informality and, 68–93. *See also* Kurdish bloc

political mobilization: civil society organizations and, 72, 77–93, 145; Kurdish language and, 88–89; Kurdish nationalism and, 1–4, 7, 13, 37–45, 66–93, 126, 180, 191, 193–99, 202n29; memorial landscape and, 195–96; neoliberal urbanism and, 191, 196; in squatter settlements, 70–93, 179; state coercion and, 193; urban analysis of, 11–13. *See also* demonstrations and protests; Kurdish mobilization

political parties. *See* pro-Kurdish party; *specific political parties*

political power: architecture and space, 9–10, 12, 201n16; central versus local control over cities, 41–43; memory and, 128; municipalities and, 41–43; political parties and, 27, 51, 76; state and, 8–9, 12

popular culture, 9, 98, 213n2

poverty alleviation projects, 84–89, 92–93, 121, 186. *See also* urban poor

private partnerships, 48–49, 65–66, 106, 183–84, 193

private schools, 106, 108

progress, 26, 51, 95, 98–102, 104, 121, 160

pro-Kurdish party: bans on, 194–95; civil society and, 12–13, 191, 197–99 (*see also* civil society organizations); formation of, 7, 34–37; Kurdish identity and, 11; memorial landscape, 126–58, *149*, 157; municipal power, 71 (*see also* Diyarbakır Metropolitan Municipality); political agendas, 34–38; post-conflict reconstruction, 180–85; public services, 7–8; recruitment in squatter settlements, 58; socialist parties and, 30–32; as a social movement, 13, 71–73, 90–91; squatter settlements and, 66–69; support for, *107* (*see also* elections); urban maneuvers (*see* wiggle room); use of term, 201n5. *See also* political articulation; *specific parties*

prosperity, 98, 102–3

protests. *See* demonstrations and protests
public housing, 48–51, 54, 56, 60, 62, 65–67, 70, 105, 179, 190

Qamishli Boulevard, 101–2
Quran courses, 89–90, 187

Rasim (informant), 67
real estate markets, 48–49, 95–98
reconstruction, post-conflict: as destruction, 159–65; infrastructure and city beautification, 170–74; Islamification of public space, 166–69; Kurdish demobilization, 185–91; memorial landscape and, 162–65; in Sur neighborhood, 174–80; urgent expropriation, 176–80, *177*, *181*, 217n27
relocation: prevention of, 58–60; of squatter settlements, 40, 56–58, 65–66. *See also* displacement
Renda, Abdülhalik, 28
republican modernism, 9–10, 20, 22–27
resettlement, 21, 28, 204n46
restaurants, 106, 112, 116, 190
revolutionary strategy, 32–34. *See also* PKK
Right to Life memorial, *129–30*, 129–33, 158, 163–64, *164–65*
Rıza, Seyid, 118, *119*
road construction, 98–104
Roboski memorial, 141–42, *142*, 157, 163
Rojava, Syria, 102
Roşna Park, 143, *144*
Roy, Ananya, 12, 71
RP (Welfare Party), 36, 43, 207n23
rural-to-urban migration: "Eastern" question and, 30; forced, by PKK-Turkish military conflict, 7, 33, 51–52, 54, 66, 73, 208n50; increase in, 205n72; in Sur's squatter settlements, 5, 51–52, 54, 73, 75; in Yenişehir, 27

Said Paşa Diyarbekirli, 19–20, 202n1
Salahaddin Ayyubi (1138–1193), 214n29
Salih (informant), 146
Saliha (municipality officer and social worker), 84–90, 138, 186
Sami (municipality officer), 135–36, 138, 147, 152–54, 156, 185–86
Şan, Ayşe, 145–46
Saturday Mothers' Initiative, 142
Scott, James, 21
secularism, 26
Selim (informant), 184

Selin (informant), 108–9
separatism, 30
Serdar (informant), 155
Sheikh Said, 118; commemoration of, 90, 138
Sheikh Said Rebellion, 7, 20, 26, 29, 151, 204n43
Sheikh Ubaydallah's rebellions, 204n48
shopping malls, 106, 112, 190
SHP (Social Democratic Populist Party), 35, 42, *107*, 207n26
Siirt, 45
Silopi, 159
Silvan, 32
sites of engagement, 11, 156, 193. *See also* memorial activism
Siverek, 32
Şırnak, 45–46, 159
Smith, Thomas, 216n3
socialist parties, 30–32
social media, 88, 134–35, 139
social networks, 70–93, 114
Solmaz, Edip, 44
Southeast Anatolia Region, 28
sovereignty, 21, 122
Soyukaya, Nevin, 59–60, 216n23
space: nationalism and, 8–11, 16; politics of, 12, 193–94
squatter settlements, 5, 47, 66, 207n31; organizing logic of, 71; political conflict over Sur, 41–43, 47, 51–69; public space in, 73, *74*; rural migrants in, 5, 51–52, 54, 73, 75, 113. *See also* urban poor
state coercion, 1, 39–41; governorship and, 47 (*see also* governorship); housing and, 68, 74; neoliberal urbanism and, 196–97; opposition to, 4; urban space and, 12. *See also* assimilation; urgent expropriation
State of Emergency (OHAL), 45–46
state oppression and violence: opposition to, 1, 4, 39; representations in memorial landscape, 127–33, 138–43, 151, 156–58. *See also* PKK-Turkish military conflict; state coercion
street names, symbolism of, 7, 23, 25, 99, 101–2, 126, 145, 167, 171–72
Street of Cultures project, 81
Sülüklü Khan (café), 115–16, 122, 213n63
Sümer Park, 110, 131–32, 212n49
Sur (inner city of Diyarbakır), 2; architecture and street layout, 52–53, 57, 73, 79, 151–52, 154, 189–91; demobilization in, 186; destruction of buildings during 2015–2106 armed conflict, 161, *161*, 174–76, 179, *181*, 192, 216n23; displaced residents, 161, 174, 179; elections, 45; historic

Sur (inner city of Diyarbakır) (*continued*)
preservation plans, 58–61, 67; history of, 5, 51–52, 208nn48–49; income levels in, 73; infrastructure, 47; Kurdish political mobilization in, 70–93, 179; map of, *65*; modernization of, 23; photographs of, *52, 74–75, 78, 83, 152*; political conflict over squatter settlements, 41–43, 47, 51–69; post-conflict reconstruction, 172, 174–84, *177, 181*, 189–91; pro-Kurdish party support, *107*; urgent expropriation in, 176–80, *177, 181*. *See also* Ali Paşa neighborhood; Lalebey neighborhood
Süreyya, Cemal, 116
surveillance, 79, 137, 161, 178, 187–88
Syria, 1, 102, 134, 208n49, 210n24

Tan, Altan, 39–40, 90
temporary workers, 54, 73
territory: national identity and, 21; nationalism and, 98; neoliberal, 196
Theodore, Nik, 95
Tigran, Aram, 131, 147–48
Tigris Valley Recreational Project, 173, *174*
TKDP (Kurdistan Democrat Party of Turkey), 32
TOKİ (Housing Development Administration of Turkey), 48–51, 54–68, 105, 189–90
tourism, 113, 175, 178–79, 190–91
Tuğal, Cihan, 11, 43, 209n6
Tunceli, 45
Tunisia, 134
Turam, Berna, 22
Türk, Ahmet, 100–101
Turkey: establishment of modern state, 21; military coups, 32, 124, 166–67, 171, 216n5; "one nation" slogan, 166, 171, 191; regions of, 28. *See also* AKP; central government; Diyarbakır; local politics
Turkish flag, 124, *125*, 161–63, 187
"Turkish History Thesis," 202n5
Turkish language, 80, 153
Turkish Municipality Association, 206n10
Turkish national identity, 20–29, 118, 156; architecture and, 9, 25–27; construction of, 9–10, 202n34; Islam and, 166–69; territory and, 21
Turkish nationalism, 20, 124–26, 171–72, 203n8

Üçkuyular, 56, 105
Uğur Kaymaz memorial, 139–40, 157, 163, 182, 214n34
Ulu Camii (grand mosque), 168, 178

unemployment, 5–8, 185, 192
UNESCO World Heritage List, 63, 173
Üngör, Uğur Ümit, 203n8, 204n45
unions, 55, 63, 71, 92
upper and middle classes, 93–94, 99, 105–7
urban activities, 11
urban development: activity reports, 103–4; by central government (*see* AKP); demobilization through, 185–91; by pro-Kurdish municipality, 94–123. *See also* infrastructure projects; reconstruction, post-conflict
urban informality, 69; organizing logic of, 71, 91–92; political articulation and, 70–93. *See also* squatter settlements
urbanization, 30–31, 42, 105
urban maneuvers, ethnography of, 13–16, 197. *See also* wiggle room
urban mobilization, 86, 160, 193
urban planning: activity reports on, 103–4; as control, 198; as empowerment, 198–99; international community, 60–64; political power and, 4–5, 194, 198–99, 201n16; Western models, 22–23, 63
urban poor, 54, 71, 73, 107; demobilization of, 186; social services and, 93; in squatter settlements, 60, 77, 79, 84–85, 179. *See also* poverty alleviation projects
"urban question," 163, 197–99
urban regeneration, 41, 48–55
urban renewal, 40–41, 47–58, 60, 64–72. *See also* urban regeneration
Urfa, 31, 54, 208n52
urgent expropriation, 176–80, *177, 181*, 217n27
Uzun, Mehmet, 153, 216n23

Van, 7, 45

Watson, Victoria, 12
Watts, Nicole, 37
Wedeen, Lisa, 10, 202n34, 211n57, 216n61
Westernism, 22–26
White, Jenny, 166, 209n11
White Butterflies Laundry Houses, 79
wiggle room (urban maneuvers), 3–4, 38, 41, 193–94; ethnography of, 13–16, 197; international support (as finding loopholes), 60–64; preservation plans, 58–60; private partnerships, 183–84
women: Kurdish-speaking, 73; memorials and, 139–42, 157; micro-entrepreneurship projects, 8, 83–87, 92–93; political participation, 87–89, 142–43, 145–46; women's liberation, 84

women's organizations, 79–80, 82–87, 92, 186, 193
Workers' Party of Turkey (TİP), 31–32, 44, 207n21
World Heritage Sites, 63, 173

Xani, Ahmed, *119*
Xizri, Huşen, 148

Yasemin (informant), 155–56
YDG-H (Patriotic Revolutionary Youth Movement), 160–61

Yenişehir, 5, 23–25, 27, 45, *107*, 110, 143
Yiftachel, Oren, 12, 40–41, 198
Young Turk movement, 203n8, 204n45
youth organizations, 2, 186, 193
YSP (Green Left Party), 35–36, 194
Yüksekdağ, Figen, 162
Yüksekova, 159

Zana, Mehdi, 31, 44–45, 206n21
Zazaki (dialect), 73
zoning, 40, 50, 59, 96–98, 103–4, 106

www.ingramcontent.com/pod-product-compliance
Lightning Source LLC
Chambersburg PA
CBHW031352230426
43670CB00006B/514